True Crime Parallels
to the Mysteries
of Agatha Christie

# True Crime Parallels to the Mysteries of Agatha Christie

ANNE POWERS

McFarland & Company, Inc., Publishers
*Jefferson, North Carolina*

ISBN (print) 978-1-4766-7946-4
ISBN (ebook) 978-1-4766-3768-6

Library of Congress and British Library
cataloguing data are available

Library of Congress Control Number 2020002051

© 2020 Anne Powers. All rights reserved

*No part of this book may be reproduced or transmitted in any form or by any means, electronic or mechanical, including photocopying or recording, or by any information storage and retrieval system, without permission in writing from the publisher.*

Front cover image © 2020 Maisei Raman/Shutterstock

Printed in the United States of America

*McFarland & Company, Inc., Publishers
Box 611, Jefferson, North Carolina 28640
www.mcfarlandpub.com*

For Tahira, Caleb, and Noah

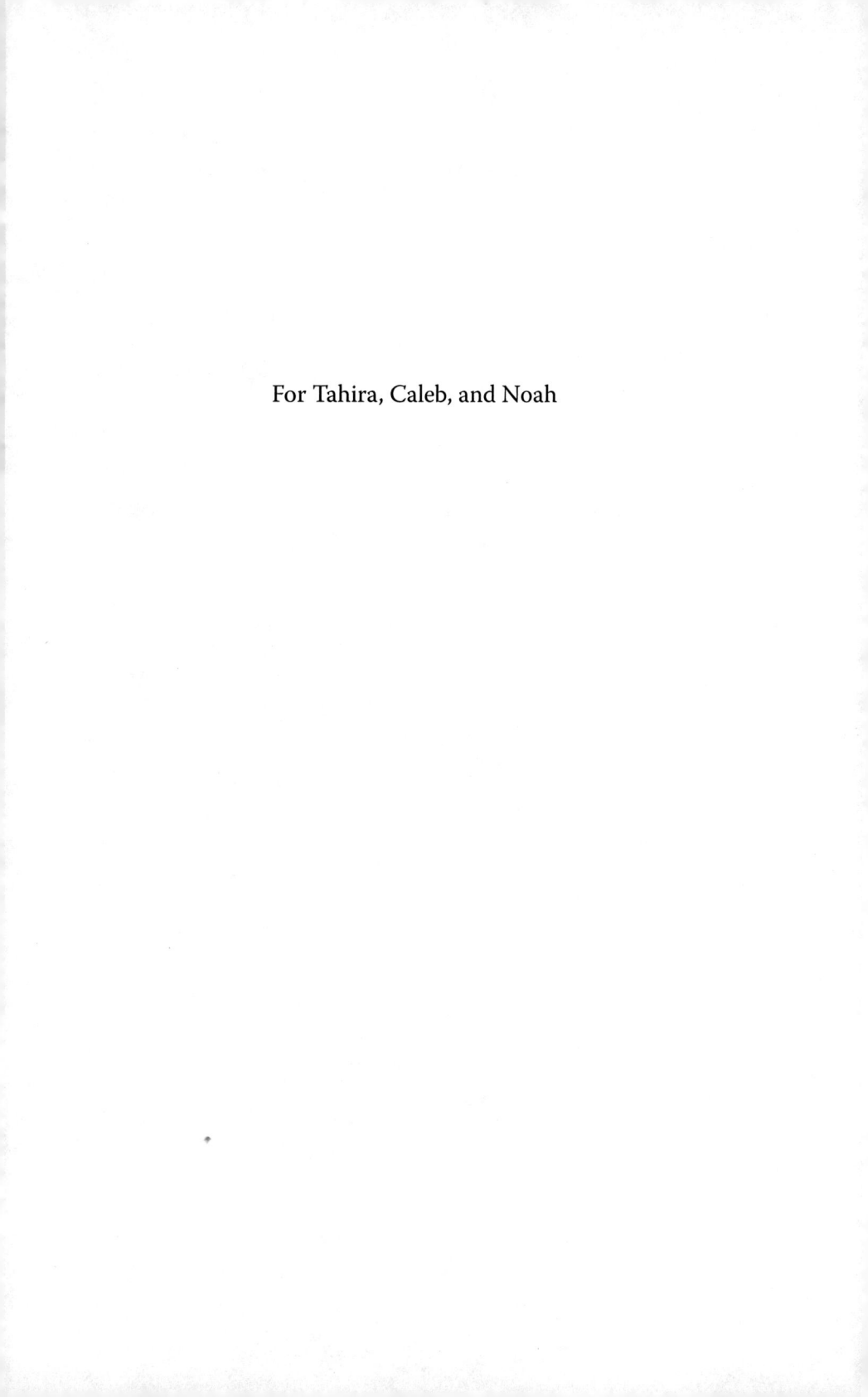

# Acknowledgments

The author would like to thank the librarians and staff of UCLA's Hugh & Hazel Darling Library of the School of Law, and of UCLA's Charles Young Research Library, for their invaluable aid in accessing their invaluable resources.

Special thanks go to Dale Stieber, Special Collections Librarian and College Archivist, and to Helena de Lemos, Special Collections Instruction & Research Librarian, of Occidental College Library, Los Angeles, for their enthusiasm and help in using the outstanding resources of the Ned Guymon Mystery and Detective Fiction Collection.

# Contents

| | |
|---|---:|
| *Acknowledgments* | vii |
| *Preface* | 1 |
| *Introduction* | 5 |
| 1. "The Rugeley Poisoner": Dr. William Palmer and *The Mysterious Affair at Styles* | 9 |
|     Dr. William Palmer | 9 |
|     *The Mysterious Affair at Styles* | 14 |
|     Dr. William Palmer + *The Mysterious Affair at Styles* | 23 |
| 2. "La Femme Fatale": Madame Marguerite Steinheil and *The Murder on the Links* | 29 |
|     Madame Marguerite Steinheil | 29 |
|     *The Murder on the Links* | 44 |
|     Madame Marguerite Steinheil + *The Murder on the Links* | 49 |
| 3. "Dope Girl": The Case of Billie Carleton and "The Affair at the Victory Ball" | 59 |
|     The Case of Billie Carleton | 59 |
|     "The Affair at the Victory Ball" | 68 |
|     The Case of Billie Carleton + "The Affair at the Victory Ball" | 69 |
|     Postscript | 71 |
| 4. "The Crime of the Century": The Case of the Lindbergh Kidnapping and *Murder on the Orient Express* | 74 |
|     The Case of the Lindbergh Kidnapping | 74 |
|     *Murder on the Orient Express* | 81 |
|     The Case of the Lindbergh Kidnapping + *Murder on the Orient Express* | 84 |
| 5. "The Kidwelly Mystery": Harold Greenwood and "The Lernean Hydra" | 89 |

| | |
|---|---|
| Harold Greenwood | 89 |
| "The Lernean Hydra" | 100 |
| Harold Greenwood + "The Lernean Hydra" | 102 |
| Postscript | 105 |

6. "An Outbreak of Sadism": The Case of Dennis O'Neill and "Three Blind Mice" — 107
   - The Case of Dennis O'Neill — 107
   - "Three Blind Mice" — 111
   - The Case of Dennis O'Neill + "Three Blind Mice" — 114

7. The "Little Man": Dr. Hawley Harvey Crippen and *Mrs. McGinty's Dead* — 121
   - Dr. Hawley Harvey Crippen — 121
   - *Mrs. McGinty's Dead* — 127
   - Dr. Hawley Harvey Crippen + *Mrs. McGinty's Dead* — 131

8. The "Balham Mystery": The Case of Charles Bravo and *Ordeal by Innocence* — 136
   - The Case of Charles Bravo — 136
   - *Ordeal by Innocence* — 140
   - The Case of Charles Bravo + *Ordeal by Innocence* — 143

9. "Poor Little Rich Girl": The Life of Gene Tierney and *The Mirror Crack'd* — 150
   - The Life of Gene Tierney — 150
   - *The Mirror Crack'd* — 157
   - The Life of Gene Tierney + *The Mirror Crack'd* — 161

10. The "Brides in the Bath" Murderer: George Joseph Smith and *A Caribbean Mystery* — 170
    - George Joseph Smith — 170
    - *A Caribbean Mystery* — 174
    - George Joseph Smith + *A Caribbean Mystery* — 177
    - Postscript — 183

*Appendix A: Christie Chronology of Mystery Novels and Story Collections* — 185

*Appendix B: Alphabetical List of Christie Mystery Novels and Story Collections* — 188

Works Cited — 191

*Index* — 195

# Preface

This book is dedicated to fans and students of Agatha Christie and her mystery-detective fiction, as well as to fans and students of classic true-crime lore.

The accounts contained herein provide fascinating insights into notorious past events that doubtless influenced Agatha Christie as she created some of her most famous works of detective fiction. This work was written for anyone who has ever wondered about the inspirations for her clever tales, or for anyone interested in the Queen of Crime's works in general. It is equally relevant for aficionados of criminology and of true crime accounts—especially accounts of vintage British *causes célèbres*.

There are reasons that Agatha Christie is the modern-day world's most successful author, outsold only by the Bible and the works of William Shakespeare. Her fans are legion, with over two billion of her detective tales sold to avid readers. Christie's appeal is essentially universal: her works are appreciated by individuals from all walks of life and from many different countries. Her dedication to the primacy of the puzzle, and to fabricating the most ingenious puzzles for the discriminating palates of mystery aficionados, and to "playing fair" with her readers, resulted in creation of highly entertaining and accessible works of fiction that can be enjoyed again and again—whether in print, in films, or in the spoken word. Her stories usually invite readers to participate in a race with the fictional sleuth of the tale, vying to be the first to unmask "whodunit." And when readers find themselves once again outfoxed by the story's detective—and by the story's author—they are likely to be more delighted than chagrined as they fall victim, once again, to the Queen of Crime's mastery of pleasurable deception.

There is no doubt that each of Christie's fiction stories is her own independent and original creation, complete with her own unique and imaginative set of puzzles and solutions. Several are also distinguished by an underlying authenticity lent by consideration of famous real-life crimes; crimes whose infamous stories are essentially ingrained in popular cultural history—especially British cultural history. Far and away the most prevalent type of crime featured in her body of work is the domestic crime: of the 66 mystery novels she produced, nearly two-thirds feature murders that occur in a family or household setting. British criminal history fairly teems with legendary domestic true crimes whose imprints have become permanently woven into the nation's cultural fabric: the names Crippen, Palmer, and many others still resonate to this day.

Present-day readers of Christie's mystery and detective concoctions are far removed in time from even indirect experience of those events. They may be unaware of the role the events could have played in affecting Christie's creative processes, and thus unfortunately miss out on rich, enlightening, and absorbing aspects that can multiply enjoyment of this remarkable author's tales many times over.

The present work repairs this regrettable circumstance, bridging the gap to recognition of famous true crimes that informed some of Christie's most celebrated and inventive creations. The public's fascination with the cases treated has been ongoing over the passing years, the decades—and even, in some cases, over the passing centuries. *True Crime Parallels* aims to allow readers to discover why much of the world—and Agatha Christie—found these long-past events so enduringly intriguing.

The true-life events occurred mostly in the hundred years roughly spanning the mid–1800s to the mid–1900s, beginning with the William Palmer case of 1856 and ending with the Dennis O'Neill tragedy in 1945. Of the events featured in the work, seven occurred in Great Britain, two in the United States, and one in France. Nine involve deliberate transgressions that ended at least one life; the tenth—the case of Gene Tierney—involves a morally problematic transgression that resulted in the ruin of at least one life.

To showcase the prominence and ubiquity of newspaper publications in proliferating information about the true-life events, many citations in this work originate from news stories published at the time of the event or later. Newspaper accounts of the true-crime histories were the most prevalent means of providing information about those crimes: readers across all class and economic strata were practically deluged by ongoing and exhaustive, day-by-day results of discovery, investigation, speculation, and resolution of the sensational murders or other malefactions—including readers like Agatha Christie. To give this work's readers an idea of both the immediate and the enduring impact over time that each true-crime case exerted—and still exerts—upon the public consciousness, profiles may include citations about the incident, taken from Christie's tales, newspaper articles, and other sources. Although American spelling conventions for the English language are used throughout, directly quoted terms, titles, phrases, etc. reflect source spelling (for example, British "labour" for "labor" or "defence" for "defense").

## Preface

The Christie tales cited include a variety of editions and print formats (for example, hardcover, paperback, large print), reflecting the plethora of editions available year after year to Christie fans. First or near-first print editions, however, were used for the ten Christie titles featured in this work. Most of these were either published in New York by Dodd, Mead for American editions, or in London by Collins for the British editions. The citations within the profiles briefly identify sources quoted, and point to full bibliographic entries at the end of the book.

# Introduction

Agatha Christie, the undisputed bestselling "Queen of Crime" among modern mystery and detective writers, was inspired by more than one famous true-crime story of the past. *True Crime Parallels to the Mysteries of Agatha Christie* celebrates this circumstance by presenting a collection of ten famous Christie creations, and discussing them together with histories of the sensational, tragic, or scandalous real-life events that colored them. Some of her most enduringly famous novels and stories were largely influenced by exciting famous true crimes. These influences were not always directly identified as such within the story but were nonetheless easily recognizable—not just to professional criminologists and crime-lore specialists but to reasonably informed, ordinary folk alike.

The detective-fiction offerings which fit this category of Christie's output either strikingly mirrored aspects of the famous real-life event, or took the event as a starting point, speculating via her fictional accounts on possible dramatic consequences. *Murder on the Orient Express*, for example, vividly recalls the infamous Lindbergh Kidnapping of 1932. That event served as a starting point, an impetus for Christie's tale: her conception of an aftermath involving survivors of a horrific crime. Exposition in the short story "The Lernean Hydra," however, echoes a progression of events in the true-crime history of beleaguered solicitor Harold Greenwood, who was tried in 1920 for the murder by poison of his wife, Mabel Bowater Greenwood. In addition, a handful of Christie's treatments seem to serve a limited social mission. Agatha Christie penned her works for entertainment, never pretending to write for social commentary. Some tales, however, send a message by providing a sort of alternate, if fictional, closure to cases where justice may have fallen short in real life; or by providing—such as in the case of the story "Three Blind Mice"—a surrogate kind of revenge for suffering survivors of some true-life crimes.

Agatha Christie's works were always original creations from her own unique imagination, never just fictionalized copies of real-life events. Her solutions or endings never repeated the true crimes' actual outcomes;

she put her own inventive stamp on the twists and surprises in the plots and storylines of every work that she created. Her genius lay in seeing the human-interest possibilities in the notorious crimes that studded cultural history, and in then connecting and translating some of those possibilities into cathartic, if fictional, experiences.

This book compares ten sensational real-life events to the Christie fictions deemed to have been partially or wholly inspired by them. Each set of elucidations is arranged chronologically by publication date of the Christie tale. Dates are therefore as important for the tales as for the crimes, in order to make it clear that Christie's relevant works were created *after* the true events. Two of the short stories featured herein—"The Affair at the Victory Ball" and "The Lernean Hydra"—appeared in newspapers or magazines long before being published in book collections; *True Crime Parallels* therefore places treatments of these tales in the chronological order of their periodicals appearances.

The analyses appear in segments, beginning with a detailed profile of a celebrated crime, which is followed by a summary of the relevant fictional Christie work. This in turn is succeeded by a comparison showing, point by point, the relationship between aspects of the true crime and aspects of the Christie tale. The point-by-point explication necessarily results in revealing much about the plot or the solution of the story—be warned! It also makes necessary a certain amount of repetition, insuring that the matchups are comprehensible to every reader, whether novice or experienced Christie (or true-crime) buff. Comparisons are thus made easier, eliminating the need to keep looking backward or forward between segments in order to find connections, or to refresh the memory.

Some accounts are more extensive than others: if Christie's tale or the real-life event is more famous or of more importance than others, its profile will be commensurately more developed. For example, *Murder on the Orient Express* is one of Agatha Christie's most well-known tales, and for that reason is given an expanded treatment. Conversely, if a classic case has plummeted from the high-profile notoriety of its heyday into comparative present-day obscurity—such as the once-sensational history of Madame Marguerite Steinheil—it is also given a lengthened presentation, in order to offer readers inclusive and detailed information about the case that may be hard to find elsewhere.

The examples of Agatha Christie's *oeuvre* contained herein also reflect different aspects of her development as she continued to mature in creating her works of detective fiction—aspects that manifest across the entire body of her work. One of these facets is a progression from the portrayals of mere mundane, flat motives for her fictional crimes—gain, love, hate, revenge, etcetera—that tended to serve as necessary excuses for the exercise of her puzzles. Another is an evolution of sorts, over time, from the "stock-character," one-dimensional feel of her character depictions to more fully-realized personages. Agatha Christie's characters are generally and essentially more "types" than individuals. However, in many of her tales, both motives and characters grow more psychologically complex as she tackled more psychologically complex issues within her cleverly-wrought puzzles; puzzles which, however, always kept the puzzle as her primary focus. Thus, the arc that begins in 1920's *The Mysterious Affair at Styles* with a basic murder for gain, committed by a basic character type from whom that behavior might well be expected, evolves into 1964's *A Caribbean Mystery*, in which Christie delivers a more subtle, mature, and sophisticated approach to the same type of crime and criminal.

# Chapter 1

# "The Rugeley Poisoner"
## Dr. William Palmer and
## *The Mysterious Affair at Styles*

This was the story that began it all: Agatha Christie's very first published detective novel. In 1916, Agatha's sister Madge had bet Agatha that she couldn't write a detective story; Agatha accepted the challenge; went on to concoct *The Mysterious Affair at Styles*; and the rest, as the saying goes, is history. Agatha Christie's work and studies in wartime medical dispensaries gave her the necessary expertise about poisons and their effects to put to good use in *Styles*, providing the first of many opportunities for her to fascinate readers with puzzles created around intriguing murders by toxic potions. The characters are simplistic types of the upper-middle, domestic, and working classes—the social classes with whom Christie was familiar—and foreshadowed the kinds of personages readers would meet in Christie's tales for years to come. The novel's story of country-house murder by strychnine appeared in 1920, sixty-four years after the sensationally infamous misdeeds of Dr. William Palmer had been bared to a horror-stricken world. His techniques for slaying earned him not only the nickname "The Rugeley Poisoner" but the title of "Prince of Poisoners" as well. Numerous aspects of Palmer's story find parallels in *The Mysterious Affair at Styles*.

## Dr. William Palmer

The infamous Dr. William Palmer of Rugeley was hanged in Staffordshire in 1856 at age 32. He was executed for the 1855 strychnine-poisoning murder of his racing crony, 28-year-old John Parsons Cook. Palmer had qualified as a physician, but had neglected his practice to follow wholeheartedly his true passions: gambling, the thrills of the turf, and, despite his marriage, marathon womanizing. Unflatteringly described as "a small, fattish man, bald, with cropped yellow side whiskers, white as a candle" ("William

Palmer" 10), Palmer hardly looked the part of a Casanova—or indeed the stereotypical conception of a lean, hard, cold-blooded murderer. Outwardly, it seemed at one time he had it all—family wealth, a complaisant wife, a son on whom he doted, a respected profession. The doctor also possessed determined intelligence, high social standing, congenial friends. He was in fact one of those deemed as "having a potentially 'successful ingenuity' had it not been turned in 'a criminal direction'" (Matlock 91). Palmer's crass crime, then, was all the more shocking because it had not been committed by a brutal, ignorant, or impoverished member of society's criminal or lower orders, but by a member of the privileged classes—one who was purportedly innately above such things. Palmer's fall was a supremely Victorian fall from grace: a disturbing and "low-life" deed surreptitiously committed by a "respectable" member of the middle class in a desperate bid to maintain an all-important façade of respectability. Its impact and its aftereffects reverberate to this day in British cultural, criminal, and legal history.

Palmer's initial good luck at gaming had soon run out, and he made the mistake of putting himself in the hands of moneylenders. The proverbial mountain of accumulating debt quickly placed him in a hopeless position from which only a timely infusion of huge sums of money could rescue him. Fear of the perilous situation pressed the outwardly coolheaded and calculating doctor into reckless, almost panicked reaction—including murder.

The two gambling friends, Cook and Palmer, both owned racehorses and had traveled together to the Shrewsbury Handicap races of November 1855, where their horses were running. They were put up at The Raven Inn. At the races Cook's horse won a very large purse, while Palmer's lost a substantial sum, continuing a downward spiral of bad gambling luck for the doctor that plunged him deeper into debt. His obligations to the tune of many thousands of pounds held him in thrall to several flint-hearted London moneylenders; and these usurious gentry were ruthless in their dealings with defaulters. Palmer knew that he could expect no mercy at their hands. He knew that they would haul him into court in a trice and, due to the harsh debtor laws of the time, see him imprisoned for his lack of ability to pay—a bitter pill for the doctor, who had been born to wealth, to swallow. In addition, he had forged guarantees for the loans, and fraud could lead to more imprisonment and even to transportation. Well before the Shrewsbury Handicap, Palmer had tried to extricate himself by fixing the horses he owned and raced, but when he was found out, the exposure "was the finish of Palmer as a racehorse owner ... this was a great blow" ("Rugeley Doctor's" 12). The doctor sank even deeper into the mire of his predicament. Young Cook was slain so that Palmer—with the imminent threat of imprisonment or transportation for fraud and other crimes menacing his freedom, his social status, and his privileged lifestyle—could quickly lay his hands on Cook's newly-collected and considerable racecourse winnings.

November 13 was a fateful day for both Palmer and Cook. Palmer, as was usual with him lately, once more lost heavily at the races; at the same time, moneylenders in London started legal action against him to recover their overdue money. Cook's luck seemed to be in: his mare, Polestar, won the large purse that was, in reality, the reason he was shortly to be slain. The elated young turf enthusiast hosted a celebration for a group of cronies, including Palmer, at the Raven Inn on the evening of November 14. One of the quaffs that Cook had happily downed was a brandy drink handed to him by the doctor. The drink burned his throat; Cook recoiled, jumped up, pointed a finger at Palmer, and accused the doctor of "dosing" him. Palmer laughed away the allegation, but that night, Cook suffered a violent attack of illness from which he was slow to recover: prosecutors would later say this was Palmer's first attempt to poison John Parsons Cook.

Whatever misgivings Cook may have had, he'd apparently dismissed by the next day, for after the races on November 15 the two "friends" traveled back to Rugeley together, with Cook carrying a large portion of his winnings with him in cash. A day or so after their arrival in Rugeley, Cook fell ill again. He was staying at the Talbot Arms, situated just across the way from Palmer's home and surgery, which made it handy for the doctor's busy, frequent visits to treat and console his crony. The pills which Dr. Palmer pressed on him not only didn't seem to help, but actually appeared to aggravate his agonizing symptoms. Curiously, however, when the elderly Dr. William Bamford of Rugeley attended and treated him, the opposite was true: Cook's pain and symptoms lessened, and his health improved. The octogenarian physician was also a good friend of Palmer, and it was Palmer's assessments of Cook's condition that Bamford accepted and relied upon not only to formulate his own medications for the ailing young man, but also to fill out the death certificate when that tragic necessity arose mere days later. Bamford would be severely taken to task for his gullibility months afterwards, when Palmer went on trial for Cook's murder.

Palmer visited Cook at his hotel on Saturday morning, November 17, and brought in a cup of coffee to his sick friend, taking it from the hotel maid, Elizabeth Mills, who was just about to deliver it. Palmer himself handed it to Cook, who took a sip and was immediately seized with the terrible symptoms he'd experienced before. The young man remained bedbound for all of the weekend, while Dr. Palmer hovered solicitously about, bearing broth, cocoa, coffee, and other nourishments to Cook as well as the pills Palmer himself prepared for the patient. But Cook's condition did not improve. The prosecution at Palmer's subsequent trial maintained that the pills—as well as the coffee, cocoa, broth, and other foods that Palmer handled—

had been laced with poison to make sure that Cook remained too ill to look after his money.

On Monday, the 19th, Palmer repaired to London, ostensibly to pick up the residue of Cook's race winnings on behalf of his ailing comrade. But as soon as he'd gotten Cook's winnings into his possession, Palmer immediately appropriated the money and dispersed it to pay down his own menacing debts. He returned to London that night—in time to devise and give to Cook another pill of his own making.

It was to come out later, in controversial testimony at Palmer's trial, that as soon as he'd reached Rugeley at about nine on the night of the 19th, he'd gone to one Mr. Salt's chemist shop and obtained from Newton, the shop's assistant and one of the doctor's cronies, three grains of strychnine. At the time of purchase on the 19th, Palmer avoided signing the poison book. In another conversation with Newton, the doctor had also wanted to know how much strychnine it would take to destroy a dog. If Newton was correct, Palmer had the substance in his possession in plenty of time to have used it in concocting a strychnine-laced pill, which, purportedly, he gave to Cook at about ten-thirty that night. Some hours after taking Palmer's capsule, Cook's screams of pain woke the entire establishment of the Talbot Arms. When the other inhabitants rushed to his aid, he was writhing and tossing in terrible pain and convulsions—but by the morning of Tuesday, the 20th, Cook seemed much better though still exhausted. Palmer, though, had been ominously busy that morn: he had gone to another local chemist and surreptitiously purchased six more grains of strychnine.

Early on the night of Tuesday, November 20, Palmer, Dr. Bamford, and Dr. William Henry Jones—Cook's own personal physician from his home town—were consulting in the patient's room about the young man's illness. Though Cook declared he wanted no more medications, Palmer and Bamford left for Bamford's office to pick up pills the octogenarian had prepared for Palmer to administer to Cook that night. Palmer then surprised the older physician by requesting that he inscribe the directions on the pillbox. Etiquette required that the attending physician—Palmer—make the necessary inscriptions for prescribed medications, but the obliging Bamford yielded once more to another of Palmer's odd requests. Dr. Palmer kept the medications in his home and his sole possession for three quarters of an hour before taking them to Cook's room, and for some reason ostentatiously drew Dr. Jones's attention to Dr. Bamford's handwriting on the box, commenting on how firm it was for a man of Bamford's advanced years. The prosecution would later say that this prepared the way to make Bamford a scapegoat should the need arise: Palmer could claim that he had no hand in preparing the pill, and that due to his advanced age the 80-year-old Bamford had mistakenly included a lethal poison in the make-up of the medication.

At about ten-thirty, Cook, though obviously unwilling, was finally persuaded at Palmer's insistence to ingest the medicine. An hour and a half later at midnight, Jones was roused from sleep by piercing screams from Cook's bed. The young man was suffering another horrendous attack, and begged Jones to send for Palmer. He managed to say that he felt he was about to be as deathly ill as the night before. True to his premonitions, Cook's body went into fearful paroxysms, his lips drawn back in a ghastly semblance of a grin. Incredibly, his body arched convulsively to form a rigid bow, with only his head and heels touching the bed. Throughout the ordeal Cook was lucid enough at intervals to communicate with Dr. Jones and the rest of the household who had gathered helplessly in his room, startled from sleep once more by Cook's agonized screams, but again unable to ease his suffering. Dr. Palmer arrived at the scene, surprisingly fully clad. According to Dr. Jones's later testimony at the trial, Palmer "made the remark 'I never dressed so quickly in my life'" (Knott 45). It would be inferred that Palmer hadn't undressed at his home at all—awaiting the word he knew would soon come, the summons to rush over and attend to Cook's recrudescent attacks. As the seizures continued, Cook requested to be turned over so as to be able to breathe. Within a few minutes of uttering these words, the tormented young man breathed his last. It had taken only a quarter of an hour from Cook's first outcry that night to the drawing of his last breath.

In the next days following the young man's death, Palmer showed an overbearing haste in wanting to get the corpse buried as soon as possible, despite having no authority to do so. The sudden arrival of Cook's stunned but capable stepfather, however, put an end to the doctor's interferences. William Stevens grieved for his son, but he was also a hardheaded man of sense. He asked to see Cook's betting book, which would have recorded the entire sum that Cook had won, and therefore the amount of money that should have been among his effects. Stevens also began to insist on a postmortem: he suspected murder, and suspected Palmer of committing it to co-opt Cook's funds—especially after no appreciable traces of Cook's cash winnings or his betting book were ever found, in spite of a thorough search of the Talbot Arms.

The postmortem was duly conducted, but practically under siege conditions. Palmer did all he dared to sabotage the proceedings and to compromise Cook's remains, but in spite of his overt and bizarre attempts, the organs were at last delivered to London's premier toxicologist of the time, Dr. Alfred Swaine Taylor. No doubt to Palmer's short-lived relief, Taylor found no signs of strychnine despite exhaustive tests of the remains. At the inquest, however, Taylor testified to extrapolating strychnine poisoning as the undoubted cause of Cook's death. There were also too many other telltale irregularities related to Cook's demise, and Palmer's probable role in it, to ignore. The inquest found that Cook had been slain by strychnine, and went further: it also found that Palmer was the slayer. William Palmer was then officially charged with the murder of John Parsons Cook.

The doctor's subsequent arrest and trial, along with revelations of other heinous crimes attributed to him, earned his case the designation of "the Crime of the Century." Several past deaths, sudden or strange, that had occurred in Palmer's proximity but had been unremarked at the time, took on sinister new meaning in hindsight. The supposed victims were "persons whose death would yield Palmer monetary gain [and who] died one after the other with monotonous regularity. Yet it was taken for granted. Nobody questioned Palmer..." ("Rugeley Poisoner" 19). These appalled speculations, combined with the shocking allegations of the Cook case, earned the suddenly infamous doctor not one but two sinister appellations: "The Rugeley Poisoner" and "Prince of Poisoners." Explosive, sensational news coverage of his suspected transgressions electrified the nation. As one news account deliriously put it, "The interest excited by this case is unparalleled in the annals of our criminal jurisprudence. It has absorbed public curiosity almost to the exclusion of all other topics" ("Rugeley Poisoning"). In fact, Palmer's notoriety grew so great that it forced acknowledgment that he could never receive a fair trial in Staffordshire. In response, Parliament quickly passed the landmark Central Criminal Court Act 1856, colloquially known as "Palmer's Act." The Act gave Palmer—and thereafter any British subject accused of a crime outside of London's Central Criminal Court's jurisdiction—the right nonetheless to a trial at the Central Criminal Court, if there was little chance of empaneling an unbiased local jury.

Palmer's case was then duly heard at London's "Old Bailey"—nickname of the Central Criminal Court—beginning May 14, 1856. The prosecution brought compelling circumstantial evidence against the doctor, including his bold, overt attempts to get his hands on every bit of Cook's winnings, and the singularly ill-advised, conspiratorial letters written to his personal friend the coroner, offering money and inducements for dismissing foul play charges at the inquest. After a sensational two-week formal trial where graphic testimony about Cook's dying convulsions and arched body—along with Taylor's insistence that only strychnine could have produced those specific symptoms—helped convince jurors of Palmer's culpability, the doctor was found guilty and sentenced to death on May 27, 1856. On June 14, 1856, that sentenced was carried out when Palmer was hanged at Stafford Prison before a crowd of over 30,000 raucous spectators.

## *The Mysterious Affair at Styles*

*The Mysterious Affair at Styles*, Agatha Christie's first detective novel, was created for the most part in 1916; but the untried, unknown author's work was shunted from publisher to publisher until The Bodley Head took a chance on it in 1920. *Styles* introduced Hercule Poirot to the world: the inimitable, dapper little Belgian detective who became known for exerting his "little grey cells" to solve the fictional crimes concocted by his ingenious creator. The tale also featured the first of several recurring appearances in Christie's works by Poirot's sidekick, Arthur Hastings, and by Scotland Yard's Chief Inspector James Japp. The novel deals with both the murder-by-poisoning of wealthy, high-handed matron Emily Inglethorp, and with Poirot's brilliant unraveling of the clever mystery. The plot involves the initial example of a now-familiar Christie device: the closed circle of suspects. Suspicion touches virtually every member of Mrs. Inglethorp's household—family members, servants, companions, visitors—nearly all of whom had open or secret opportunity to provide the elderly matriarch with a fatal dose. Nearly all of them, too, harbored the more or less obvious motive of hope for monetary gain.

*The Mysterious Affair at Styles* enthusiastically presents a profusion of characters, encounters, misunderstandings, and clues, together with a tight sequence of simultaneous or misconstrued events that spill around—and over—each other, contributing to a perception that Christie's first novel is over-full and over-complex. Yet, although the story's exposition lacks the clarity and smoothness that would later mark her works, nearly every oddity and circumstance in this maiden effort is scrupulously presented to the reader, and brilliantly elucidated by Poirot at the conclusion.

Christie's tale is set in England during the height of World War I—or the "Great War," as it was then known. The crime takes place in a grand manor situated in Essex, marking Christie's first venture into golden-age, country-house mysteries. As the story opens, Hastings, the tale's narrator, had been wounded in Western Front action. A chance meeting with old acquaintance John Cavendish resulted in Cavendish's inviting Hastings to spend his sick leave recuperating at Styles Court, the Cavendish family's imposing estate in the village of Styles St. Mary.

As they reminisced about the youthful holidays Hastings had spent at Styles, John revealed that his septuagenarian stepmother Emily had three months earlier met, and then subsequently married, a much younger man, one Alfred Inglethorp. The family wealth was Emily's to control absolutely. The long-deceased father of John and his brother Lawrence had died a wealthy man, but, having been in life completely under the thumb of his masterful second spouse, had left the bulk of his riches to her instead of to the sons by his first marriage. Even Styles, although it would come to John in due course, belonged to Emily for her lifetime. The Cavendish brothers had resented being dependent on their stepmother, though John had been the beneficiary of her will before she met Inglethorp. Emily, however, had a frequent habit of changing her will, and the brothers feared that on her death Alfred Inglethorp would inherit the money they deemed rightfully theirs.

The horrors and realities of war do not impinge very much on the narrative of *Styles*, but the storyline does indeed acknowledge its existence. The war had forced economies and privations on everyone, and members of the Styles household had found it sensible to reside under one roof and to do whatever else they could do to help the war effort on the home front. This included saving paper at Styles—a circumstance forcing two separate situations that would later guide Poirot to inspired deductions about the murder: the first involving a valuable clue to a missing document; the second revealing a shocking blueprint for murder.

John and his wife Mary, as well as the unmarried Lawrence, lived at Styles with Emily and her new spouse. Much as the situation chafed, there was no denying that living at Styles relieved the brothers of the necessity to support themselves. Moreover, both brothers were now effectively penniless and in debt, although each had previously qualified for a proper occupation. Lawrence had trained as a doctor but instead now chose to pursue an as-yet-unrewarded writing career, just as his brother John had forsaken his profession as a barrister for the life of a country gentleman. Two other persons, unrelated to the family, also resided at Styles. Cynthia Murdoch, orphaned young daughter of an old friend of Mrs. Inglethorp, dwelled there reliant on the generosity of its charity-minded matriarch. Emily's devoted companion Evelyn Howard also made her home at the manor. She was outsized, outspoken, bighearted and gruff-voiced, and was affectionately known to the family as "Evie." The manor's servants included the equally devoted parlormaid Dorcas and the housemaid Annie, whose recollections of fateful events would later play a major role in pointing Poirot to the shocking truth behind Mrs. Inglethorp's slaying. Each and every one of these actors of the piece would have his or her part to play in both creating and resolving the life-and-death drama that waited in the offing.

Besides the thorny issue of Emily's remarriage, other disharmonies disturbed the routine tenor of existence at Styles—a fact that Hastings sensed as soon as he arrived at the manor. Still, there was no getting away from the fact that the main focus of uneasiness and ill will in the atmosphere remained centered on Alfred Inglethorp. Strangely, Inglethorp seemed the only one oblivious to the barely concealed wariness or contempt that the inhabitants of Styles—except for his wife—exhibited towards him. Hastings himself took an instant dislike to the man, finding him unnaturally wooden and out of place, with a startlingly improbable black beard and gold-rimmed pince-nez that gave him an even more unreal appearance. However, Hastings found other individuals in or about Styles Court to be much more congenial. He liked Lawrence and Cynthia, and was somewhat smitten by the beautiful, mysteriously intense Mary Cavendish. But he took a rooted aversion to a constant visitor to the manor: Dr. Bauerstein, who often left his abode in the village to venture out to Styles. Bauerstein, an internationally famous toxicologist, seemed somehow out of place in that bucolic corner of the world. He also sported a beard much like Inglethorp's, which made it easy for Hastings to dislike him even more.

Christie brings readers to the novel's principal crime via a series of events in July marked by their significant dates and times, beginning with Hastings' arrival at Styles on July 5. On the July 6 evening after Hastings' arrival, a momentous upheaval occurred in the manor's household. Evie and Emily had quarreled bitterly about Alfred Inglethorp, with Evie flatly warning her friend that she was an "old fool" being taken advantage of by her husband, who was, as gossip had it, having an undoubted affair with Mrs. Raikes, the good-looking young wife of a village farmer. Alfred Inglethorp, Evie had bluntly declared, was only after Emily's money, and "would as soon murder her as look at her" (Christie, *Mysterious* 24). This was too much for the affronted Emily, who immediately ordered her companion off the premises. An equally angry Evie promptly packed her bags. But, alone for a minute with Hastings before leaving, she surprised and flustered him by suddenly adjuring him to keep watch over her friend Emily: Alfred Inglethorp, she said, was not the only one victimizing the old lady—almost all of the individuals in the household were "sharks" as well, out for what they could get of Emily Inglethorp's money. Her departure left a strangely bereft feeling over the house, as if its commonsense and stabilizing mainstay had been suddenly wrenched away.

On Tuesday, July 17, ten days after the disconcerting exit of Evelyn Howard, tragedy was preparing to strike the household at Styles Court. Mrs. Inglethorp was recovering from tiring community-minded exertions of Monday, July 16, the day before; she was quite unaware that cold-blooded murder had now marked her out in relentless earnest. Nor had Hastings, or other unsuspecting inhabitants of the manor, any inkling of the turmoil that was shortly to engulf them all. In fact, the day began as pleasantly and as routinely for them as any other that summer: Emily had returned briskly to her charitable pursuits; and that sunny afternoon, Hastings and Lawrence had visited Cynthia and toured her dispensary. There, an unusually sociable Lawrence showed a mild doctorly interest in the poisons cabinet, and the two men capped off their visit by sharing a "cheery tea" with Cynthia before accompanying her, near the four o'clock hour, back to Styles.

On the way to Styles they stopped in the village, where Hastings literally bumped into an old friend at the local post office—the celebrated former Belgian police detective, Hercule Poirot. The little man embraced Hastings with glad fervor, overjoyed to meet again a comrade from happier days. Poirot and Hastings had become acquainted in Belgium, and Hastings had been so impressed with the little man's sleuthing prowess that he'd developed a yen to become a detective himself. The war had forced many Belgians to seek temporary havens in England, and Emily Inglethorp magnanimously provided housing in Styles St. Mary for seven of the displaced refugees; Poirot was one of their number.

Witnesses' versions of the next several encounters at Styles would go far, when the time came, toward steering Poirot to the method behind the murder of Emily Inglethorp. After Hastings, Lawrence, and Cynthia had chatted briefly with Poirot and had reached Styles towards five that evening, the trio had come upon an obviously upset Mrs. Inglethorp. She was heard to ask Dorcas if a fire had already been lit in the boudoir fireplace, as the parlormaid had earlier been instructed to do. Later on, Poirot would realize just how significantly that lighted fire—in the midst of a hot summer evening—would figure in the tragic events that followed. Moments later, close after that five o'clock hour, Hastings was on his way to a pre-supper tennis match with Cynthia when he passed Mrs. Inglethorp's window and caught snatches of an angry exchange within. Mary Cavendish was desperately demanding that her mother-in-law allow her to see some unnamed object, which Mrs. Inglethorp was pointedly refusing to do. Much later it would be revealed that Mary herself had also accidentally overheard a significant conversation a little earlier in the day; a conversation that led her to the argument with Mrs. Inglethorp—and to actions afterwards which would dramatically color ensuing events.

When Hastings caught up with Cynthia, he found her fairly agog with excitement. He learned that at around four that afternoon—an hour or so previously—there had been another overhearing of an agitated conversation that day. Dorcas had passed Mrs. Inglethorp's closed door and had picked up on an angry quarrel inside the lady's bedroom. The parlormaid had afterwards revealed what she'd heard to Cynthia, and now the girl was ready to share excited conjecture about that quarrel with Hastings. Dorcas had divulged that there'd been a "row" between Emily and Alfred Inglethorp, and Cynthia was eagerly hopeful that it heralded Inglethorp's imminent downfall and departure. The girl wondered what the quarrel could have been about; Hastings thought to himself that very likely it had involved insinuations Miss Howard had made before her departure—insinuations linking Alfred Inglethorp's name with that of the comely Mrs. Raikes. When Poirot later questioned Dorcas about the quarrel she'd overheard, the parlormaid would remember that the indignant Mrs. Inglethorp had vowed at that time that "no fear of scandal between husband and wife" (71) would keep her from doing what she had determined to do. Significantly, Dorcas would also recall to Poirot that Mrs. Inglethorp had repeated that phrase to her an hour later, near five o'clock when Dorcas had brought her distraught mistress a cup of tea. Emily had been clutching a paper that looked like a letter; she had looked sickly and shaken, and distractedly confided to Dorcas that she was in a turmoil of indecision: "scandal between husband and wife," she had said, "is a dreadful thing" (72). After the murder Hercule Poirot would bring to light the import of that repeated phrase as he unraveled the meanings behind July 17's tangled order of events.

Supper was at seven thirty that fateful night of July 17, and the sequence of activities attending the meal and its aftermath were minutely gone into during the subsequent murder investigation. For Poirot, several meaningful timepoints became markers on which he based his conclusions about the family's movements, and thereafter his conclusions about the case. Along with the tangible but puzzling clues he unearthed, the importance of these activities became threads he employed to weave the random strands of the murder into a right-side-up and coherent whole.

Mrs. Inglethorp had continued nervous and upset at the meal, leaving the table early and abruptly. Near eight o'clock, she requested Mary to send a cup of coffee to her in her chambers and retreated to her boudoir. The coffee was ultimately delivered to her by Alfred Inglethorp and would come to be suspected of containing the lethal dose of strychnine that killed the mistress of Styles.

The timeline to death marched inexorably on. At five in the morning, when late night July 17 was becoming the small hours of July 18, Hastings found himself being urgently shaken out of slumber by an anxious Lawrence Cavendish. His stepmother was ill, Lawrence said; she was in serious distress in her locked bedroom, and no one was able to get in to help her. The ensuing events seemed to happen with nightmare swiftness and ineluctability. Hours before, the household had retired for the night in its normal fashion, but by the time Hastings arrived at Emily Inglethorp's door, all of Styles' inhabitants had been startled from sleep by her outcries and had now gathered outside that door, listening helplessly to the sounds of distress within. They had quickly sent for Emily's personal physician, Dr. Wilkins; but by the time they finally broke the locked door down, the physician had not yet arrived. Rushing into the room, the group espied Mrs. Inglethorp on her bed, exhausted from the seizures which were just subsiding as they crowded around the bedside. At that moment she was able to gasp out a few breathless words of apology and to say that she was now better—but almost immediately a new wave of seizures overwhelmed her, sending her into throes of agonizing and powerful convulsions. At one point the ferocious paroxysms saw her body arched so powerfully that only her head and heels were in contact with the bed.

Just then Dr. Bauerstein suddenly materialized in the doorway; his eyes riveted on the figure contorted on the bed. In those fleeting but intense few moments, Mrs. Inglethorp stared at him, uttered the words

"Alfred—Alfred—," and then dropped back lifelessly onto the bed. Bauerstein bounded in to attempt reviving her just as Dr. Wilkins finally hurried onto the scene—but it was apparent to the shocked witnesses in the room that Mrs. Inglethorp was beyond medical help: the matriarch of Styles Court was suddenly and frighteningly dead.

Bauerstein explained his unexpected presence, fully dressed at that very late-night hour, by saying that he'd happened to be passing Styles' gates when he'd learned of the commotion inside and of the urgent clamor to get hold of Dr. Wilkins. Now somberly taking Wilkins aside, Bauerstein confided to him that he was convinced that Mrs. Inglethorp had died of poisoning: he hinted at strychnine since the symptoms he'd witnessed proclaimed it; the death was therefore a case for the authorities. Wilkins scoffed at the toxicologist's melodramatic reading of Mrs. Inglethorp's demise, but nevertheless agreed to a postmortem. Hastings, already certain that Mrs. Inglethorp had been murdered, urged the Cavendish brothers to bring in Poirot to investigate. Despite Lawrence's vehement opposition, arguing that murder was out of the question, John reluctantly decided to do so. Before hurrying off to advise Poirot of the tragic tidings, Hastings rushed to the manor's library and found "a medical book which gave a description of strychnine poisoning" (52).

Poirot willingly joined the investigation into the sudden and unsettling death of his benefactress. The postmortem that Bauerstein had demanded took place that very night of July 18—and proved unequivocally that Mrs. Inglethorp's death was in fact due to strychnine poisoning. John had earlier that day notified Evie Howard by wire of her friend's death. Grief-stricken and angry, she had set out for Styles at once, arriving with loud and bitter accusations of Alfred Inglethorp on her lips. The entire household at Styles apparently joined her in that conviction: Alfred Inglethorp had obviously murdered his wife to inherit her money. And he'd boldly done so by poisoning her coffee prior to leaving on the night of her death.

And soon it was obvious that Scotland Yard believed it too. Inglethorp himself, strangely obtuse, appeared to be the only one unaware of his imminent danger of arrest and ultimate execution for murder. The man obstinately refused to provide authorities with the alibi that he hinted he possessed—giving the impression that it involved an intrigue with Mrs. Raikes—and his lips must remain sealed. But Poirot found Inglethorp's behavior baffling and worked to counter its effects.

Tracing the trail of Emily's cup of coffee was of primary importance in the investigation. Alfred Inglethorp had handed his wife her cup of coffee that evening before her death; therefore, the brew—and Inglethorp—remained primary suspects. After supper that night, minutes after eight o'clock, Mary had asked Cynthia to take Mrs. Inglethorp's coffee to her, but

Alfred had intervened, saying that he would take the coffee to his wife instead. He then filled a cup himself, and took it out of the room. Lawrence also left the dining area in Inglethorp's wake. Unexpectedly, Dr. Bauerstein appeared at their door and was invited to join the family for coffee. Mrs. Inglethorp at that point called to Cynthia to bring her "dispatch," or documents, case to her. That case, which Emily habitually used to lock away all her important papers, would shortly come into play as an essential spur to Poirot's Sherlockian feats of deduction about Emily Inglethorp's movements and motives just prior to her slaying. At that eight o'clock hour of the 17th, then, Emily was clearly seen holding her unsampled cup of coffee in her hand. Consequently, nearly every member of the household, as well as visitor Dr. Bauerstein, was present between seven-thirty and a little after eight—the time that Emily asked for and received her coffee. Moreover, the cup had afterwards rested on a hall table for a short space of time, easily accessible by anyone in the household; therefore, nearly all of Styles' occupants at that time had the opportunity of poisoning her coffee at one time or another. These and other accumulated facts afterwards became matters of extreme interest as Poirot worked to determine a true step by step progression of events toward the slaying.

On Friday, July 20, the inquest was held at the village inn, the Styles Arms. In sensational inquest testimony, young Mr. Mace, the very new assistant at a Styles St. Mary chemist's shop, identified Alfred Inglethorp as the person who'd acquired strychnine from him just a short time before Mrs. Inglethorp's poisoning. Inglethorp had used the excuse that he needed it to get rid of a dog, and had even signed the poison book with his own name. Investigating authorities, in the persons of Scotland Yard's Superintendent Summerhaye and Detective Inspector Japp, arrived on the scene ready to arrest Inglethorp on the available evidence of his guilt. He had, after all, bought the poison; he'd given Emily the coffee; she had made her will in his favor even before marriage. Therefore, as the one who had the most to gain, he figured as the likely slayer. Despite the accumulated evidence, however, Poirot's instinctive reaction was that something was out of kilter. He therefore advised his law enforcement associates to proceed slowly, and before Inglethorp could be charged and tried for murder, succeeded in holding them off.

Apparently that restraint had been a fortunate choice by the authorities, for suddenly Scotland Yard had reason to turn its official attentions from Alfred Inglethorp to John Cavendish. The motive advanced for John was the same motive that had been advanced for Inglethorp: murder for gain. Investigation extrapolated that John had argued bitterly with Emily, but had been at pains to hide the fact. He was deeply in debt, and it was known that Emily had refused to increase his allowance. It was reasoned that after the quarrel with John, Emily Inglethorp had actually made a new will in Alfred Inglethorp's favor. Officials alleged that John Cavendish had killed his stepmother and burned the new will. It had been he who had disguised himself as Inglethorp to obtain strychnine from the local chemists. He was easily able to fool Mr. Mace, who was unfamiliar with the inhabitants of Styles Court. Items John had used for that imposture—fake pince-nez glasses and a fake beard much like Inglethorp's real one—had actually been ferreted out at Styles where John allegedly tried to conceal them. And a bottle of strychnine from that same shop was found hidden in his room. The collected facts pointed one way: toward the guilt of John Cavendish.

The mass of pat evidence against the elder Cavendish brother made Poirot as uneasy as the evidence against Inglethorp had done earlier. So did the plenitude of strychnine sources that suddenly erupted in the case. From the moment Dr. Bauerstein had insinuated strychnine on the night of Emily's death, that poison in one form or another seemed to crop up everywhere. There had even been strychnine in the daily tonic that Emily took: Lawrence grasped at this fact to argue strenuously the theory that the medicine had killed her, thus making her death not a murder but a terrible accident. However, circumstances and medical testimony showed that her regular tonic was a harmless concoction. Alfred Inglethorp—and then John—had been accused of buying the poison from the village chemist. It had been found among John's effects. Several individuals at or around Styles also had access to strychnine, and any of them might have had motive, means, or opportunity of one sort or another to dislike or kill Mrs. Inglethorp, including Lawrence Cavendish, Cynthia Murdoch—and even Dr. Bauerstein.

Hercule Poirot conducted his own meticulous—not to say finicky—approach to the case. If a new will had indeed been written, why, then, had the document been subsequently and deliberately destroyed? And by whom? The answer to these perplexing questions, Poirot knew, would be the key to the whole seemingly impenetrable conundrum. Other clues came into play as Poirot strove to unravel the complex mystery: the dregs of a cup of cocoa, for example, had been discovered in Emily's room. Had that cup contained the poison? Poirot had also come across Emily's dispatch case, and found it had been forced open. Why? What had it contained, and who had abstracted its contents? He'd also come upon a harmless-seeming cardboard medicine box—obviously an empty container for the bromide sleeping powders which Mrs. Inglethorp was in the habit of taking—but very strangely, there was a peculiarity in the box's labeling. Again, why?

Poirot worked feverishly to crack the frustrating case. For the fastidious and detail-minded detective, there existed far too many eccentric clues and unexplained oddities in the affair, and throughout the hectic investigation, he'd clung to his own creed of order and method to see his way clear.

The solution to the crime, he knew, would have to provide satisfactory answers to the puzzles and loose ends that pervaded the mystery. He'd been certain that every item connected with the slaying of Emily Inglethorp must have had meaning, and order besides. And, in his impressive debut effort, he dazzlingly proves this to be true.

While John Cavendish underwent the ordeal of his sensational trial for murder, Poirot toiled nonstop behind the scenes in his quest to find the true solution to the case—whether that truth led to John Cavendish's guilt or not. And when a chance remark from Hastings spurred the stymied detective to a new view of things, everything fell into place. Breathlessly, at the eleventh hour, he unearthed the cleverly hidden key to the mystery and an even cleverer outline for murder—just in time to thwart the success of a cold-blooded and chillingly ingenious enterprise.

In the very first of her trademark "gatherings of the suspects" at the story's conclusion, Agatha Christie carefully allows her Belgian sleuth to clarify the implication—or lack of it—behind the freely-dispensed clues and red herrings strewn throughout *The Mysterious Affair at Styles*. The purposes of the summation gathering—to name the surprise malefactor; to explain the motives and workings behind the crime, and to showcase the inimitable skill of the tale's detective—are all fully realized in Christie's first venture into this type of exposition. The "closed circle of suspects" at the story's beginning has itself come full circle, having evolved at the story's end into the "gathering of the suspects" and the explication of events. By the conclusion of the novel, readers learn, among other things, the roles that Emily Inglethorp's coffee and cocoa played in the unfolding story, and how misunderstandings regarding certain overheard conversations drastically affected the mystery. Poirot also adroitly details the significance of the burned document, of the letter kept in Emily's dispatch case, and of another altered missive. He clears up the confusion wrought by Dr. Bauerstein's enigmatic presence; the significance of the beards in the tale; and the clever psychological import behind each use by Emily Inglethorp of the phrase "scandal between husband and wife." All in all, *The Mysterious Affair at Styles*, despite its moments of novice-author coltishness, successfully heralds the stream of brilliant performances that will ensue in decades to come—from both Hercule Poirot, the highly engaging creation, and from Agatha Christie, his highly inventive creator.

## Dr. William Palmer + *The Mysterious Affair at Styles*

Several powerful aspects of the William Palmer affair correspond with important facets of the narrative in *The Mysterious Affair at Styles*. Even in her first detective work, Christie demonstrates clever mastery of storytelling, embedding in her tale several striking patterns embodied in the complex Palmer case. The technique communicates an energy of underlying real-life validity to patterns of her own original work of make-believe.

In *Styles*, Mrs. Inglethorp's poisoner chose strychnine to do the deed, as had the Victorian era's most notorious killer: suspected mass poisoner Dr. William Palmer of Rugeley. Desperately in need of funds, the high-living Palmer coolly decided in 1855 to slay his young gambling and racing associate, John Parsons Cook, in order to get hold of Cook's considerable cash from recent winnings at the horse races.

Palmer committed murder to claw his way out of a pit of inescapable debt brought on by his massive losses on the turf, hoping thus to avoid the unforgiving penalties of social disgrace and imprisonment which, in the harsh Victorian culture, would inevitably accompany his downfall. His story is a nightmarish history of murder. The respected, once-wealthy doctor had left the practice of medicine to pursue racing, gambling, and philandering. Cook, on coming into an inheritance, had also given up his career as a solicitor to live a life of leisure. In *Styles*, two principal characters also abandon their professions to follow more congenial occupations. The first, a prime suspect in the crime, had also left his position as a lawyer for a more leisurely life. In addition, he, too, was also in deep debt for which he could find no ready cure—except, perhaps, murder. The second personage also left his medical career for another pursuit; these two fictional circumstances echo the factual circumstances involving Cook and Palmer in real life.

Palmer's dismal tale began in November 1855, after he and his crony Cook had attended the Shrewsbury Handicap horse races together. Cook, after winning big at Shrewsbury, suddenly fell uncustomarily ill after accepting a brandy from his friend Palmer, who had suffered drastic, irretrievable losses at the track. Nevertheless, Cook traveled next day, November 14, with Palmer back to the doctor's hometown of Rugeley, registering at the Talbot Arms, just across the way from Palmer's own home. In *The Mysterious Affair at Styles*, the name of the local inn, the Styles Arms, would recall the inn of the true-life Palmer case.

In the true-crime affair, Dr. Palmer was a constant visitor to his friend at the inn, especially to offer medical treatment when Cook's recently-arising bouts of sickness arose again—oftentimes after the young man had received coffee, cocoa, food, or medicine from the hand of Dr. Palmer. Within the pages of Christie's tale, coffee, tea, and medicine also figured largely as suspected means of delivering poison to the novel's victim. Christie's novel also presents a foregrounded, extremely dense timeline leading to Emily Inglethorp's death, especially for the dates of July 16, 17, and 18. This matches the extremely significant, activity-packed dates in mid–November 1855, which led up to the death by strychnine of John Parsons Cook. On November 15 Cook was seized with a most virulent attack, a strange and sudden illness that incapacitated him for a day or so—this after drinking coffee that Palmer had brought to him. Despite the "attentions" of Palmer, and the additional, well-meaning treatments of Palmer's aged friend Dr. William Bamford of Rugeley, the young man was forced to take to his bed—and in a very few days was dead.

Christie tellingly echoed the manner of Cook's dying in her own fictional scenario for the death of Emily Inglethorp. John Parsons Cook had died in his bedroom at the Talbot Arms. He'd been jolted awake by sudden agony in the middle of the night of November 20, 1855, and was soon plunged into horrific convulsions and other tormenting symptoms. In a matter of a quarter of an hour from his first cry, he had perished. The scene was witnessed and attended by several inmates of the hotel: friends and servants who'd been suddenly startled from repose by his terrible outcries. They had then run to his room to aid him, but were helpless to do so as he perished dramatically before their very eyes. Palmer had been hastily fetched from his home, but it seemed as if he'd been strangely on the alert and ready for the call: he'd been suspiciously awake, fully dressed, and on the spot near the Talbot Arms at the post-midnight hour that Cook was racked by the paroxysms of his final, fatal attack.

The scene of Cook's demise is essentially mirrored in parallel fashion in Christie's novel. Mrs. Inglethorp dies in convulsions in the middle of the night, in her bed at Styles Court. Like Cook, she, too, had been wakened by terrible convulsions and severe pain. The scene is witnessed and attended by inmates of the house: family and servants who'd been suddenly startled from slumber by her outcries. They had rushed to her bedroom, but were helpless to aid her, and she dies in a matter of moments before their very eyes. Strangely, Dr. Bauerstein, a famous London toxicologist, suddenly appears on the scene, and is at once struck by the nature of Mrs. Inglethorp's telltale paroxysms. Even more strangely Dr. Bauerstein had been, like Palmer, suspiciously awake, fully dressed, and on the spot at the post-midnight hour that Mrs. Inglethorp woke up to her fatal attack—circumstances that placed him in a highly suspicious light.

At Palmer's murder trial, Cook's hometown physician, Dr. William Henry Jones, gave testimony that quickly identified strychnine as the agent of Cook's death. Jones testified that Cook "was suddenly seized with violent convulsions ... his body was so twisted or bowed that if I had placed it upon the back it would have rested upon the head and the feet" (*Most Extraordinary Trial* 26). Both the prosecution and defense at trial would demand repeated recitals of these disturbing manifestations from witnesses, each faction seeking to use the witnesses' descriptions to sway the jury to that faction's interpretation of them. In *Styles*, her maiden detective-story effort, Christie describes Mrs. Inglethorp's decease with more specificity and graphic detail than she would usually employ in her later writings, emphasizing the convulsions which arched Mrs. Inglethorp's body in the characteristic way that attends poisoning by strychnine. Much as Dr. Jones had delineated Cook's symptoms, Hastings reports of Mrs. Inglethorp's demise that "the convulsions were of a violence terrible to behold.... A final convulsion lifted her from the bed, until she appeared to rest upon her head and her heels, with her body arched in an extraordinary manner" (Christie, *Mysterious* 46).

In the real-life Palmer saga Cook's bereft stepfather William Stevens, suspicious of the sudden death and especially of Palmer's part in it, forced a postmortem on Cook's remains. In the fictional world of *Styles*, Dr. Bauerstein also forces a postmortem examination on Emily's remains when his suspicions lead him to insist on an official autopsy. The inquiry into Mrs. Inglethorp's dubious demise is held at the village inn, the Styles Arms; and the attendant sensationalism triggers massive and pervasive newspaper publicity. This echoes the unfolding scandal and inquiry into Cook's even more dubious but very real demise: the attendant scandal and its ever more gruesome revelations exploded on the national scene, providing an unprecedented flow of fodder for pervasively sensationalist news coverage throughout the country. An inquest was held in December 1855 at the Talbot Arms, the village inn where Cook had died.

The fact of Emily Inglethorp's fictional murder was irrefutably established by Christie from the first; interest was directed toward following Poirot's sleuthing journey to arriving at the true solution of "whodunit." Christie therefore provided a plentiful array of seemingly viable and likely suspects. In the aftermath of John Parsons Cook's real-world death, apprehensive Rugeley locals as well as city officials suspected right away that the young man had been murdered; but there was never a doubt for them as to who had committed it. The only difficulty lay in displaying sufficient cold, hard, reasonable proof of William Palmer's guilt in an English court of law— enough proof to convince an English jury of the doctor's culpability.

That "proof" was brought by Palmer's nemesis, Dr. Alfred Swaine Taylor, London's most eminent forensics analyst of the epoch. The famous toxicologist declared at both the inquest on Cook's death and at the later trial that he believed the young man to have died from the fatal effects of strychnine poisoning, despite the fact that his own analysis of Cook's remains had failed to detect the substance. Taylor never wavered in his insistence, even though others—including the elderly and naïve Rugeley medical man Dr. Bamford—were positing natural disease as cause of death. In *Styles*, Dr. Bauerstein is one of the "greatest authorities of the day on the subject of toxicology" (127), corresponding to the real-life Taylor. Bauerstein emulates

Dr. Taylor in holding adamantly to his own conviction that Mrs. Inglethorp died due to poisoning by strychnine, although others, including the lady's own somewhat gullible personal physician, Dr. Wilkins, stridently emphasize death due to natural causes. Wilkins' clueless assessment of the nature of Emily's death matches the true-life Dr. Bamford's obliviousness in the case of Cook's death.

There are other salient resonances between situations in the fictional *The Mysterious Affair at Styles* and in the true-crime Palmer case. Among them, missing documents and conspiratorial letters play large roles. In the Palmer affair, Cook's betting book and his money went missing immediately after his death. Finding either of these belongings—especially in Palmer's possession or vicinity—could well have illuminated the doctor's motive for murder, affording prosecutors surer and harder evidence, rather than mostly circumstantial proofs, in their drive to convict. But these items were never found. Similarly in Christie's work the sapient Poirot deduces a missing will—one which Emily Inglethorp had lately written. Because such a document could shed light on motive for murder, investigators search both Mrs. Inglethorp's rooms and the rest of Styles Court most assiduously—but the missing document is never found; and for a reason cleverly extrapolated by Poirot.

In the true-crime case, Palmer composed and posted a set of clandestine, conspiratorial letters which were, unfortunately for Palmer, nosed out by the prosecution and exposed at his trial. The extremely unwise missives revealed transgressions that added greatly to the weight of circumstantial evidence against the doctor. In addition, Palmer had sent letters just before Cook's death to Dr. Jones; letters which contained deliberately misleading information about Cook's illness and its causes. In the pages of *The Mysterious Affair at Styles*, a murderer also writes a clandestine conspiratorial letter which Poirot's astute investigation brings to light, revealing a stunning crime; while another letter, which had been altered to plant deliberately misleading information and thus protect a killer, is also exposed.

Another small but telling detail in Palmer's tale is echoed in *Styles*. An anomaly attends the labeling of a cardboard medicine box; the one containing the pills that Cook ingested on the night of his death. The receptacle bore a suggestively suspicious peculiarity: the instructions for taking the medication were not written in the hand of Dr. Palmer—and they should have been. In the fictional counterpart, Poirot discovers an intriguing cardboard box that had contained Mrs. Inglethorp's medicine; it, too, bears a suspicious peculiarity in its labeling, providing the detective with much suggestive food for thought.

William Palmer was tried for Cook's slaying beginning May 14, 1856. Stunning events unveiled at Palmer's inquest and trial hearings find resonance in several important facets of *The Mysterious Affair at Styles*. For example, at Palmer's trial a true sensation of the day occurred when Newton, assistant to local chemist Mr. Salt, belatedly and controversially revealed on the witness stand that he'd supplied strychnine to Palmer earlier on the night that Cook died. Newton further testified that he and Palmer had discussed what amount of strychnine it would take to poison a dog to death.

Christie in her novel delineates courtroom scenes where Mace, the local chemist's assistant, delivers the "sensation of the day" (137) during inquest testimony. The contrite young man reveals information that he, too, had withheld before: he had provided strychnine to a resident of Styles Court who was later deemed a prime murder suspect. The chemist's assistant also testifies that he and the suspect had talked of using strychnine to poison a dog.

While Christie never allows a doubt that Mrs. Inglethorp was murdered, and murdered by the use of strychnine, William Palmer's trial became an intense sparring match between the Crown and the defense, focused on two contending medical points of view. In fact, Cook's symptoms became "the battleground of the case" (Knott 11). The prosecution argued that the tetanic convulsions, Cook's ability to communicate verbally, and other manifestations attending Cook's death were irrefutably due to deliberate strychnine poisoning; the Palmer defense argued that the convulsions and other symptoms had been caused by natural disease—and that Cook had perished from natural disease alone. Each side therefore showcased, and argued extensively over, every minute aspect of the 15-minute ordeal which Cook experienced before he drew his last breath. Despite the circumstantial nature of the prosecution's case, it was Dr. Taylor's unshaken medical testimony asserting strychnine as the cause of Cook's death which carried the day. William Palmer was found guilty of Cook's murder, sentenced to death on May 27, 1856, and hanged on June 14, 1856.

In *The Mysterious Affair at Styles*, the victim's death from strychnine, complete with descriptions of the convulsions, Emily's ability to communicate with witnesses, and the "bowed" effect of the body, was also showcased. However, the sole question of the novel remained: who, among the possibilities, had deliberately poisoned Mrs. Inglethorp to death by deliberately-administered strychnine? In the pages of Christie's story, Scotland Yard decided on a culprit, who was duly put on trial. Poirot, on the other hand, as the novel's principal detective, was charged with the entertaining and engrossing task of proving out, for the reader's delectation, whether the authorities' choice had been the correct one—or if a cunning and startling twist on the solution lay in the offing. And this task, in his first appearance, the little Belgian detective carries out with the flair and uniqueness that would come to be familiar, if more refined, to Christie aficionados for many more tales to come.

## Chapter 2

# "La Femme Fatale"
## Madame Marguerite Steinheil and *The Murder on the Links*

Agatha Christie's third novel generates a very "French" feel: not only does most of the action of the murder mystery take place in France, but Christie invests many of the characterizations and actions of the story with her version of a very "Frenchified" sensibility—including motives for murder and revenge. She invokes elements of *le crime passionel*, although neither the inciting crime of the past nor the principal murder of the main plot can lay claim to being a true crime of passion. However, the "French feel" is justified: Christie based the tale on a scandalous true crime that had stirred all of France and much of Europe fifteen years before publication of *The Murder on the Links*. Many points of the murders involving the notorious Mme. Steinheil—"L'Affaire de l'Impasse Ronsin" or "L'Affaire Steinheil" as the events came to be known—were echoed in Agatha Christie's fictional account.

## Madame Marguerite Steinheil

In the early morning hours of May 31, 1908, Remy Couillard, servant of the French painter Adolphe Steinheil and his family, discovered the murdered bodies of Steinheil and of Steinheil's widowed mother-in-law, Emilie Japy. They had been brutally slain during the night at the family's Impasse Ronsin villa near Paris's rue Vaugirard. Both had died of strangulation. Steinheil was found on the floor of one room, thrown brutally back from a kneeling posture, seemingly garroted from behind by a ligature about his neck. An alpenstock—a staff with an iron-tipped head, used for mountain climbing—was discovered near the body. On a bed in a separate room, Mme. Japy had been asphyxiated when the wad of cotton-wool cloth that had been shoved into her mouth forced her dentures down her throat.

## Chapter 2. "La Femme Fatale"

The painter's 17-year-old daughter, Marthe, was fortunately away from home the night of May 30, visiting with relatives of Pierre Buisson, her fiancé; but Steinheil's wife Marguerite had slept in Marthe's bedchamber that night, and Couillard found her alive but tied down to her daughter's bed, apparently suffering from effects of prolonged terror, pain, and shock. When sufficiently recovered, Mme. Steinheil faltered out to summoned police an account of murderous interlopers who had overpowered, bound, gagged, and repeatedly threatened her. These appalling robbery-murders once more catapulted the affairs of the beautiful Marguerite Steinheil—fascinating cynosure of "All Paris"—for a second time in 10 years into the scorching glare of all-too-public social and political notoriety.

Marguerite-Jeanne Japy, called "Meg" by her intimates, was born into the family of wealthy industrialist Edouard Japy on April 16, 1869. Favored by her father, she was reared to regard herself as someone special. This treatment perhaps fostered the self-centered behavior that was to surface so tellingly later in her life—behavior which helped impel her into perilous situations, and which almost certainly aided her in surviving them. Meg married artist Adolphe Steinheil, who was some 20 years her senior, in 1890. A daughter, Marthe, was born of the marriage in 1891. There can be little doubt that Meg was socially ambitious from the outset, desiring to take her place in the ranks of *le Tout Paris*—All Paris; those who "mattered" in the sophisticated life of the vibrant French capital. She established a *salon* which was frequented by the socially prominent as well as the leading politicians and artists of the era: Emile Zola and Jules Massenet, among others, formed part of her coterie.

Another adherent of the charming Mme. Steinheil was Felix Faure, president of France's Third Republic from 1895 to 1899. He had become a central figure in the Dreyfus Affair: the controversial 1894 trial and conviction for treason of Jewish army officer Alfred Dreyfus. Unforeseen as it was at the time, this circumstance was later to become a matter of importance in the fortunes—and misfortunes—of the Steinheils.

Faure had refused to grant review of the Dreyfus Affair, even after findings of widespread perjury and anti–Semitism on the part of Dreyfus's accusers had set up a clamor for justice. Militantly nationalist and anti–Semitic factions of both the government and the country's press, who had actively fomented prejudice against Dreyfus, welcomed the conviction and imprisonment on Devil's Island; many of their compatriots, however, decried the injustice of both the charge and the verdict and campaigned vigorously for revision. Even after Zola's 1898 publication of *J'Accuse*—the famous indictment of the Dreyfus conviction, and the corruption and anti–Semitism behind it—had created a furor that helped to heighten the controversy to fever pitch, Faure and his nationalist regime resisted reopening and reviewing the case.

Dreyfus's principal persecutors had included Major Hubert Joseph Henry, and Major Ferdinand Walsin-Esterhazy—who was himself, in due course, found to have contrived false evidence and testimony against Dreyfus. Henry was also discovered to have withheld genuine exculpatory documents and to have forged falsely incriminating ones in the case. As relative truth finally emerged, lives and careers and reputations were destroyed: Esterhazy fled in panic to Belgium and then to England; Henry admitted his crimes and then committed suicide in August 1898. In the irresistible wake of that suicide, Dreyfus was retried in September 1899, and although again found guilty, was pardoned; a 1906 appeals court finally cleared him completely.

Felix Faure and Marguerite Steinheil had first met in 1897, when Adolphe Steinheil had secured a governmental contract as painter. Soon thereafter, the president and the painter's wife began a clandestine love affair. But their liaison was not to remain secret for long. When later events made it necessary to characterize their relationship, Meg had at first claimed that she and Faure had met only to hold "consultations" of a "political nature" at the presidential palace. During these consultations at the Palais de l'Élysée, she claimed that her only function was to offer political counsel to the president, as his confidante and one of his few trusted advisors. Marguerite sought to clarify and quash the issue by declaring repeatedly that, in her role of faithful presidential "consultant" and "confidante," she did indeed pay visits to the presidential palace that might seem surreptitious to outside observers, but she did so only to advise Faure on matters of state. These explanations of her visits, however, were never for a moment credited by palace staff or others in the know, either at the time the visits took place or later. Their worldly view of the truth of the matter was given unexpectedly dramatic credence on February 16, 1899.

On that date, during a daytime tryst with Mme. Steinheil in a private room of the Palais de l'Élysée itself, Faure suffered a massive seizure. Earlier that afternoon, Meg had slipped into the palace through a side door to visit the president, as was her wont; they had, as was also their custom, closeted themselves in a private room for the "consultation." Suddenly, staff members heard alarmed screams from Marguerite. They rushed in to find both Faure and Meg in states of undress and dishevelment that spoke of an interrupted sexual encounter, and the president of the republic *in extremis* on a couch. Faure died later that same day.

The true character of her encounters with Faure was now indisputably revealed, though Marguerite held desperately to her original assertions as long as she dared. Tabloid and opposition press, political opponents of Faure, and social enemies of Mme. Steinheil gleefully wallowed in the scandal, devising ribald puns and irreverent jokes about the tragic but embarrassingly compromising situation, and exploiting the near farcical circumstances of the president's inglorious demise to the full. Journalists pounced on the publicity bonanza, hounding Meg's every step, hungry for other titillating morsels and revelations. This was effectively a preview of things to come: though it could hardly be suspected in 1899, the circumstances of the president's death, and his involvement with the Dreyfus Affair, would come to figure prominently in the drama surrounding the murders of Adolphe Steinheil and Mme. Japy nearly 10 years later. The perceived link to these events would be Marguerite Steinheil.

In the wake of Faure's bizarre death the ensuing scandal branded Marguerite Steinheil a *courtisane intrigante*, a notorious woman whose façade of upper-class social propriety had been torn away, and her true nature bared for all to see. In the wake of this all-too-public disgrace, Adolphe Steinheil was described as "a man deep in depression who had thought of divorce from Meg in 1898 after the horrid finish of the affair with President Faure but who could not overcome his desperate love for her..." (Martin 55). In an attempt at salvaging her reputation just after the president's demise, Meg added embellishments to her story that included dramatic and impressive details meant to render her prior assertions more believable. The true reason for those meetings, she now claimed, was for the purpose of assisting Faure in writing his secret political memoirs, and in preparing other sensitive governmental and political papers which at all costs had to be kept confidential. The president was in fear of opposition spies, even within his own regime, and had given Meg the further confidential task, she said, of hiding these precious documents away and safeguarding them from his enemies. But the circumstances of the president's sudden death were too sensational, too amazingly scandalous, too portentous for the nation as a whole to be easily dismissed with contrived and highly-colored explanations for which there was no real evidence. Despite her efforts at deflecting censure, opportunistic accusations against the adulterous Meg quickly surfaced in newspapers across the social and political spectra. Anti-Marguerite consensus disbelieved her entirely, and consigned her manufacturing of apocryphal "writing sessions" with Faure to diversionary tactics, used by the scheming woman merely to cover her illicit relationship with the president. Some publications went so far as to charge Mme. Steinheil with the political murder of Faure: "'She was in the pay of the Dreyfusards'" raged Henri Rochefort, editor of the nationalist newspaper *La Patrie*, "'...and the Dreyfusards knew that so long as Faure lived there would be no Revision. So they commissioned the woman Steinheil, his mistress, to assassinate him'" (Macdonald 1107).

On the morning of May 31, 1908, however, the long-ago Faure episode was merely a vaguely-remembered and dormant backdrop to the terrible immediacy of the violent deaths, just the night before, of Mme. Steinheil's husband and her mother. The authorities and the media, barely confronted with these horrific new developments, had not yet had time to absorb them into connections with the old. In the late morning hours of that last day of May in 1908, for the few hours remaining before the press and the public would rouse their memories and begin to link the present shock with the shock of events past, Mme. Steinheil would hold center stage. The future course of the investigation was in her hands. Whatever she said or did at that moment would determine trend and focus from press, public, police, and politicians for at least an appreciable time to come. Marguerite was fully alive to the implications of her situation and when recovered enough from her ordeal to provide details, she was ready to meet the occasion in her own inimitable way.

Madame Steinheiil had a surreal and harrowing tale to tell police. She declared that she had been harshly wakened from sleep by marauders demanding money and household valuables. They had brutally and painfully gagged and trussed her. There had been four of the vicious intruders, all garbed in long black robes, like "Russian popes." There were three men and one woman. Madame Steinheil had not known of the fates of her husband and mother in their separate chambers, but had been put in sustained fear of her own life throughout. One of the three men wore a red beard while the other two were disguised with black beards. One of the intruders was a red-haired woman whom Marguerite had recognized, she said, as one of her husband's former models. The invaders were obviously bent on robbery—and murder as well: they threatened death if their demands were not met. The red-haired woman had urged her confederates to kill the terrified Marguerite, but one of the men, Marguerite said, took pity on the captive whom they mistook in the poorly lit room for the teenaged daughter of the house.

At first authorities had seemed to accept her explanation of events, but they had only concealed for the moment their skepticism of Mme. Steinheil's somewhat fantastical narrative. She had of course been besieged by the press from the moment that news of the murders reached the public: popular and factionalist newspapers not only bruited the current tragedy but also, inevitably, began raucously to recall her former connection with President Faure and his sensational demise. Meanwhile, her own current horror story was duly splashed across the headlines and columns of newspapers in France, Europe, and abroad.

Madame Steinheil was not unaware of her precarious situation as the days passed and no hint of the perpetrators she had described was ever traced. Her circumstantial descriptions of the marauders provided fodder for skeptical commentary from newspapers inside and outside of France. "Indeed," observed the *Auckland Star* with tongue-in-cheek restraint, "so precise is her description of all four [of the murderers] that the chief detective declares it to be worthy of M. Bertillon himself" ("Tragedy" p. 15).

The growing and overt or veiled hostility of the press and of public opinion were threat enough, but Marguerite also sensed the much more dangerous reticence that underlay the authorities' guarded reception of her story. It seemed clear to her that they suspected her of having something to do with the murders. Yet her account of the crimes had effectively kept officials and even much of the press at bay: though they may have disbelieved her story, they had no real proof of anything that could negate it.

She was in a fix. Journalists had seized hold of this new sensation surrounding the woman who had lent herself to so much profitable copy in the past, and had practically camped out at her homes, fairly imprisoning herself and Marthe wherever they tried to take refuge. Popular and factionalist press seemed hourly to grow bolder, resurrecting with a vengeance her former connection with President Faure and with his compromising death. These segments of the press had no hesitation in splashing their contempt and accusations across the headlines. Recrudescent nationalistic elements took up their old war cries to fan the flames of public outrage once more against Meg, reviving accusations that she had poisoned Faure at the instigation of his "Dreyfusard" enemies. The rapacious singularity of press persecution and intrusion that Marguerite Steinheil suffered during the entire affair prompted the *Times of London* to protest. "If, in England during a criminal trial," ran its report, "one-hundredth part of the articles which have appeared in the Steinheil case had been published, those who were responsible would soon have been put under lock and key" ("Steinheil Case" 5).

The days continued to pass since the crimes had rocked the peace of Impasse Ronsin. Police investigations failed to turn up anything tangible enough to move the inquiry forward. Authorities may have disbelieved her version of events, but Mme. Steinheil was still their only witness to the deeds, their only real lead; a state of affairs that proved a two-edged sword for both police and for Marguerite herself: they were both stuck with her story. The authorities were forced to wait it out in the hope that something would break; Marguerite, it would seem, had only to outwait the police. That course might have been the wise one to take, but Marguerite Steinheil was not known for her wise decisions. As she felt the threat of suspicion closing in on her, she acted to disarm it. Increasingly baited by a cynical popular press, vilified by either side of the politically partisan newspapers, feeling public and police suspicion hardening almost palpably against her, Marguerite Steinheil panicked. She felt the pressure of the derisive disbelief around her, voiced and unvoiced. Too anxious and agitated to let the matter rest, she rashly and hastily commenced to dismantle her own official statements bit by bit by bit. Tentatively at first, beginning by repudiating her identification of the "red-haired" woman robber, Meg went on to bigger and better things some days later. She attempted a few frantic preemptive strikes by making sudden changes to her story, and then anxiously progressed to telling patently obvious lies. From there she took to backtracking and confusedly revising her own revisions. The ruses she essayed were so ill-conceived that they inevitably spawned even graver suspicion against her in their wake.

At the time of Faure's death a decade before, Marguerite had initiated a pattern of evasion when she had tried to shelter behind delayed "revelations" about the president's "secret documents." Her contentions had held just a tinge of "what-if" believability. Given the seething factionalism of official France at the height of both the Dreyfus Affair, and of Faure's failed attempt at empire-building in the Fashoda Incident, the president might well have tried to safeguard himself against political repercussions. Such documents as Meg claimed that Faure had secretly composed and hidden away would have furnished compelling political protection indeed for the president—if they truly existed. Conversely, if he had indeed exposed political plots or plotters in the documents, that circumstance would surely have constituted motive enough for intriguers' attempts to acquire them from Mme. Steinheil. They would not hesitate to obtain them by any and every means—even by robbery and murder; even after a dormant span of 10 years. Such was the interpretation Mme. Steinheil did her best to impress on the minds of any and all of her latter-day inquisitors. To drive home the point, she began to insist on a connection between the search for Faure's "secret papers" and the Impasse Ronsin murders.

Marguerite perceived, however, that the bare recital of her version of facts needed much more substantiation, if that version was to serve its purpose of liberating and exonerating her. As the pressure mounted in the waiting game between herself and the authorities, the resourceful Meg one day dropped a desperate bombshell: she confessed to a serious sin of omission from her first statements to police. She had deemed it time to reveal more details—long-suppressed, unsuspected, and thoroughly intriguing details— about the connection between the Impasse Ronsin murders and Faure's secret papers. With charming feminine contrition, Meg revealed that she had not told the complete truth about the robbers' demands on that night of the slayings. The invaders had known a secret. They had known of Faure's papers—and also about a five-strand pearl necklace that Faure had given her. "I said that I had been asked for the money and the jewels, but I did not add that I had further been asked for the pearls and the papers..." she admitted (Steinheil 179).

After hearing her tale many wondered if she fabricated the story to distract investigators from seeking a more personal motive on her part. But there was at least one modicum of truth in Meg's revelation. It had indeed transpired that, in the days of their liaison, Felix Faure had made a present to his inamorata of a 5-strand pearl collar, or necklace: "le collier presidentiel," as the newspapers came to term it. Marguerite disclosed that just after giving her the pearls, Faure had for some reason become quite agitated about the necklace and had begged her to keep it as hidden away and as confidential as the "political papers" he'd entrusted to her. On the night of the robbery-murders, the deadly intruders had *not* limited their demands to the household money and valuables, as Meg had at first declared. They had on the contrary made it clear that they knew of and were determined to get hold of both the documents and the pearls.

To Meg's way of thinking her narrative surely demonstrated that she herself could not have committed the crimes, which—it should now be plain to see—had obviously been perpetrated by her political enemies. Or by the enemies—or even the proponents—of Faure himself, who either wanted to hide or to reveal the proofs of some damaging intrigue in which the president, his supporters, or his enemies had figured. The killers could not otherwise have known of the necklace or the manuscripts without some inside political knowledge. But Mme. Steinheil's detractors scoffed at her logic. Did such papers, they asked cynically, or such pearls even exist? Did such a passage ever occur between Meg and the intruders? Did even the *intruders* exist? If so, why had she concealed this all-important information from the police? Was it because (as disparagers would later claim outright) the story was a further fabrication, a ploy to shunt authorities off her track by justifying their continued chasing after a quartet of mythical killers?

Meg also "revealed" that after Faure's death a mysterious German agent had made surreptitious visits to Marguerite and her husband, and had purchased some of the necklace's pearls one by one, as well as the "documents" which Faure had placed with her for safekeeping (123).Was this truth or self-serving invention? Even nationalist and strident anti–Marguerite segments of the press and public showed a willingness to believe, at least half-way, in the existence of the "German" and the papers, if only to justify their animosity towards the so-called "Tragic Widow." Once again they took to braying their mantra: Faure's papers, they charged, had been seized by pro–Dreyfus forces because they proved indisputably that Dreyfus had truly been guilty all along. Marguerite herself had indeed poisoned Faure 10 years earlier, used as a willing tool by the Dreyfusards to destroy the president's adamant opposition to Revision. But Marguerite's own explanation for failing to divulge much earlier to police these remarkable aspects of the crimes was dramatic yet simple: Fear had held her back. She had feared for her life, and for that of her daughter, if the murderers or intriguers took revenge for revealing the highly-charged, highly-political aspects of the crimes.

During the weeks and months that followed the murders, Marguerite Steinheil continued to make alterations to her declarations surrounding the mysteries of the fatal night. With jaw-dropping rapidity and rashness, she adjusted her methods according to the way she judged press, prosecution, or public opinion to be shaping for or against her at the time. Whenever a lie or omission was uncovered or questioned too closely, Marguerite desperately tried to draw attention away from it by substituting another that was even more outrageous.

Her next move was so extraordinary that it must surely have been impelled by a sudden surge of fear, an irresistible urge toward self-preservation alone. Meg suddenly decided to flail out against the net tightening around her by the simple expedient of fastening the crime on a decidedly specific Someone Else. She elected one of her own servants for this honor.

Marguerite planted one of the pearls from the presidential necklace in Remy Couillard's wallet. She then staged finding the gem in Couillard's possession, complete with credible witnesses to the discovery, and declared to the world that the pearl had been part of the valuables stolen by the murderers on the night of the crimes. Therefore, Couillard must have been, had to have been, one of those disguised murderers on that fatal night. But her efforts were clumsy and easily disproven. It was incontestably shown that she herself had taken that selfsame pearl to a jeweler for resetting on a date *after* the murders—so the gem could never, in the way she had claimed, have been stolen from her on the night of the crimes, by Couillard or anyone else.

Only momentarily daunted by this setback, Meg then unhesitatingly turned her accusations on another of her servants, Alexandre Wolff—son of her elderly housekeeper Mariette Wolff. This time her charges were even more quickly discounted, as Alexandre promptly proved a thoroughly credible and convincing alibi. Marguerite Steinheil's convoluted, easily scuttled untruths compounded the effects of her suspicious behavior. Without doubt her lies helped to pave the way for the long-expected arrest, which for months had been looming on the horizon. The blow finally fell on November 26, 1908. Madame Steinheil was at last arrested for the two murders at Impasse Ronsin and hustled away in police custody. Her detention marked the beginning of a yearlong pretrial incarceration at notorious Saint-Lazare Prison.

Marguerite Steinheil's trial-by-jury for the double murder began on November 3, 1909. Enormous public and media interest blazed anew. State officials reasoned that Mme. Steinheil had either acted alone, drugging her mother's and husband's nightcap drinks and then dispatching her victims; or she had been complicit in their slayings. The presiding judge of the court, Charles-Bernard de Valles, and Avocat-General Paul Trouard-Riolle led for the State. De Valles, as dictated by French law, acted as both judge and chief prosecutor of the case. Marguerite's defense was led by prominent young Maître Antony Aubin, assisted by Benjamin Landowski. From the outset of the process, de Valles had been plainly and openly antagonistic towards Marguerite, terming all her testimony a tissue of lies. The case against her and the prevailing public sentiment regarding the notorious defendant were summed up in his words:

"'You have stated that on the night of the crime you were bound down and gagged by three men in black robes and by a red-headed woman, who entered your room with a dark lantern and then—after they had bound and gagged you and after you yourself had lost consciousness—assassinated poor M. Steinheil and the unfortunate Mme. Japy. Nobody believes you; your story is a tissue of falsehoods. It was you, who with the help of accomplices, murdered your husband and your mother'" (Macdonald 1107).

The case that the prosecution must prove, then, centered on the crucial question: had Marguerite Steinheil murdered her husband and mother, either alone or with the help of an accomplice or accomplices, and then staged the "robbery" to escape detection of her crime? Prosecutors emphatically alleged that the answer was "Yes"; Mme. Steinheil had indeed committed these crimes and in the most heartless and calculated manner. They intended to prove their contention to the jury by establishing a motive understandable enough and cogent enough for the panel to accept, a motive as old as humanity. Marguerite Steinheil's reason for this heinous double crime, they claimed, was to rid herself of a husband she had never loved, as evidenced by her many affairs; and then to realize her desire to wed another man.

After Faure's death, Marguerite had engaged more or less discreetly in other affairs with a number of other prominent men, to which by then her husband seemed to have become inured or indifferent. By 1908 Meg had entered into a secret *affaire de coeur* with Maurice Borderel, an extremely wealthy and respected industrialist of the Ardennes; she was later to say of him that he was the only man she had ever truly loved. The encomium seemed to imply a motive for murder, and the prosecution seized on it. Marguerite's desire to be rid of her uninteresting husband comprised the "strongest point" in the State's case against her. "Madame Steinheil," the prosecution flatly claimed, "had murdered her husband in order to be free to marry 'the rich chatelain, M. Borderel'" (1111). The relationship with the industrialist, along with her other illicit liaisons, had come back to haunt both Mme. Steinheil and her succession of lovers—during the trial and long afterwards.

Marguerite had met widower Maurice Borderel in February 1908, and had soon become his mistress. As details of their liaison were laid bare at the trial, an obviously distressed and mortified Borderel testified that it was true that they had loved each other, and that Marguerite had "mentioned" marriage; however, he had definitely negatived even the possibility of such a union. Although he loved her, he didn't want to bring a stepmother into the lives of his children. He went on to maintain staunchly that he never thought for a moment that Marguerite could be guilty of murder. His tearful and fervent declaration of belief in her innocence impressed jurors and spectators alike with its sincerity and fundamentally Gallic chivalry.

The prosecution chose not to rely solely on the primary motive to prove its case. The State hacked away at Mme. Steinheil's prior statements, highlighted her damning lies, and attacked the credibility of her defenses. Why had she alone survived the attacks on the night of May 30, 1908? "How do you explain that you were not made to share the fate of your mother and your husband?" prosecutors sneered. "How do you explain the fact that [the killers] could spare you when you were a dangerous witness—one who would be the more formidable, more implacable and relentless because the victims were your own mother and husband?" (Steinheil 169). Madame Steinheil had given a reason for the unlikely forbearance of the killers at the beginning of the investigation, stating for the record that she thought the marauders had shown mercy because they'd mistaken her, in the poor light of the bedchamber, for her young daughter. But the murder indictment itself had scoffed at the mere suggestion: "She thought she was spared," it read, "because the assassins, taking her for Marthe, took pity on her youth. Such a confusion is most unlikely, for Mme. Steinheil could not be taken for a young lady barely seventeen." Prosecutors went further into the unlikelihood of Mme. Steinheil's being spared in a true robbery, firing more questions at her, defying her to convince the jury of her story. To these queries Mme. Steinheil replied wonderingly that she herself didn't understand the killers' leniency. She didn't know, she further added, if the robbers intended at all that she should survive, since she had been trussed up in a way that "meant death to me at the slightest movement" (169).

This statement gave the State an opening to launch an all-out attack on the very question of her binding and gagging, and they swiftly tore away ferociously at this further weakness in her declarations. She had claimed that the robbers had silenced her and cruelly tethered her to her bed. But, the prosecution countered, none of the cotton-wool wadding found at her bed or anywhere at the crime scene showed any evidence that it had ever been in her mouth. As for the bindings around her neck, arms and legs, prosecutors declared, "On May 31st, at 6 A.M., Rémy Couillard saw that you were bound, but the ropes were tied in so indifferent a manner that they left on your wrists and ankles only superficial marks, marks that were not lasting. It was also found that the rope round your neck was rather loose" (169).

Madame Steinheil's answer to the inference? There were no such bruises, she responded, because she simply had not moved. She had not dared to do so.

Couillard had also testified that Mme. Steinheil had—uncharacteristically—prepared rum nightcaps or "grogs" for her husband and mother on the night of the murders, and that immediately after they imbibed the drinks she had made sure the glasses they'd used had been washed and rinsed clean. Had she drugged the painter and his mother-in-law? Had she—or an accomplice—then murdered them, and staged the robbery? The prosecution flatly insisted that that had indeed been the case. To the question "Was it a habit in your house to take 'grogs' at night?" Mme. Steinheil admitted, "No, it was not a habit … the evening of May 30th I was very tired.… I had said I would drink a hot 'grog' before going to bed, and my husband and my mother said they would do the same. That was why my husband or I told Couillard to bring up some hot water, sugar, the bottle of rum, and three glasses" (163).

Another servant also testified that Marguerite had asked—again uncharacteristically—for an alpenstock to protect herself on the night of the murders. That alpenstock had been found near the body of Adolphe Steinheil. Had she or an accomplice used it to subdue or kill the painter? Monsieur de Valles declared that the heartless Mme. Steinheil had undeniably done all these things. But though the prosecutorial bombardment was hostile, insulting, and unrelenting, the beleaguered Mme. Steinheil steadfastly if histrionically denied all guilt of the slayings.

When confronted during the trial with the proven lies and fantastic intricacies she had fabricated after the murders, Marguerite Steinheil would frequently excuse her less-than-forthcoming behavior by sheltering behind a façade of anguished motherhood, or of mortification over exposure of her promiscuity. She had been afraid for her reputation, afraid for Marthe's happiness, afraid for her own and Marthe's safety, their very lives. She had panicked from the very first, she explained. "I did not want [my real friends] to … know that I had not been faithful to my husband. And above all, there was Marthe, my only child, my beloved daughter!" (179).

Marthe's "happiness" had been a constant theme in Mme. Steinheil's rationalizations whether in newspaper interviews, in her statements to investigators, in her trial testimony, or in her *Memoirs*. According to Meg, Marthe's happiness had hinged on her ignorance of her mother's amatory activities, and her continued belief in her mother's innocence of the murders at Impasse Ronsin. But most of all, the happiness of Marthe seemed to depend on the love of her fiancé. "[Marthe] was engaged to Pierre Buisson," Meg explained in her *Memoirs* (179). "If I mentioned the pearls and the documents, the truth about my 'friendship' with [Faure] was sure to be

... disclosed ... even to my own child, and to her betrothed. There would be a terrible scandal, my daughter's marriage would be broken off.... I fully realised the danger of mentioning the pearls and the documents, and so I held my tongue." Marguerite's fears on this score proved to be at least partially well-founded. Marthe's engagement was eventually terminated by her fiancé, whose family had been unable to withstand the scandal and the implications of an alliance with Marthe and her mother. The relationship had collapsed under the pressures of incessant hounding by the press and the shocked speculations and ostracism of society.

Meg's trial lasted for 10 days, during which time the public seemed to be as captivated by the unfolding revelation of her illicit love life as it had been appalled by the murder allegations leveled against her. All France and much of Europe were abuzz, enthralled by the shocking yet fascinating details of the salacious doings of certain members of the *haut monde*. Not the least fascinating of these fascinating details was the sheer number of affairs in which Meg had been embroiled, and the identities of the illustrious paramours who had been her partners—including a king of Cambodia. The trial tantalized and piqued the avid interest of the French public unlike any other. Public admission to the trial proceedings was hard-won; but once inside, the performance of the accused did not disappoint. Many highly-placed individuals from France and abroad, such as Robert Scarlett, brother of England's 5th Baron Abinger, joined other eager onlookers crowded into the courtroom to witness the exciting drama playing out before them. Madame Steinheil, dressed in dramatic black, fought fiercely to avoid conviction. She was "an extraordinary woman, Mme. Steinheil.... Imagine Sarah Bernhardt in some supremely tragical role—pathetic, threatening; tender, violent; despairing, tearful; wrecked with indignation, suffering, and exhaustion, and you will gain an idea of the 'Tragic Widow's' demeanour during the ten days of her trial" (Macdonald 1105).

The State, largely unimpressed with the defendant's performances, continued to hack away at every aspect of Meg's vulnerabilities. To the charge that she was immoral, she fairly flamed out, "'Yes, I have been a bad woman. Yes, I have been an immoral woman. Yes, I made false, wicked accusations against Remy Couillard and Alexandre Wolff. But I am not an assassin, a fiend. And only a fiend could murder her mother'" (1106).

The prosecution countered with incessant badgering and reiteration of the unsatisfactorily-answered questions before the court. Madame Steinheil's assertion that the killers had mistaken her for Marthe, and had spared her because of her perceived youth, was derided over and over again at scathing length. The prosecution continued to slash away at more of her testimony, scoffing, over and over again at the absurdity of the "brutal" gagging and binding that could never have occurred, yet from which she had pretended to suffer so much. What, they asked repeatedly, was the true reason she had given nightcaps to her husband and mother that night? For she herself had admitted that it was an unusual thing for her to have done.

But Marguerite clung stubbornly to repudiation of all involvement in the crimes at Impasse Ronsin, although the State continued to rain pitiless scorn on all her testimony. Her responses to queries were ready and unabashed, if not always completely convincing, meeting every blistering attack of M. de Valles or of M. Trouard-Riolle with either haughty calm, tempestuous defiance, or disarming weariness. Beneath it all she maintained always a subtext of suppliant feminine vulnerability in the face of the presiding judge's aggressive and bullying tactics. Meg made herself the very picture of lone, frail, defenseless but proudly defiant womanhood, cudgeled mercilessly by the marshaled and offended male might of the State. Though at times she stormed or wept, she admitted her false accusations against Couillard and Alexandre Wolff in a different key altogether: a softer womanly appeal to the jury, begging for sympathy and understanding of the anguished frame of mind induced by the bullying tricks that had led her to that folly. "In Sarah Bernhardt's melodious voice, she thus addressed the jury—'Gentlemen, I am deeply repentant for all the wrong I have done. Please realise that I was mad—that I was being tortured—when I made those false, atrocious accusations. I was being tortured by the examining-magistrate and by the journalists who invaded my villa...'" (1106).

There was no doubt that the worldly-wise Marguerite Steinheil unabashedly aimed all her defenses and her femininity at manipulating the men that made up the all-important jury. She was fighting for her life with every womanly wile in her arsenal—and it paid off. The trial, with all its draining hoopla and stormy emotion, came at last to an end on November 14, 1909, ten days after its start. Madame Steinheil was acquitted.

The State, with all the will in the world to condemn her, had adduced no proofs strong enough to convince the jury to convict. The evidence was weak, the motive insufficient—at least, so it seemed, to the minds of the Gallic panel that judged her case. No one, the jurors surely must have told themselves, would arrange such a horrible crime in so puerile a fashion and for such tenuous motives as those put forward by Meg's prosecutors. And certainly not such a womanly woman as the defendant who—though undoubtedly an adulteress—felt just as she ought to feel about respecting her own mother and shielding her husband and daughter from the scandal of her actions! The French public seemed to agree—at least with the supposition that the State had not proved its case. On announcement of the verdict, an immediate and approving pandemonium broke out, a roar of support from well-wishers who had been captivated, not necessarily by any belief that true justice had been truly served, but more by Meg's success in brazening out a perilous ordeal. The din of approbation reverberated deafeningly both inside and outside the courtroom as import of the verdict struggled to reach Meg's consciousness through the daze of apprehension she must have been suffering. When she finally realized she had been freed, she fainted. She was quickly secreted out of the court and whisked away to a sanatorium, but journalists hot on the trail quickly found her and continued to beleaguer their prey, practically baying at the heels of Marguerite, her daughter, and anyone else unfortunate enough to have been even remotely connected with the crime or trial. As a result of the ordeal, Marthe Steinheil's betrothal to Pierre Buisson was not the only sad casualty of the "Affaire Steinheil." Maurice Borderel, reputation ruined, was forced to sell his estate and quit the Ardennes. Others whose peccadilloes had been publicly revealed, as well as many innocents unfortunate enough to be touched by the crime or its aftermath, suffered social, political, or economic devastation. Factionalist newspapers howled that the judges had been "bought," while more reasoned responses of the French press saw the trial as an indictment of "antiquated" French criminal trial procedures: "There is a singular unanimity in the opinions of the Paris newspapers," reported the *Times of London*, "as regards the significance of the acquittal of Mme. Steinheil … [the newspapers] express the idea that the action of the jury is the virtual condemnation of the Magistrature" ("Steinheil Case" 5).

Yet, despite the fact that Mme. Steinheil had been acquitted, the murders *had* occurred. Some person, or some persons, had committed them. No one else had been seriously considered for the crime, not even the black-robed foursome of Mme. Steinheil's original declarations. Did Marguerite Steinheil get away with murder? Common reason might say that it was so. Was she indeed a "fatal woman"—a "femme fatale" in both senses of the term, with not only many lovers in her past but also as many as three deaths to be laid at her door? Decidedly she exhibited the childish self-centered tendencies, the shallow thinking of one with a narcissist bent. Was she someone who believed her own charm would always save her from harm—or from the consequences of her harmful actions? Could she have persuaded herself that murder had been necessary to obtain the happiness she deserved? Unless some heretofore concealed or lost information comes to the fore, posterity is not likely ever to know the entire true story of the "Affaire de l'Impasse Ronsin."

But Marguerite Steinheil herself, whatever else she may have been, was also resourceful and resilient, a true survivor. Others may have suffered irretrievable damage of an emotional, social or economic nature, but Marguerite appeared to escape every one of these consequences. Shortly after the trial's end she fled to England, where she landed on her feet yet again, and in a fittingly flamboyant manner. Meg lived in England under the name "Mme.

de Serignac," an alias which seemed effectively to shield her true identity until she herself was willing to unveil it. Her reminiscences, entitled *Mes Memoires* (*My Memoirs*), were published in 1912. The work—an essentially romanticized exculpation of her behavior and motives—nevertheless offered insight of a kind into her mind and character.

A few years after the trial, before Lord Justice Charles Darling, Mme. Steinheil came out from behind her assumed identity to bring suit for libel against author Hargrave L. Adam and his publisher, Thomas Werner Laurie. Contending that their portrayal of her in the book *Woman and Crime* (Adam 309–18) was detrimental and untrue, she was successful in her action. In June 1917, she married Robert Brooke Campbell Scarlett, 6th Baron Abinger. He had reportedly fallen in love with her several years before their marriage—when he had attended her trial for murder. Marguerite lived as Baroness Abinger with her husband in apparent harmony until his death in 1927. In 1938 Mme. Steinheil's name resurfaced in news accounts when she brought another libel suit against an English writer ("Baroness Libelled" 4). So successful had Marguerite been in hiding her presence and her true identity in Britain, that author Guy B. Logan had apparently assumed that the notorious Mme. Steinheil was long dead ("Suit" 5). He had therefore felt free to include passages in one of his works comparing her to notorious American murderer Ruth Snyder (Logan 966) and other descriptions of Mme. Steinheil as a killer. Marguerite's suit, to prove both that she still lived and to refute his assertions that she'd ever been found guilty of murder, netted her a "handsome amount" in damages from an out-of-court settlement with the writer and his publishers. Thereafter she lived relatively quietly until her July 1954 death at age 85, in a London nursing home.

## *The Murder on the Links*

*The Murder on the Links* (first published in May 1923) is Agatha Christie's second novel featuring the exploits of Hercule Poirot. In this work the natty little detective also shares a second collaboration with Arthur Hastings. The association is fateful for Poirot's "Watson" in more ways than one, for it is during the investigation of the strange case that Hastings meets "Cinderella," the love of his life and his future spouse.

*Links* is a complicated affair, as is perhaps not surprising in an effort from a newly-minted mystery novelist. It's a story connected by several subplots, past and present; and by many characters with circuitous motives and movements—but a clear-cut main story is still discernible within the busy interplay of plot and subplot. Poirot is drawn into the episode when he receives a letter entreating him to take on a case in France. The sender writes that his life is in imminent danger, and begs for Poirot's help to avoid this fate. The detective's jaded palate is piqued, not so much by the request for help—the celebrated little sleuth received such requests every day—but by the calculated postscripted fillip added to the hitherto restrained missive. In what was obviously meant to strike Poirot as suppressed desperation breaking through the request's forced calmness, the writer had scrawled: "For God's sake, come!" (Christie, *Murder on the Links* 22). The letter's author signed himself "Paul Renauld," whose name Hastings instantly recognized as that of a "well-known South American millionaire fellow" (23). Losing no time, Poirot and Hastings hie themselves to the Villa Geneviève, Renauld's estate in Merlinville-sur-Mer, a fashionable spot between Boulogne and Calais in France. During the train journey Hastings meets a fascinatingly lively and mysteriously elusive young woman whom he dubs "Cinderella"— and with whom he falls in love.

On their way to the villa Poirot and Hastings encountered a beautiful girl who, Poirot noted, watched them with "anxious eyes" (31). When they arrived at their destination, they were greeted with the stunning news that Poirot's client, M. Renauld, was dead. He and his wife, Éloïse, had been viciously assailed early that very morning, and although the wife survived, the unfortunate Renauld had been cold-bloodedly murdered. It seemed that M. Renauld's somewhat disingenuous letter had not understated his peril after all.

Poirot conferred with his French colleagues, old friend Commissaire Lucien Bex; M. Giraud of the renowned Sûreté; and the Examining Magistrate, M. Hautet. Giraud was extremely hostile to and contemptuous of Poirot and of his methods, but M. Hautet welcomed the celebrated detective into the investigation, sharing with Poirot and Hastings all that he knew of the case. Hautet also gave them official carte blanche access to witnesses, the crime scene, and the evidence in the case. When Mme. Renauld recovered sufficiently she had agitatedly told the police as much of the terrible events that had befallen her husband and herself as she knew. The information gathered so far was that M. Renauld and his wife had been attacked in their home while they slept at about two o'clock in the morning. Their assailants were two bearded, foreign men. Her husband had been kidnapped at knifepoint after she had been viciously bound and gagged and left on her bed. At about nine in the morning servants had found Renauld's body in a shallow grave on a nearby golf course; a little later they had discovered the frightened and suffering Mme. Renauld in her bedroom. The police had then been alerted. Poirot had accompanied officers as they questioned Mme. Renauld, and to test her story, he discreetly examined her wrists. The deep, painful marks of the ropes where they'd bitten into her flesh attested to the truth of her tale. Officials surmised that the miscreants had gained entry through the front door, which had somehow been left unlocked. The

## Chapter 2. "La Femme Fatale"

police had discovered the unfortunate Renauld's body, clad only in nightwear and, strangely, his son Jack's overcoat. He had been fatally stabbed in the back, lying in a freshly-dug grave on the premises of a nearby golf course. When police later took Mme. Renauld to the crime scene to identify the body, she had fainted with obviously genuine grief and horror at sight of her beloved husband's corpse.

The Villa Geneviève's residents had included the Renaulds; their young son Jack; M. Renauld's secretary, Gabriel Stonor, and five servants. At the time of the murder, three of the household had been absent: Jack Renauld, who'd been sent to South America on business, the secretary, Stonor, who was attending to affairs in England, and the vacationing chauffeur. On questioning the remaining servants Poirot and the police had elicited some interesting information: there had been ructions and high emotions at the Villa Geneviève the day and night preceding the murder. Two domestics gave conflicting but potentially significant information concerning Paul Renauld's furtive reception of a visit from "a woman" that day. One servant declared that the seductive owner of the neighboring villa, Mme. Daubreuil—rumored to be Renauld's mistress—had paid a clandestine visit to M. Renauld after Mme. Renauld had gone to bed for the night. But the second servant insisted that it was another woman altogether who had shown up at the Renauld home, an unidentified stranger who was younger than Mme. Daubreuil. The stranger had been embroiled in a stormy but curtailed interview with an impatient Renauld. In addition M. Renauld had engaged in a loud and hot-tempered quarrel with his son Jack just before the younger man had gone angrily off to catch his train.

Stonor, on his return to the villa, revealed his opinion that Mme. Daubreuil was blackmailing M. Renauld—there was no love affair between them, as many believed. Investigators found that Mme. Daubreuil had indeed been paying large amounts into her bank accounts before the tragedy, and also that Paul Renauld had changed his will just before his death, cutting off his son entirely and leaving all his fortune to his wife.

Poirot and Hastings, along with M. Hautet, paid a visit to Mme. Daubreuil at her home, the adjoining Villa Marguerite, to question her about the murder and her ostensible relationship with M. Renauld as his mistress. They learned that the girl with the "anxious eyes" whom they had encountered on arrival was Mme. Daubreuil's daughter, Marthe, and that the young woman was indeed anxious to find out from Poirot if any specific person was suspected of the murder. She and Jack Renauld were in love and wished to marry, but Jack's parents had adamantly, even violently, opposed the match. Perhaps, the detectives mused, that circumstance explained the anxiety Poirot had seen in her eyes: Marthe may have feared that Jack had slain his father in the heat of an argument over his son's engagement. Meanwhile, Mme. Daubreuil waxed haughtily indignant at imputations of an affair, but Poirot was convinced that he had seen the handsome woman's face somewhere before—and in connection with another murder case.

And then Hastings, on a solitary tour of the crime scene on the golf links, suddenly ran into his "Cinderella" of the Calais train. After allowing her to coax him into smuggling her into the investigation rooms, he afterwards discovered that the girl had disappeared—and the murder dagger with her.

While Poirot was pursuing his inquiries in Paris another corpse turns up on the Renauld grounds, this one with a dagger through its heart. The man was much like Paul Renauld in general build; well-dressed but obviously a tramp. Examination showed that he had perished of an epileptic fit, that his death occurred before Renauld's, and that, strangely, he had been stabbed *after* death. The imperious Giraud arrested Jack Renauld for the murder of his father, citing circumstantial facts: Jack had been cut out of the father's will and they had argued and fought over Jack's determination to wed Marthe Daubreuil. But Jack's love for Marthe had cooled by then, and he had returned to a former sweetheart. A series of misunderstandings and errors had caused both the young man and the sweetheart to suspect each other of slaying Paul Renauld. In addition the smitten Hastings managed to obstruct justice for a time, attempting to shield his own "Cinderella" after mistaking her for another. Then Jack himself had been released, when his sweetheart had confessed to the murder to protect the man she loved.

Christie weaves into *The Murder on the Links* an interesting thematic design as well as an intricate puzzle of detection. As in a veritable Shakespearean "Comedy of Errors," she vigorously expands on the theme of "the double" in the narrative, reiterating it throughout, which enriches at the same time that it complicates the character-rich terrain of the tale. The plethora of bodies, lovers, and mistaken identities notwithstanding; however, Poirot had uncovered much about "Paul Renauld" and his unsavory history. In Paris 22 years earlier, there had been a notorious murder case singularly similar to the Renauld slaying. One Jeanne Beroldy, a bold young beauty, had gone on trial for the murder of her inoffensive and much older husband. She had at first claimed that Arnold Beroldy had been dispatched by two masked men with beards who had entered the Beroldy home the night of the murder, cruelly binding her hand and foot before cold-bloodedly killing her husband. But authorities had been made suspicious of the wife when they discovered that she had not been tightly tied up at all. The bindings were faked: they had been too loose to leave any marks at all on her arms or legs, thus giving the lie to her story of being brutally attacked and incapacitated. After she went on trial for the murder of her husband, a letter had been sent to the police by Mme. Beroldy's lover, the missing Georges Conneau, who had vanished after the murder. Conneau confessed that it had been he, in complicity with Mme. Beroldy, who had stabbed Beroldy to death so that he and Beroldy's captivating wife could be together. His confession was prompted by jealousy and revenge: he'd discovered that Mme. Beroldy had intended to jilt him to marry another man instead. Conneau had been supplanted by a rich American, and had only learned that bitter fact from recent newspaper accounts of the trial. At that sensational juncture Mme. Beroldy, without turning a hair, immediately repudiated her former testimony naming bearded marauders, and pointed the finger of blame solely at a passion-maddened Conneau. She called on all her allure and femininity in an all-out emotional appeal to the gallantry of the men on the jury—who, against all odds, duly responded by acquitting her. Then she, too, with her little daughter, had disappeared from the scene. Poirot found "Paul Renauld" had indeed been the alias of the absconded Georges Conneau, who had gone on to amass a fortune in Chile. He also learns that Mme. Daubreuil was the alias of the notorious Mme. Beroldy; and that, when Conneau had finally dared to return to France, the greatest of fatal coincidences had landed him literally next door to his hated ex-mistress.

The now-respectable Renauld was easy prey for Mme. Daubreuil's blackmail. To escape his tormentor, he had devised a desperate expedient: when a tramp had died of an epileptic fit on his villa grounds, Renauld had seized the opportunity to fake his own demise, and arrange it so the tramp's body would be taken for his own. He restaged the scenario that he and Mme. Beroldy had concocted decades earlier, when they had plotted to kill Arnold Beroldy. Now, however, he was plotting with his beloved Éloïse—not to kill but to save his new life from the predatory claws of "Mme. Daubreuil." Madame Renauld, who knew of his past and who loved him enough to go through with the charade, now played the role that the trussed-up Mme. Beroldy had played decades before. This time Renauld took care to bind her so tightly that no ruse would be suspected. Madame Renauld's reaction to the sight of the body at the golf-links grave had been true shock and grief: instead of finding the body of the tramp as she expected, it was sight of the murdered body of her beloved husband that had met her gaze. Renauld's plans had been derailed by a vastly dangerous intriguer who had managed to turn Renauld's own plot against him.

Toward the conclusion of the novel Poirot solves the intricate puzzle of who killed Paul Renauld—and why, although the motive had been obscured by multiple suspects and their intertwining entanglements. True to her hallmark of unmasking the "least likely" killer in her mystery and detective tales, Christie unveils a most surprising murderer as Poirot races against time, playing a thrilling and dangerous game to expose the miscreant—and to prevent by a hairsbreadth the killer's last slaying.

# Madame Marguerite Steinheil + *The Murder on the Links*

*The Murder on the Links* (1923) was Agatha Christie's third detective novel, but the second featuring Hercule Poirot, and she explains in *An Autobiography* how she came to create it: "[*Murder on the Links*] must have been written not long after a *cause célèbre* which occurred in France.... It was some tale of masked men who had broken into a house, killed the owner, tied up and gagged the wife—the mother-in-law had also died, but only apparently because she had choked on her false teeth. Anyway, the wife's story was disproved, and there was a suggestion that it was the wife who had killed her husband, and that she had never been tied up at all, or only by an accomplice" (267).

Christie's memory for detail is admirably good: her précis of the case, which was dubbed "L'Affaire de l'Impasse Ronsin" by France's press, almost exactly encapsulates one of the most sensational murder cases ever to leave its mark on early 20th-century French culture: the case of Mme. Marguerite Japy Steinheil, who went on trial in 1909 for the 1908 murders of her husband, artist Adolphe Steinheil, and her mother (or stepmother), Emilie Japy. Christie in her *Autobiography* also admits, "I can't remember the name of any of the participants by now" (267); but that circumstance was not entirely remarkable. Despite the fact that the case made quite a stir in Britain as well as in France, Europe, and abroad at the time it happened, it may have later slipped through the cracks of English popular-culture memory. After all, Britain, at that time and just afterward, had spawned its own just-as-notorious and sensational icons of British true-crime and trial lore. The cases involving Dr. Crippen's *cause célèbre* of 1910, or George Joseph Smith's 1915 case of the "Brides in the Bath," for example, never strayed far from British criminological recollection.

The true-case scenario of the "Steinheil Affair" thoroughly imbues the plots of *The Murder on the Links*, but even in this early effort—only her second novel featuring Hercule Poirot and Arthur Hastings—Agatha Christie plants her own inimitable imprint on the story, making it indubitably her own and foreshadowing great things to come from her mystery-and-detection-dipped pen. In addition, Hastings meets in this novel his "Cinderella"—his future wife—who plays an unexpected but important role in the story.

The Steinheil saga began prosaically enough. In 1890, middle-aged, minor French artist Adolphe Steinheil married the beautiful 21-year-old Marguerite Japy. A year later the birth of a daughter, Marthe, completed their little family circle. Marguerite—or Meg—had been born to privilege as the daughter of a very wealthy businessman, and the height of her ambition was to mingle with, and to lead, the elite political and artistic scene of Paris of the time. She succeeded: famous writers and composers, along with prominent and powerful statesmen of the day, formed part of her *salon* or her court.

No doubt discussions of the era's political controversies filled the hours at her salon. Among those discussions would surely have been heated debates over the infamous Dreyfus Affair of 1894. Jewish military officer Alfred Dreyfus had been convicted of treason on largely trumped-up and anti–Semitic charges; the "Dreyfusards," an outraged and outspoken faction of prominent citizens incensed at the injustice of it all, clamored for revision of the conviction by Felix Faure, president of the republic by 1895. Faure had refused; he and his party remained staunchly opposed to revision until Faure's strange death in 1899—a death that famously involved Marguerite Steinheil. She had become Faure's mistress by then, a fact that had remained relatively discreetly concealed until the day that, in a room of the Presidential Palace itself, Faure fell victim to a seizure in the middle of a tryst with his "confidante." The president of the French republic died only hours after that collapse.

The scandal was immediate and explosive. Madame Steinheil attempted to deny the compromising true nature of her relationship with Felix Faure by maintaining that their meetings had been strictly political: they had been writing his memoirs in secret. Faure was afraid that his enemies would interfere due to dangerous political revelations in the documents, she claimed, and he had entrusted these all-important papers to Mme. Steinheil's confidential care. This hardly credible explanation was met with hooted disdain by the tabloid press—and by nationalist factions who claimed that Meg had been a paid spy for the Dreyfusards. The manner of Faure's death resulted in ribald discredit that marked Meg as a publicly-exposed adulteress, but the resilient and strong-willed young woman hardly seemed to suffer among the powerful males whose society she courted. Her marriage to Adolphe Steinheil notwithstanding, in the years succeeding Faure's death she quietly took on several other lovers from high positions and stations in life—including at least one from the ranks of foreign royalty.

But on May 31, 1908, the disreputable Meg fell into her most dangerous scandal yet. In the early morning hours of that day, one of her servants, Remy Couillard, had entered the bedroom area of the Steinheil home at Impasse Ronsin, a street in Paris. To his horror he had discovered the slain bodies of Adolphe Steinheil and of Emilie Japy, Meg's mother. They had both died of strangulation. A gag shoved down Mme. Japy's throat had forced her to choke on her own dentures. Seventeen-year-old Marthe had fortunately been away for the night, but Marguerite Steinheil herself was found lying gagged and tied by rope to Marthe's bed. When police arrived, the exhausted and terrified Mme. Steinheil told them a tale of prolonged terror. She'd been awakened the night before by murderous thugs looking for money, jewels, and other valuables. They'd tied her hands and bound her to the bed, gagging her into the bargain. Throughout the ordeal she'd known nothing of what had become of her husband and mother, as they had been in separate rooms. There had been four of the intruders, all dressed in long black robes like "Russian popes." One of the gang had been a woman. The men were roughly disguised: two of them wore black beards while the third sported a red one.

Madame Steinheil's description of this scene recurs in *Links*, with subtle and telling variations. The signature patterns are the same: in the middle of the night, the "heroine" is bound and gagged by murderous intruders, but left alive while her husband is mercilessly killed by bearded ostensible robbers in pursuit of something valuable. The tableau not only appears in the true-life Steinheil Affair that inspired the fictional *Murder on the Links*, but is also twice represented in that novel. Agatha Christie showcases throughout the work an insistence on the theme of "the double" in various configurations, of which two-fold representation of the "bound and gagged" scenario is one of the most conspicuous. She features the scene on two distinct occasions separated by many years, in different locations with different sets of characters playing the principal roles—for reasons that turn out to be both very similar, and yet at the same time very different. The reception accorded Mme. Steinheil's story in the real-life event was as skeptical as that given to the replicated versions in the novel. Meg Steinheil's descriptions were hardly believable; still, for some weeks, authorities sought high and low for the villains of her descriptions, with no success. Eventually authorities turned their attentions more fully on Meg. To deflect their suspicions she resurrected the "secret papers" ploy she'd used at the time of Faure's death ten years before. She "confessed" that she had not been entirely candid with police about the intruders' demands on the night of the murders. What the marauders had really been after, she declared, were Faure's "secret documents" of a decade earlier. They had threatened her into silence about their objectives, and she had been afraid to tell authorities the whole truth; afraid not only for her own life but for her daughter Marthe's safety as well.

In the novel, it is this juncture that forms Christie's jumping-off point from the true-crime history of the Steinheil affair—which, she writes in her *Autobiography*, "struck me as a good plot on which to weave my own story"—to the commencement point for her novel's main story. That point, Christie notes, "start[ed] with the wife's life after she had been acquitted of the murder" (267). The story proper of *Links* thus begins two decades after the murder in Paris of an insignificant little French wine merchant named Arnold Beroldy. First mention of this event occurs late in the novel, at the time when its significance becomes evident in Christie's storyline.

## Chapter 2. "La Femme Fatale"

As the novel opens, Poirot has been enticed to France on another matter altogether, but one which will eventually connect to the past Beroldy affair. The Belgian detective's interest had been awakened after he'd received a curious letter from a Monsieur Paul Renauld, whose name Hastings recognized as that of a millionaire industrialist who'd made his wealth in South America. Renauld writes that he fears he is about to be murdered, urging Poirot to come to his aid before it is too late. But when Poirot and Hastings arrive at the Renaulds' northern France villa in Merlinville-sur-Mer, it is indeed too late: Renauld has already been brutally stabbed to death, his half-dressed body found lying in a grave on a golf course near his grand home, the Villa Geneviève. He and his wife had been attacked in their home just the night before Poirot's arrival. When Mme. Renauld has sufficiently recovered from her own ordeal to talk to officials, Poirot instantly recognizes in her a *"maîtresse-femme"* despite her shaken state. She manages to impart to police and Poirot a careful summary, recounting as much as she knows of the circumstances leading to her husband's death. The couple had been asleep in their bedroom and violently awakened around two o'clock in the morning by two masked and fierce intruders. One was a tall man, black-bearded; the shorter one wore a red beard. The red-bearded man gagged her and bound her viciously hand and foot while the other menaced M. Renauld with a dagger snatched up from Mme. Renauld's dressing table. The terrified and distraught woman had been near to fainting during the ordeal, but had nevertheless recognized a South American dialect used by the interlopers. They were demanding some sort of "secret" item from her husband, threatening to kill him outright if he didn't immediately produce it and turn it over to them. A frightened M. Renauld had tried to convince them that he didn't have what they wanted, but the intruders ferociously overrode his protests, forcing him to huddle into an overcoat and accompany them to some undisclosed destination.

The story seems fantastical to Mme. Renauld's listeners, and Poirot senses some kind of restraint in her studied account. Is she telling the truth—or at any rate all of it? The little detective tests the veracity of Mme. Renauld's statements in his own way: he notes the cruel bite marks of the ropes on Mme. Renauld's wrists and limbs. They are real; she has truly been very brutally bound. And when she is taken to identify the body of her husband, her poignant shocked grief and anguish are too genuine to be doubted. Yet there was something that seemed to Poirot to be somewhat off-key.

Poirot and Hastings continue to delve deeper into the mystery of Paul Renauld's strange death. Gossip had coupled the dead man's name with that of a beautiful and mysterious widow, Mme. Daubreuil, who lived next to the Renaulds at the Villa Marguerite with her lovely young daughter, Marthe.

## Madame Marguerite Steinheil + *The Murder on the Links* 53

Poirot and Hastings had encountered the beautiful Marthe when they first arrived in Merlinville-sur-Mer; and the little detective had been struck by the "anxious eyes" of the young woman. When Poirot and Hastings interview Mme. Daubreuil at her home, they do not entirely believe her indignant protests that she had not been Renauld's mistress. When Gabriel Stonor, Renauld's secretary, suggests to Poirot that the clandestine relationship between Renauld and Mme. Daubreuil had been based, not on an illicit amour, but on blackmail, with the mysterious woman as blackmailer, Poirot begins to see light. The story Mme. Renauld had told of her ordeal the night of Paul Renauld's slaying stirs a chord of memory, and Poirot tracks it to its source: the story of one Mme. Beroldy, who many years before had stood trial in Paris for the sensational murder of her husband. Poirot unearths a newspaper photograph of the lady. It shows the notorious Mme. Beroldy of the past case, and the intriguing Mme. Daubreuil of the present case, to be one and the same woman. Hastings also remembers the case; his recollection of the sensational newspaper coverage of the Beroldy trial reveals the important background of the present situation. At this stage in Christie's story, the nexus manifests itself between the tale that Mme. Renauld had recently recounted, and the tale that Jeanne Beroldy had told two decades before, detailing the murder of Arnold Beroldy. The circumstance helps elucidate for Poirot the true order and purpose of events in the slaying of Paul Renauld, the case at hand. Detection proper now begins for solving the principal problem—the mystery of Paul Renauld's murder—which Christie skillfully superimposes on the Steinheil true-crime substratum beneath it.

Hastings recalls that twenty years earlier, and some months before his slaying, middle-aged wine-merchant Arnold Beroldy had brought his adored, much-younger wife Jeanne and their baby daughter Marthe from the relative provinces of Lyon to live in the big city of Paris. His beautiful and determined wife's ambitions outgrew not only the walls of their small apartment and the resources of their minuscule bank account, but the confines of their stultifying marriage as well. One of the couple's Parisian friends, young lawyer Georges Conneau, fell completely under the spell of the fascinating Mme. Beroldy. They began a secret love affair. The hotheaded, infatuated young man conspired with her to murder the inconvenient husband, and thus to free his mistress to live happily ever after with him. They carried out a plan to make it seem that the hapless Beroldy had been killed by robbers. Madame Beroldy prepared the way by spreading beforehand a tale among their acquaintance that her husband had become deeply involved in dangerous politics. He had gone so far, she confided to them, as to agree to keeping in his own custody a "secret document" whose contents were so compromising that they would rock all Europe were they to fall into the wrong hands. And therefore she, his wife, was now afraid for her brave husband's very life.

Sure enough, the Beroldys' daily servant arrived one morning to stumble on a shocking scene: M. Beroldy stabbed to death in his bed, and poor Mme. Beroldy trussed up like an animal on the floor, bound hand and foot and obviously in pain from hours of enforced suffering. She brokenly revealed to police a harrowing tale: two masked men had frightened her out of sleep during the night, then bound and gagged her. They had viciously demanded of her husband that he hand over to them a "secret document"; he had refused. The intruders had then pitilessly stabbed him to death. Afterwards the culprits had callously rifled his effects and finally departed, taking away with them a cache of papers and leaving Mme. Beroldy in her terrorized and tethered state. Madame Beroldy had later described the assailants to police as heavily bearded men whom she recognized as Russian.

Officials did not entirely believe in the woman's bizarre tale: her bindings, for example, had been quite loose, leading to the conclusion that they had not been as cruelly administered as the lady claimed they'd been; and no trail to the melodramatic bearded Russians was ever found. Police bided their time. They then suddenly arrested Jeanne Beroldy for the murder of her husband, citing also an unknown accomplice.

In the real-life Steinheil Affair, on November 26, 1908, Marguerite too was inevitably arrested for the murders of her husband and mother, probably with the help of an accomplice. Nearly a full year later in November 1909, Meg finally went on trial for the crimes. The ferocious trial judge, who, in accord with French law, also served as main prosecutor, went after Mme. Steinheil with all the savagery he could muster. She'd been charged with the murders of Adolphe Steinheil and of Mme. Japy, either acting alone or with an unknown accomplice. The bindings she'd shown had been loose and unconvincing; there was no mark on her from the ropes she claimed had held her motionless and in agony for the long hours of that fateful night before she was discovered. In addition the gag she swore they used on her showed no signs of ever having been in her mouth.

The heartless crimes had been committed, prosecutors contended, to free her from the older, dull, unambitious husband she loathed so that she could marry her true love: widower Maurice Borderel, a much-respected, quite ordinary, and very rich French businessman of the Ardennes. This respectable man had not figured among the catalogue of Mme. Steinheil's other more flamboyant and prominent lovers. She'd been Borderel's mistress since February 1908, and had been known to declare that he was the love of her life. On the witness stand Borderel, obviously shocked and shaken by the scandal that had overtaken him, testified in obvious mortification that he and Meg had indeed been lovers, and that Meg had indeed talked of their marriage. But, he declared, there could have been no question of marriage between them: he wanted no stepmother for his children. The distressed Borderel's honesty and discomfiture was so apparently genuine that the court and jury—and the spectators who hung on his words with bated breath—had no difficulty in believing in both his testimony and in his guiltlessness as accomplice in the slayings.

In *The Murder on the Links* Christie's antagonist Jeanne Beroldy endures a fictionalized but duplicate litigation experience. Her trial, too, was a public and press sensation. All Paris, all Europe, was abuzz with the scandal and the sudden turn of events when she had been so summarily arrested. The populace turned out in force to witness the hearing, where fierce prosecutors avidly attacked all of Mme. Beroldy's defenses and her character besides. They proved that the bindings which she claimed had incapacitated her on the fatal night had been faked, probably by her still unapprehended, unknown accomplice and lover. And for motive the authorities had discovered "another man" in Jeanne Beroldy's life—but that man was not Georges Conneau, who had effectively disappeared since the time of Arnold Beroldy's murder.

The enterprising Jeanne had, before the slaying, met and captured the heart of an unworldly middle-aged American millionaire, Mr. Hiram P. Trapp. Conneau was unaware of the existence of the other man. Conneau was even less aware that, even while Jeanne was leading him on and inciting him to murder, she had as her real objective marriage to the wealthy American. The absconded Conneau, along with the rest of the world, learned through newspaper accounts of Mr. Trapp's place in Jeanne Beroldy's life. When the fiery young lawyer read of his mistress's treachery in using him as a mere besotted dupe to get to Mr. Trapp's millions, he exacted revenge by writing the court and exposing their murder plot. He then vanished completely into thin air.

The excitement caused by Conneau's revelation increased the trial's sensation level a hundredfold, but Mme. Beroldy was more than equal to this surprise twist of fortune. On trial for her life, Jeanne called on all her powers of persuasion, playing her seductive beauty for all it was worth. She immediately dropped all pretense of bearded Russian interlopers, casting all blame for the slaying onto a passion-crazed Georges Conneau. Jeanne Beroldy also swore that she had forced herself to keep silent about Conneau's true role in the killing because of fear—fear of scandal; fear for her safety and that of little Marthe; fear of losing her reputation forever and having her child grow up tainted by the mother's shame.

Madame Steinheil at her trial had originally used the self-same ploys, which Christie later placed in the arsenal of the devious Mme. Beroldy. Yes, Meg admitted, she had lied; but she had been in a panic; she had feared for her life and for her daughter's life. More, she feared how scandal would affect her innocent Marthe's standing in society were it to become known about her mother's licentious lifestyle. She hadn't wanted the young girl to know of her mother's parade of lovers, of the kind of secret life her mother led. But despite this Marthe had indeed ultimately suffered because of the scandal: she had been engaged to the son of a respectable family, but when Meg's escapades and the murder charge became public knowledge, the virtuous fiancé and his family saw to it that the engagement was broken. Christie reflected this circumstance in the novel, when the engagement of the fictional Marthe, daughter of Mme. Beroldy, to the son of the Renauld house was vehemently opposed by his parents.

Marguerite Steinheil continued to bare her soul on the witness stand. Playing for the highest of stakes, Meg pulled out all the stops, falling back on the considerable appeal and feminine wiles that had made her career up to then so successful. She did not hesitate to exploit a womanly vulnerability, engaging the Gallic sympathy of a jury-box full of susceptible males. Whenever the situation seemed to call for it as she gave her testimony, Mme. Steinheil wept, stormed, or whispered out her responses to contemptuous prosecutors who scorned and baited her.

And in the end it all paid off. On November 14, 1909, Marguerite Steinheil was acquitted of the murder charges. The courtroom spectators erupted into a spontaneous roar of approval and congratulation at the verdict, while the keyed-up Meg swooned away in the best "helpless female" tradition. She had fought her way through a perilous ordeal, and—guilty of murder or not—she had won. Madame Steinheil, seemingly indomitable, left France for England soon afterwards, electing to live there under an assumed name. In June 1917 her true identity was revealed when she very publicly entered into marriage with Robert Scarlett, 6th Baron Abinger, who, it was said, had fallen in love with Meg Steinheil years earlier—when he had been one of a number of aristocrats who'd attended her murder trial. Like the proverbial nine-lived feline, Meg had landed on her feet once again.

Within the pages of the novel, Christie's audacious Mme. Beroldy saved herself in much the same way as her real-life alter ego had done. Jeanne Beroldy had unleashed the full effect of her beauty coupled with apparent feminine contrition, vulnerability, and passion onto the judge and the members of the jury. As she testified, she sobbed out her confessions as Meg Steinheil had done. And in the end Christie's fictional jury had responded as gallantly to Jeanne Beroldy's artful protestations as the real-life jury had responded to those of Marguerite Steinheil. It had been a narrow escape, but Mme. Beroldy was acquitted, amid cheering and outbursts of support from impulsive court-room onlookers. She lost no time, however, in whisking herself and her child both out of Paris, and out of the public eye, immediately thereafter.

And now here she was, twenty years later, resurfaced in France and somehow connected to a murder eerily like the one of two decades before.

Poirot put his little grey cells to work. How did the Beroldy slaying of so long ago relate to the present-day murder of Paul Renauld? It was obvious that Mme. Daubreuil/Beroldy was involved. But so was Mme. Renauld—their stories of being bound and gagged while ruthless thugs seeking a valuable "secret" murdered their husbands were too similar to be merely coincidental. The two women were in no way in league with each other, but, Poirot knew, there had to be some real link between the cases. That connection turned out to be Georges Conneau. Madame Beroldy's lover and accomplice of twenty years earlier was not only Georges Conneau, but also Paul Renauld, the husband of the redoubtable Mme. Éloïse Renauld and the slaying victim of mere days ago. The murderer of Arnold Beroldy had come full circle and was now himself murdered. But by whom?

With his added knowledge Poirot deduces and verifies the chain of events that must have led to Conneau/Renauld's killing. With the complicity of his loving wife, Renauld had counterfeited his abduction and murder in a desperate try at escaping a blackmailer's clutches. Mindful of the fact that too-loose bindings had betrayed the conspirators in the past Beroldy slaying, Renauld had been careful that the ropes used to tether his wife on the night of the fake abduction were extremely tight—tight enough to convince police of the truth of their tale. But all their effort came to nothing when an unknown entity had entered the game, a killer who had struck Renauld down, turning the desperate ploy of his simulated death into reality.

Poirot next manages to sift through the confusing configuration of characters, subplots, and motivations to arrive at a suspenseful finish. The indomitable detective points an unerring finger at last to identify the surprising least-likely killer of Paul Renauld, while he orchestrates a final ruse that brings things to a head—and summary justice to a most unlikely murderer.

Agatha Christie includes definite stylistic and thematic details in the story. She sometimes inserts names connected to her inspiration true story into her fictional narrative, and in *Links* she retains the name of Mme. Steinheil's daughter Marthe for the "Marthe" of the novel—Mme. Daubreuil's daughter. As well, she takes Mme. Steinheil's given name to entitle the Daubreuil estate, calling it the Villa Marguerite.

By the end of the novel, Agatha Christie has repeated the theme of "the double" throughout its narrative, manifesting it in a variety of ways: the use of a set of twins; a profusion of mistaken identities and of double identities; and in significant cases of personages living double lives, to name several examples. A striking manifestation of the theme is in the symbolism regarding humankind's dual nature, with its conflicting facets of good and evil.

This aspect is personified most graphically in the character of Conneau/Renauld, since the "evil" Conneau is also the same man who has become the "good" Renauld. The novel also features instances where two separate individuals represent each warring half of dual nature: the "good" Mme. Renauld and the "evil" Mme. Daubreuil symbolize good and bad aspects of the beloved and "loving" woman—and of the "good" and "bad" mother. In a way, Poirot and Giraud also exemplify the same kind of dichotomy, with Poirot representing the good way of detecting and Giraud the bad. Christie caps the "doubles" theme and the Shakespearean comic motif running subtly through the tale toward the end of her novel, when Hercule Poirot, in the role of Cupid, lightens the mood by informing his friend Hastings "I have arranged you a marriage." In fact, in the true style of Elizabethan drama, the novel ends with twin marriages in the offing—that of Hastings to his new-found soulmate, and of a much-tried young protagonist to his regained love.

# Chapter 3

# "Dope Girl"
## The Case of Billie Carleton
## and "The Affair at the Victory Ball"

"The Affair at the Victory Ball" was Christie's very first published detective short story, appearing in a September 1923 issue of *The Sketch*, a weekly London newspaper. The story later appeared in the 1951 collection *The Under Dog and Other Stories* and in 1974's *Poirot's Early Cases*. Reflecting, in typically muted Christie fashion, the panicked preoccupation of the society of the time with the suddenly-revealed threat of cocaine addiction among the nation's brightest and best, "The Affair at the Victory Ball" puts its focus on the puzzle. Motive and characterization are basic, but the settings provide color and vitality. Facets of the cautionary tale, involving the death of young and successful Billie Carleton five years before the story's appearance, provide the tale with much of its circumstantial realism and infrastructure.

## The Case of Billie Carleton

The enduring claim to fame—or infamy—of music-hall comedienne Billie Carleton rests more with her death, and the manner of her death, than with any legacy she left as a young music hall star.

She died of a reputed overdose of cocaine on November 28, 1918, only hours after leaving the festivities of the gala Victory Ball. Her dramatic passing cut short her tenure as an up-and-coming musical variety actress in the lively, Edwardian-London theatre scene of the day.

She was born Florence Leonora Stewart in London on September 4, 1896. The birth certificate listed her mother as one Margaret Stewart, a chorus girl, but only a blank line represented the identity of her unnamed father. She later adopted her professional alias, and, following in the show-business footsteps of her mother, set out at 15 to make a name for herself as an entertainer. Her ill-fated star seemed to rise and fall with the waxing and waning of World War I: starting out in the 1914 stage-show chorus of famed producer Charles B. Cochran's *Watch Your Step*, her pert sparkle and prettiness earned her the first solid role of her short career when Cochran tapped her for a featured part in the production. But even at that early date she was already involved with drugs, and Cochran, on learning of her experimenting with opium, cut her out of the show entirely. However by 1917, at age 21, she was back on the boards and near the pinnacle of her brief career, with a featured role in the musical *The Boy*. In early 1918, she appeared in *Fair and Warmer* with Fay Compton—a popular stage and film actress descended from a long line of prominent English actors and stage professionals. Audiences took to Billie's petite beauty, and her charmingly fairylike yet vivacious presence. She sailed from strength to strength, and in August of that year she was tapped to star in *The Freedom of the Seas* at the Haymarket Theatre. A *Times of London* review, in muted praise, noted that her part in the production was "merely to be sprightly" ("Freedom" 9), and that she was.

When the Armistice of November 11, 1918, announced an end to the draining and deeply troubling "Great War," which had erupted in Europe in 1914, all of Britain was more than ready for it. Almost immediately a mood of explosive buoyancy, infused with the high spirits born of relief, began to resurge in England, burgeoning throughout the country in outbursts of triumphant celebration.

The fancy-dress Victory Ball of November 27, 1918, was just such a celebration. Held at London's Royal Albert Hall, the event attracted nearly 4,000 of the world's political, royal, and high-society glitterati, who lit up the venerable edifice with over-the-top opulence and festivity. The fashionable and the famous of several nations thronged the Hall that night, led by duchesses, countesses, and other high-born patrons. Garbed in such costume conceits as "Britannia" and "England" and "Air," the jewelry-bedecked partygoers made the most of their revelry, long into the night.

Britain's entertainment-world stars of the epoch were also out in force, rubbing elbows with the cream of social and political power. An international array of celebrities was represented as well, including American actress Irene Castle. For, at this time in history, the Western world stood at the eve of the Jazz Age, and on the very cusp of the cult-of-celebrity era. Onto this stage frolicked the West End darling of the moment, Billie Carleton, dressed in frothy and daringly revealing chiffon wisps. With her was her Anglo-French fashion-designer friend—who was, whispered some, more than a friend. His was the hand that had created her audacious costume, and he himself sported one of his own designs as well. His name was Raoul Reginald de Veulle, and he had garbed himself that notable night as a particularly conspicuous Harlequin.

Hours before, Billie had finished her performance at the Haymarket Theatre, supped afterwards with friends—actress Fay Compton and Dr. Frederick Stewart, who was Billie's personal physician and money manager as well—and then had gone on to the Victory Ball. She had spent some time mingling and celebrating riotously with her entourage and with other revelers: just what activities she'd engaged in, and with whom, was destined later to become a matter of solemn moment and speculation in a court of law.

On leaving the celebration in the wee hours with fellow actors Lionel Belcher and his paramour, Olive Richardson, Billie repaired to her apartment near the posh Savoy Hotel, where she entertained her friends at an opium-smoking party. She then went to bed, to all seeming in a normal frame of mind and health. But later that afternoon her maid, who thought it was about time to awaken Billie, was horrified to discover the lifeless body of her mistress lying in her bed. Doctors called to the scene suspected a drug overdose; in support of this inference investigators found a little gold box containing a suspect white powder on Billie's bedroom table; a powder which was later identified as cocaine. A supply of the drug Veronal was discovered as well.

Cocaine and opium, though previously legally obtainable, had been effectively outlawed in Britain since the Defence of the Realm Act (DORA) of 1914, which when further enacted in 1916 had summarily made unauthorized possession of those substances a criminal offense. By the time of that milestone legislation, Billie was probably already well on her way to dependence on these and other substances. Though money to pay for her habit was sometimes hard to come by, she had no problem finding suppliers of the drugs she craved in her immediate circle. Reginald de Veulle seemed to be her primary dealer.

Billie Carleton had first made the acquaintance of "Reggie" de Veulle in 1915, when she began modeling his show-business costumes and creations. He supplied her—and himself—with opium and cocaine through London's East End connections, notably via dealings with young actor Lionel Belcher and a rather unorthodox married couple: Ada Lo Ping, a woman of Scots birth, and her elderly Chinese husband, Lo Ping Yu. These three were quite at home in the drug culture of the time: Belcher himself smoked opium, took both cocaine and heroin, and dealt in drugs as well as used them; Ada Lo Ping presided over drugging parties, "cooking" the opium for these clandestine gatherings; Lo Ping Yu, a physically frail near-invalid who had been an opium addict since childhood, kept an opium den in Limehouse.

History has it that Billie Carleton, at barely 22, died of an overdose of illicitly obtained and illicitly used cocaine, which she had sought out and taken of her own volition: suicide was deemed improbable, although later adduced as a possibility in trial. Central questions arose from her death. If she did indeed die of cocaine poisoning, where and when did she obtain the drug, and who supplied it to her? Had she gotten hold of the drug that killed her before, during, or after the Victory Ball? If during the ball, who, among that sophisticated throng, had furnished it? Circumstantially, any of a large cast of characters could possibly have done so, but probabilities narrowed the list to some who were more likely than others. Her close social circle included several candidates, and they had all, like Billie herself, made the scene at the Victory Ball. Had it been fellow actor Lionel Belcher? Or her costume-designer, more-than-friend, Reggie de Veulle? His jealous wife? Or could it have been Billie's own doctor, who had been known to provide her perhaps too liberally with more conventional—and legal—sedatives and sleep-inducers?

Press and public opinion nominated Reggie de Veulle for this distinction. Though of highly respectable British stock (his father had been a Vice Consul to France; his grandfather, Sir John de Veulle, had served as Bailiff/Magistrate of the Isle of Jersey), Reggie's Anglo-French heritage was compromising, and he was looked on as a deviant, a predator of "foreign" descent who ruthlessly victimized the vulnerable of the nation, as symbolized by poor Billie Carleton. He was depicted in newspapers as, among other things, sexually ambivalent: epithets such as "effeminate" and "mincing" were used to describe him. Despite his 1916 marriage to Pauline Gay, a fashion designer five years his senior, he had engaged in at least one homosexual liaison in his past. This aspect of de Veulle's history had been made public when, some years earlier, his relationship with a "gentleman admirer" had been brought to light in an unsavory legal action concerning sexual blackmail. De Veulle had become involved with an older businessman named William Cronshaw during his acting days, and had been instrumental in introducing Cronshaw to another young man, Frederick Powers. Frederick's parents, John and Rose Powers, subsequently threatened to divulge to Cronshaw's family and associates the businessman's immoral relationship with their son—unless they were handed £10,000 as reparation to prevent the socially-damning disclosure. While these enterprising parents were learning from Justice Charles Darling that their suit could well be considered an attempt at blackmail, testimony also incidentally revealed the fact that de Veulle had not only brought Cronshaw and young Powers together, but had also received large sums of money from the businessman. De Veulle was also a known cross-dresser, and had once been discovered at a party where he and others were dressed as women; the incensed citizens who made the discovery then routed the participants by hurling stones at them. In his equally disreputable present, de Veulle and his wife threw "doping" parties at their Mayfair residence at which Pauline de Veulle, though present, claimed not to have indulged. Mrs. de Veulle's own relationship with

Billie was reportedly strained and distant, marked by her abiding jealousy of Billie's relationship with her husband.

When news of the decease of Billie Carleton and its shocking circumstances hit the headlines, the resultant scandal acted as an explosive catalyst. A British population aghast at the turn of events took a hasty, headlong leap into a pitched battle against what it saw as an intolerable moral threat to its way of life. Ethereal Billie Carleton was virtually apotheosized as the poster girl for that threat—the threat which Reggie de Veulle was selected to embody. The public at large seemed to feel that half-hidden forces of moral evil had suddenly sprouted and spawned in society's very midst, and yet society had been largely blind to it. One colonial newspaper, in what seemed like blandest understatement compared to other press fulminations, opined in its introduction to condemnation of the state of affairs that "every now and then, the public are surprised at the revelation of some widespread offence which had not been suspected" ("Drug Scandal" 10). In the Carleton affair, response to that surprise resulted in incensed public outcry; in sensational and sometimes hysterical news coverage; in charges of laxity on the part of law enforcement; and in opportunistic and sanctimonious political harangue—all of which decried the drug counterculture whose widespread existence had barely been suspected up to that time. These reactions precipitated a paranoid, panicked backlash against certain stereotyped segments of society and its under classes—a backlash which seemed to spawn more injustices than it cured.

Billie's heretofore concealed lifestyle was inevitably laid bare, as were the lives of her drug-scene cohorts. Notwithstanding her posthumous elevation in the public mind to near-martyr status, investigations revealed her to have been a quintessential party girl of that dawning flapper era; one who sported nearly all the credentials thereby entailed. Not only was she kept by at least one older sugar daddy—a doting and free-spending wealthy gentleman by the name of John Marsh; not only did she love a good time and indulge in opium and morphine and cocaine; but she also consorted with "degenerates" like drug dealers, drug takers, and drag queens—and Reggie de Veulle was perceived as all three of the latter rolled into one, and more besides.

Billie's perky charm had made her a West End favorite by the time of her demise, but her rising star had been extinguished before reaching any appreciably permanent heights of fame. Her untimely death had definitely opened the door to scandalous revelations of drugtaking and loose living—irretrievably sordid behavior by the moral standards of the day; behavior which should have dimmed her luster in the eyes of the populace. Still, shocked public and press reaction ("Billie Carleton's Tragic Death" 1), based on her youth, looks, and the effervescent girl-next-door façade she had projected in her public persona, followed hard on the starlet's disturbing demise, and she became for many the very symbol of endangered and unprotected young British womanhood at risk in a too-lax world.

On learning of Billie's peccadilloes, the country was left with a new phantasm of fear to contend with, inflamed by the Chicken Little rhetoric of both the sensational tabloids and the censorious establishment press. The message, loud and clear, was that decency and the English way of life was under attack, threatened by this peril which had somehow been allowed to get out of hand. This danger was insidiously perpetrated against the best of the nation, especially its young women, by a lowlife, degenerate, and foreign underclass element, whose motivations were greed and lust underscored by a subtext of class hatred and class envy. This pernicious element's *modus operandi* was ruthless exploitation and degradation, which ultimately and inevitably led to ruin and death. Guileless or unprotected young women were especially vulnerable, preyed upon by older seducers and alien cynics who led them into immorality, and who then secured subjection of these hapless victims by drug dependence. Newspapers continued to ratchet up the panic factor by conjuring up frightening scenarios. A glance at headlines in even moderate newspapers revealed the journalistic trends used to either excite or confirm the public's worst fears, whether they were sentimental ("Drug Victim" 5) or xenophobic ("Drug Cocaine" 3) or moralistic ("The Drug Scandal" 10) or sensational ("'Dope'" 3). One publication even managed to appeal to nearly all prevailing fears and moods by compressing its message into one resourceful caption: "Beautiful 'Billie Carleton': Her Strange Weird 'Life' and Sudden and Lamentable Death; Allegations as to 'Amazing Orgies'; Did 'Billie' and Her 'Unholy' Associates Try to Revive Madame de Montespan's 'Black Mass'?" ("Beautiful" 8).

For decades thereafter, Billie Carleton's "dope-induced" fate was dredged up each time a young woman's accidental death or suicide from cocaine addiction made the headlines. As Kohn points out, "The major application of Billie Carleton's name was as a point of departure for drug stories. Until well into the 1950s, these narratives conventionally began with a reference to tragic Billie Carleton, who epitomized the sorry fate of the drug victim" (114).

The inquest into the cause of Billie Carleton's death took place at intervals between December 3, 1918, and January 19, 1919. The highly publicized proceedings helped translate the public's pugnacious mood into official action. In the out-for-reform aftermath of Billie's death, de Veulle's dodgy lifestyle, as uncovered by official and unofficial investigations, fitted him perfectly for the role of scapegoat in the affair, and the legal inquiry provided the perfect vehicle for casting him firmly in that role.

Westminster coroner Ingleby Oddie conducted the inquest, on which he had at first sat alone. As press and public interest had intensified, resulting pressure required that any serious accusations to come be brought to the attention of a full inquest jury. After an earlier adjournment, the probe resumed on December 12, 1918. A jury had by then been empaneled which continued the hearing as if the panel had been convened from the outset. The change must have seemed an ill omen to de Veulle, Belcher, and other vulnerable witnesses; especially when Mr. Oddie was careful to cite a legal—and chilling—mandate for the move: the possibility of manslaughter charges emerging from the inquiry. A parade of important witnesses gave testimony over the course of the procedure. May Booker, Billie's maid, testified that on the morning after the Victory Ball she had found her employer in a deep stertorous sleep from which she never woke. Medical examiner G. A. Hammerton deposed as to the cause of death, stating, "an overdose of cocaine would be likely to produce the signs he found when he made a postmortem examination" ("Miss" 3). Lionel Belcher, in dubious testimony, admitted to seeing de Veulle greet Billie at the ball, but thought it "impossible that de Veulle could have passed cocaine to her" (3). After the Victory Ball, he (Belcher), Billie, and another friend had left the festivities and gone to her place at the Savoy.

The actor denied seeing anything of Billie's little gold box on the night of the ball, and had no explanation to offer for the Veronal found in Billie's bedroom, but admitted to having participated in doping parties. Belcher cited gatherings at the apartment of an Egyptian named Don Kimful; another hosted by de Veulle at his home; and still another hosted by Ada Lo Ping where she was in charge of cooking the opium at her domicile. These "orgies" had all been attended by himself, de Veulle, and Billie Carleton, along with various others. Belcher also revealed that he had taken Billie, at her request, to an opium den in Chinatown.

The inquest concluded on January 19, 1918, with a verdict reflecting a xenophobic and rush-to-judgment mentality. The coroner's inquest not only found that Billie Carleton had met her death through an overdose of cocaine, but that Reginald de Veulle had provided it to her "in a culpable and negligible manner." De Veulle's hardly exemplary character and background, his drug trafficking, and his sallow, "unmanly" appearance no doubt made it easy for the jury to have seen him as a villainous outsider who deserved to be punished for the death of the young starlet. He was forthwith charged with both the manslaughter death of Billie Carleton, and with conspiracy to supply a prohibited drug under the Defence of the Realm Act. Ada Lo Ping and her husband were also charged, under DORA's Regulation 40B, with supplying opium to Billie between August 21 and October 14, 1918. The places where they did so included 16 Dover Street, Piccadilly—the abode of Reggie and Pauline de Veulle, where "on [one] occasion disgusting orgies took place extending from Saturday night until early in the Sunday afternoon" ("Chinatown" 5).

Reginald de Veulle's manslaughter trial began on April 2, 1919, at London's Old Bailey, with Mr. Justice Salter on the bench, Sir Richard Muir leading for the Crown, and Huntly Jenkins in charge of de Veulle's defense. Muir, in the prosecution's opening statement, asserted that Billie Carleton had died from an overdose of an illegal drug (cocaine) and that the drug had been provided to her illegally. "Therefore," Muir insisted, "the … urgent point before the Court for consideration, was: 'Who did supply that drug to Billie Carleton?' The case for the prosecution was that the prisoner De Veulle was the person who supplied it" ("Case" 3). The nation's press swarmed the proceeding in a frenzy of reportorial zeal, splashing every sensational detail of the trial—real, implied, or simply imagined—across its pages for the delectation of its fascinated readers.

The little gold box found near Billie's deathbed played an all-important role in the course of the drama. The prosecution's case depended heavily on establishing a clear link from de Veulle to Billie and to the cocaine found in that little box at the time of her death. The tiny container, designed as a lady's accessory for holding smelling salts and the like, had been used by Billie to keep and transport her cache of cocaine, as witnesses testified. On the day of the ball, Billie had inadvertently left the box at home on her dressing table. At about nine that night, she had telephoned from the Haymarket Theatre to her maid, May Booker, at Billie's apartment. The maid was asked to bring the box to her mistress at the theatre. May Booker located the box, looked inside it, and found it empty. She then duly delivered it to the theatre, where the container was placed in Billie's handbag. When next it figured, investigators had found the box at Billie's bedside immediately after her death. The little box was proved to have contained cocaine. The residue, the prosecution alleged, of a supply that had killed Billie Carleton: a supply Reginald de Veulle had delivered to her. De Veulle "strenuously denied" doing so; Lionel Belcher at the inquest had also declared that de Veulle had had no opportunity to pass cocaine to Billie at the ball.

By the time of the manslaughter trial, Belcher had obviously decided to protect himself by recanting lies told at the inquest. Not only did he repeat revelations of names, dates, and places for the opium-smoking parties hosted by himself—or Billie, or the de Veulles, or others—but he now declared that de Veulle had in fact brought cocaine to the Victory Ball and had even taken a sniff of it himself in one of the Hall's men's rooms. On the strength of this testimony, then, de Veulle had indeed had a supply of the drug at the ball; a supply that could have contained a quantity destined for Billie Carleton. Furthermore, Belcher now claimed that he had actually seen de Veulle interacting with the starlet during the Victory Ball, although he had denied this at the inquest. He had lied about it, he said, to shield de Veulle.

Other trial testimony went over old ground, and fine-tuned timelines and events. At eleven-thirty the night of the gala, Billie had left the theatre for supper with Fay Compton and Dr. Stewart, and an hour later departed for the Victory Ball. On May Booker's evidence, there was no cocaine in Billie's gold box when the maid delivered it to her after nine. But on arriving with Belcher and Olive Richardson at her apartment around three-thirty that morning, Billie had apparently been in possession of the substance during the ball: Belcher testified that Billie had confided to him she'd been disturbed by some jealous accusations from Pauline de Veulle at the gala, and "being upset about it she had taken a good sniff of the cocaine" (3). If so, Billie had seemingly acquired cocaine sometime between the delivery of the little gold box to her at the theatre, and her departure from the Victory Ball to her apartment. And to the authorities, Reginald de Veulle seemed indicated as the scoundrel who had supplied it to her. Perhaps only too aware of the strong public and political revulsion against him, de Veulle had barely been able to totter to the dock, where he reacted nervously throughout the first day's proceeding on the verge of physical collapse. When, at his own request, de Veulle was treated on the spot, the examining physician had to concur with the defendant's self-diagnosis of being near to fainting, and therefore unfit to continue the proceedings. The hearing was duly adjourned. When the trial had resumed and wound down to its conclusion, the defense's rebuttal had asserted that there was no real proof that Billie had died of an overdose of cocaine—Veronal and other substances as well had been found in her rooms after her death—but even if she had so perished, there was certainly no real proof that de Veulle and de Veulle alone supplied it. The defense was apparently successful, despite the general public's widespread belief in de Veulle's guilt. In the event, the manslaughter charge against Reginald de Veulle ended in acquittal on April 5, 1919, after less than an hour's jury deliberation, and despite the perceived fact that Mr. Justice Salter had clearly summed up heavily for conviction.

On April 7 De Veulle returned to the Old Bailey before Mr. Justice Salter to answer to the lesser charges of drug trafficking. The fashion designer pleaded guilty to conspiracy with Ada Lo Ping to procure "large quantities of cocaine" ("Billie Carleton's Death" 2) between January 1918 and November 28, 1918, and was given a sentence of eight months in prison. Ada Lo Ping received a sentence of five months imprisonment; Lo Ping Yu, on trial at another venue before another judge, received only a fine of £10. His wife served her term, and afterwards died of tuberculosis at age 29, within months of her prison release.

At Reggie de Veulle's sentencing, Mr. Justice Salter made no bones about his disgust towards the defendant's involvement in drug-dealing and all that it led to for its victims: "Traffic in this deadly drug," he rebuked the man before him, "is a most pernicious thing. It leads to sordid, depraved, and disgusting practices ... [followed by] disease, depravity, crime, insanity, despair, and death" (2). The underlying fear in these hyperbolic sentiments—that the vitiating effects of widespread drug addiction could take up where the war left off and continue to devastate for generations the very fabric of British society—was to reverberate in the social consciousness for decades to come. Billie Carleton's tragedy was re-echoed again and again in ensuing years, again and again sounding an unsettling warning knell: in 1922, dancer Freda Kempton died in a cocaine-related suicide. Aristocratic heiress Elvira Barney, a drug-abusing and notorious party girl, survived a sensational murder trial in 1932 for killing her lover, only to end up dying alone in a Paris hotel four years later. Socialite actress Brenda Dean Paul's futile struggle against cocaine addiction and her slow, pitiful decline and poignant death were chronicled in newspaper accounts from her first arrest in 1931 until her demise in 1959.

Between the unsettled, uncertain wake of one devastating war, and the slow uneasy buildup to another, drug use proliferated throughout the culture, from the lowest classes to the highest. Embittered middle and upper class English youth, adrift in a limbo of restless uncertainty, clung to it in an orgy of disillusioned hedonism. Cocaine and other drug use was part and parcel of the lifestyle of Britain's "Bright Young Things" of the 1920s and 1930s, serving as a defiance and repudiation of the old order, the old values that had failed them so spectacularly during and after the Great War. The aftermath of the hostilities had brought unwelcome and permanent changes to British society's old guard, fueled by new social values born of disenchantment; by new economic realities born of hardship; and impacted by the influx of new immigrants of differing races, cultures, and values. The British social order would never be the same again.

## "The Affair at the Victory Ball"

The short story "The Affair at the Victory Ball" finds Poirot investigating a murder committed during the climax of festivities at the fashionable, annual event known as the Victory Ball: a fancy-dress gala celebrating the triumphant end to the Great War, or World War I. The victim, young and wealthy Viscount Cronshaw, had arrived at the ball with a company of friends. The group consisted of his fiancée, the beautiful and fascinating actress Coco Courtenay, who was also the theatrical world's darling of the moment; Cronshaw's impecunious uncle—and heir—The Honourable

Eustace Beltane; an American friend, the vivacious widow Mrs. Mallaby; and the pleasant young actor Christopher Davidson accompanied by his shrewd-eyed wife.

The little group had attended the masquerade elegantly and cleverly costumed as various members of the Italian *commedia dell'arte*, but much as the comedic garb they wore masked their persons, the seeming congeniality of the party masked roiling contentions and motives underneath. The crusading, anti-drug trafficking Cronshaw was dressed as Harlequin; the secret cocaine addict Coco as Harlequin's beautiful and enticing Columbine. Uncle Eustace wore the attire of Punchinello, with Mrs. Mallaby as corresponding Pulcinella; while the Davidsons were costumed as Pierrot and Pierrette.

Something must have caused suppressed emotions and conflicts to erupt, for even the group's forced gaiety seemed to have gone wrong during the course of the revelry. Coco and Cronshaw were observed to quarrel with each other and to be on tense nonspeaking terms as the evening progressed, despite the anxious but discreet efforts of Davidson and the archly merry ones of Mrs. Mallaby to reconcile the rift. Their efforts were signally unavailing: Coco stormed off, imperiously dragooning Davidson into taking her home. Cronshaw had remained at the ball but continued unsociable and aloof from the remaining members of his party, who only glimpsed his moody presence now and then and from afar, recognizable by his distinctive costume.

Then, at unmasking time his body was discovered in a deserted supper room, stabbed to the heart. To compound the tragedy, on the following morning Coco's maid found her mistress dead in her bed of a cocaine overdose. Was her death caused by suicide, accident—or was it also murder, and somehow related to the Viscount's slaying? Her demise seemed too opportune to the murder of Lord Cronshaw to be merely a poignant coincidence. At the scene of Lord Cronshaw's murder a small decorative enamel box had been found, filled with cocaine and with the name "Coco" inscribed on it in diamonds. Cronshaw's fist was discovered to be clenched fast in death around a pompon undoubtedly from one of his party's costumes.

Unluckily for the clever killer, Inspector Japp had urged Hercule Poirot and Captain Hastings onto the case. Poirot would later use the significance of both the box and the pompon to round out a tale of criminal drug trafficking, and to expose and trap a cold-blooded, pernicious killer.

# The Case of Billie Carleton + "The Affair at the Victory Ball"

In "The Affair at the Victory Ball," the character and actions of "Coco Courtenay" parallel those of Billie Carleton, the young English musical-theatre star of the early 20th century. The fate of young Lord Cronshaw is the main concern of the tale; it is his murder that draws Hercule Poirot into the investigation. Coco's probable murder provides background to events that befall the Viscount, but it is her story that harks back to that of the unfortunate Miss Carleton.

The sensational case of Billie Carleton's drug-related demise occurred in 1918. In the tale, the fictional protagonist Coco Courtenay, a young and beautiful and popular theatrical star, perishes much the way that Billie Carleton—a young and beautiful and popular theatrical star—perished in real life. The settings for the deaths of both began at a Victory Ball held in grandiose venues (the "Colossus Hall" in the short story, equating to the gigantic Royal Albert Hall in the true-life event), where both connected with providers of the quantity of cocaine which would later be blamed for killing them. Each had most probably obtained her supply of cocaine at the Ball itself, or directly after it. Each had died, after going home from the Ball to their abodes, from a self-administered overdose that could have been suicide or accident. In the fictional account, another cause-of-death option is added: the chilling possibility of deliberate murder.

Both ladies kept their supplies of the drug in small ornamental boxes; and these dainty containers—an enamel one for Coco and a gold one for Billie—would play significant roles in the investigations that followed their deaths. Both died in bed of suspected cocaine overdoses; and both deaths were discovered by their maids the following day. In the Carleton case, Reginald de Veulle, Billie's "decadent" friend of Anglo-French extraction, was Billie's costume designer and principal drug supplier, and the hapless De Veulle would ultimately be blamed for Billie's death.

To the society of the time, drug-related deaths constituted proclamations of complete moral degeneracy and irreclaimable social disgrace, and foreign drug dealers were seen as the principal purveyors of these horrors. The shadowy figures were execrated as insidious predators who gloried in leading the promising youth of the nation—such as the charming, "vulnerable" Billie Carleton—to the certain degradation and ruin of drug addiction. Dealers brought to account were treated as tantamount to murderers of the most monstrous kind. A frightened Reggie de Veulle, whose partially French heritage seemed to qualify him as "foreign," consequently faced a manslaughter trial conducted in a vengeful atmosphere—an atmosphere electric with intense public outrage. He nevertheless continued desperately to insist that he was neither guilty of supplying Carleton with the fatal dose of cocaine at the ill-starred Victory Ball, or with any other drug. Near miraculously, his lawyers were able to wrest from the trial a grudging acquittal for their client on manslaughter charges.

Though the pertinent query in "The Affair at the Victory Ball" was "who killed Lord Cronshaw and Coco Courtenay?" There was also an important underlying question: who supplied Coco with the cocaine at that celebration? The answer to the latter query would also, as Poirot well knew, supply the answer to the former. As is unsurprising in Agatha Christie tales, almost any character could have qualified as the culprit. Likewise, in the Carleton case, the question of who had provided the drug to Billie, and when, was also of overriding importance. Besides de Veulle there were demonstrably several other candidates for the role of possible supplier. The accused's jealous wife, for example, had been present at the Ball and at Billie's after-party. Billie had also had frequent contact with a husband-and-wife team of opium den proprietors, Ada Lo Ping and Lo Ping Yu, her spouse. Popular actor Lionel Belcher confessed to both using and selling drugs—but did not, he swore, provide any to Billie Carleton at the Victory Ball. However, Belcher had attended the Ball with his love interest of the moment, and had admitted that he had interacted there with Carleton. In addition the actor and his date were also later present at the post-ball party at Billie's apartment.

In the fictional work the personas of several factual twosomes—the de Veulles, the Lo Pings, and Belcher and his lover—were economically melded into a composite couple, the glib husband-and-wife team of Christopher Davidson and his spouse. In addition there was the loose pairing of Mrs. Mallaby and Eustace Beltane.

The story also echoed another theme appearing in the real-life occurrence: Reginald de Veulle reputedly attended the Victory Ball of 1918 dressed in his own design—a stylized Harlequin costume. Christie's tale elaborates on this detail by adorning her narrative with five more masks of the *commedia dell'arte* in addition to that of Harlequin: those of Columbine, Punchinello, Pulcinella, Pierrot, and Pierrette.

Across the body of her work, Agatha Christie seemed to have a fondness for naming some of her characters for real persons—and at times those real persons' names were more or less related to a true crime that inspired some part of her work in hand. The first victim of the fictional tale, Lord Cronshaw, shares another connection with the broader context of the Carleton case: de Veulle had once been involved in a criminal lawsuit for sexual blackmail; one of the lawsuit's principals was named William Cronshaw.

# Postscript

*In addition to exploring the hazards of **cocaine** trafficking in the storyline of "The Affair at the Victory Ball," Agatha Christie also examined consequences of cocaine use or addiction in several other works. References to the substance occur superficially or fleetingly in such stories as* The Murder of

Roger Ackroyd *and* Death in the Clouds, *but there are other tales in which the drug takes on a much larger role.*

*For example, cocaine smuggling is behind a plotline in Christie's* Hickory Dickory Death *which the author outlines in detail (178–188). While investigating a case of eccentric pilfering in a hostel for university students, Hercule Poirot discovers that cocaine is one link between a savaged backpack and tourism to the Continent by the hostel's students.*

*In* Lord Edgware Dies, *Poirot mentions cocaine only in passing as he explains to Captain Hastings how he had spent his day. In Chapter 25 the detective refers obliquely to the substance, disclosing to Hastings that he had just passed an hour "in a ladies' Beauty Parlour." That remark refers to the much-more developed roles that both cocaine smuggling and a beauty parlor play in Christie's tale "The Ambassador's Boots" (231–250). That story, from the collection* Partners in Crime, *features the lively sleuthing of young married detectives Tuppence and Tommy Beresford.*

*In her short story "The Horses of Diomedes" (775–790), Christie imaginatively outlines a surreptitiously clever means of distributing cocaine among users in upper society's ranks. She takes direct aim at drug dealers' cynical and ruthless methods of exploiting weaknesses of abusers while she also proffers a sobering yet humane look at brittle victims—users and suppliers alike—haplessly caught up in the toils of drug trafficking. The two aspects are personified in the character of the confused and vulnerable young Sheila Grant, who not only has begun to take the drug herself, but is also suspected of supplying it to others. Sheila is, however, fortunate enough to have been befriended by one of Hercule Poirot's associates, Dr. Stoddart. The doctor is attracted to Sheila and fights to save her from herself. He enlists the help of Poirot to find and destroy the hidden predators manipulating substance abuse among members of Sheila's social set before it is too late.*

*Stoddart provides a sobering description of cocaine's psychological and physiological effects—a description clad in both the moralistically monitory wording of the era in which the tale was written, and in the clinical knowledge bred of Christie's expertise in chemicals and poisons:*

*"'Cocaine is stuff that starts off making you feel just grand and with everything in the garden lovely,'" the doctor explains. "'It peps you up and you feel you can do twice as much as you usually do. Take too much of it and you get violent mental excitement, delusions and delirium'" (776).*

*In* Peril at End House, *the focus of the novel is not on cocaine, but on Poirot's solving of the vexing mystery of who is attempting to kill young, pretty, and vivacious "Nick" Buckley—and why. Nevertheless Christie features cocaine significantly in the plotting of the work. When a member of Nick's house party is shot dead by the unknown killer, Poirot is forced to reckon with the dangers of cocaine on his way to protecting Nick and ferreting out a crafty killer; for the sophisticated Nick and her equally sophisticated crowd of pleasure-seeking companions have long been playing a risky game of flirting with recreational cocaine abuse. In fact, Nick's best friend "Freddie" Rice struggles in quiet desperation, well on the road to becoming a hopeless addict.*

*In an exciting episode of the novel, Christie wields the drug like a murder weapon: the novel's unknown killer has sent Nick a box of chocolates poisoned with cocaine (170). Later, after Poirot dramatically reveals the murderer's startling identity, cocaine serves another deadly purpose when the exposed killer opts to use it to commit suicide rather than face the gallows.*

## Chapter 4

# "The Crime of the Century"
## The Case of the Lindbergh Kidnapping and *Murder on the Orient Express*

The book was published in 1934 as *Murder on the Orient Express*, but had been printed in serial form in the U.S. in 1933 (in the magazine *The Saturday Evening Post*) as *Murder in the Calais Coach*. A basic motive drives the tale, but is allied with complicated characterizations which begin with "typed" depictions, but, ultimately, reveal strong emotions beneath the façades. The tour-de-force detective story remains one of Christie's most famous and imaginative works, taking as a starting point for its plot the tragedy in the U.S. of the 1932 Baby Lindbergh murder.

## The Case of the Lindbergh Kidnapping

On the night of March 1, 1932, between eight and ten that night, little Charles Augustus Lindbergh, Jr., was abducted from his second-floor nursery bed at his parents' Hopewell, New Jersey home. The child was a few months from his second birthday, having been born to American aviation hero Colonel Charles A. Lindbergh—the "Lone Eagle"—and his wife, socialite Anne Morrow Lindbergh, on June 22, 1930.

A little after ten that night, the child's Scottish nurse, 27-year-old Betty Gow, had discovered that the child was missing and had alerted his parents. After hastily checking the nursery and house, Colonel Lindbergh immediately seized a gun and began a search of the estate grounds. A ransom note was found on the window sill of the nursery room, written in apparently illiterate English, and with apparently Germanic linguistic and spelling errors. The note demanded $50,000 ransom for the child, and was encoded with two interlinked circles: one red, the other blue, creating an oval in the middle, and punched with three square holes, one outside each circle and one inside the oval. This symbol, the note went on, would appear on and verify the authenticity of subsequent communications from the kidnappers. Local and state police had been notified, and their initial investigations found traces of muddy footprints in the nursery, but no fingerprints. They also discovered parts of a broken ladder outside the nursery window.

In the hours and days after the abduction the members of two households, the Lindbergh and the Morrow ménages, were extensively and rigorously questioned. They included servants of the Lindberghs' Hopewell home and those of Next Day Hill, the Morrow estate in Englewood. Next Day Hill was the domicile of Anne Lindbergh's widowed mother, Mrs. Dwight Morrow, and Mrs. Morrow's two other daughters, Elisabeth and Constance.

Colonel Lindbergh had quickly assumed a *de facto* role as leader of the investigation. He had gained lasting fame and adulation when, in 1927, he'd become the first man to fly solo across the Atlantic in a single-engine plane—his own aircraft, *The Spirit of St. Louis*. His status, as both iconic American hero and father of the abducted child, led authorities to defer to Lindbergh's co-option of command. Notable among these authorities was Colonel H. Norman Schwarzkopf, Sr., of the New Jersey State Police, nominally the head investigator of the case. Colonel Lindbergh called on persons in high and low places for help in locating his son. News of the kidnapping galvanized and gripped the attention of the nation and much of the world. Early on, knowing time was of the essence, Lindbergh and some officials had begun speculating about the possible identities of perpetrators of the crime. They conjectured that organized crime was behind the seizing of the child: prime among suspects considered were minions of Al Capone and members of the "Purple Gang" ("Kidnaping" 2). Some officials also held fast to another theory, that at least part of the abduction was an inside job, and one or more of the domestic servants at the Hopewell or Morrow estates could be implicated. A compelling reason for the suspicion was the opportune timing of the kidnapping: it was entirely by accident that the child was at Hopewell on the night of the abduction at all, since his parents' normal practice would have been to have taken him to the Morrow estate. At the last minute it had been decided to spare the child the disturbance of moving him, since he was suffering from a cold at the time. How did the kidnappers know that, on that night of all nights, he would be sleeping at Hopewell? And why did the family dog, Trixie, fail to bark if the abductor had been a stranger?

Chief among the suspected servants was Betty Gow. Who, police asked themselves, would know better about the boy's movements than his nanny? And, on learning that the baby would be remaining at Hopewell, the nanny had telephoned a message to Henry "Red" Johnsen (or Johnson), the Norwegian-sailor boyfriend she'd been seeing for about a year, to inform him of the change in plans and to cancel their date for the night. Or had she called to urge him to the deed, now that unexpected opportunity had arisen? Johnsen had necessary knowledge of the layouts of both estates, having driven Betty back and forth between them on several occasions. But although Gow came in for a good deal of mistrust, the other domestics weren't neglected on her account. Other Lindbergh household servants who came under suspicion and almost incessant interrogation included a British couple: cook Elsie Whately and butler-chauffeur-caretaker-factotum Oliver Whately, her husband.

The Morrow household provided an even greater number of potential suspects. They were given the same inquisitorial treatment as their counterparts at Hopewell. Among others, the domestics at Next Day Hill included: chauffeur Henry Ellerson, gardener George Cowe, English butler Septimus Banks, English housekeeper Mrs. Grimes-Graheme—and English house-parlor maid Violet Sharpe.

Investigations of the servants and their backgrounds were thorough and far-flung. Juicy tidbits for the sensational press were dredged up and splashed all over the newspapers, as was information on virtually anything and anyone connected—however tenuously—to the families, the crime, or the investigations. A volatile atmosphere of shocked hysteria and explosive outrage colored the intense interest in the case; and hysteria continued to reign supreme in public reactions to the kidnapping long after the first wave of stunned disbelief had subsided. It was "the Crime of the Century," and any "outsider" linked to it at all came under a gauntlet of suspicion by officials and the general public alike. The domestics' dirty linen was exuberantly aired in the media: it was revealed that Septimus Banks, despite impressive credentials as past butler to notables such as Andrew Carnegie and Lord Islington, was a drunkard. He had been dismissed several times from the Morrow service because of it. Mrs. Morrow, however, had each time relented and allowed him to return to his duties. His liaison with Violet Sharpe had at one time resulted in a pregnancy, which had been terminated by abortion. The English housekeeper, Mrs. Grimes-Graheme, was found to be proficient in procuring kickbacks from the household's suppliers. George Cowe pilfered gasoline from his employers; and chauffeur Henry Ellerson threw parties at the Morrows' pool when they were away from home (Kennedy 87). Did these depredations and dishonesties also mean they were capable of abducting a young child and holding him for ransom?

Authorities continued their dogged marathon questioning of the household employees. Schwarzkopf persisted in a belief that the "questions he had asked [the servants] the very first day were still not fully answered." The domestics, he felt, provided far too much a probability for guilt than the men of Colonel Lindbergh's fixation on organized crime. "Had Betty Gow," he ruminated, "been duped by an ingratiating thug? ... Had Henry Ellerson, a nomad with a thirst for booze, finally succumbed to his wild streak? Had Banks, demoralized by poverty and liquor, sold his honor for a 'gentleman's cut'?" (Hertog 196).

Betty Gow's boyfriend, Henry Johnsen, had apparently disappeared right after the abduction, and a feverish hunt for him ensued. Officials discovered that he was in the country illegally. When he was finally run to earth, investigators found a milk bottle on the seat of his car. Had it been intended as food for the kidnapped child? But it turned out that Johnsen's suspicious "disappearance" amounted to no more than a brief visit to an out-of-town relative, and the milk bottle merely the evidence of Johnsen's own taste in beverages. His alibi was subsequently found to be perfectly true: his exculpation was patent. In addition, evidence of Betty Gow's demonstratively genuine attachment to the baby prior to his abduction, and her equally genuine distress afterwards, finally convinced investigators that she too had had no hand in the crime.

Violet Sharpe, however, proved more promising material. Her unimpressive looks seemed to match her rather lackluster personality: she had "short, dark hair and sparkling brown eyes. Her protruding front teeth and round, rosy working-girl's face gave her the look of a chipmunk. Overall, she was plump and somewhat bottom-heavy" (Fisher 4). Violet also had a reputation as a rather hysterical young woman. Her appearance and peculiarity notwithstanding, everyone in the Morrow household nevertheless took it for granted that someday Violet would marry Septimus Banks. As far as investigators were concerned, however, the Morrow family's house-parlor maid's odd behavior singled her out almost from the first. She was nervous and abrupt when questioned, grimacing and gesturing unexpectedly and inappropriately throughout the first interview. Still, given the terrible reason for the interrogation, her behavior was initially put down to understandable anxiety and stress. It had been she who had taken the telephone message from Betty Gow, the message stating that the baby would be spending the night at Hopewell. On questioning, she declared to officials that she had been at the movies when the boy was taken. But subsequent inquiry into her alibi proved she had lied. She had instead been picked up by a young man that night, carousing with him and another couple at a local road house during the time she stated she'd been taking in a film.

Given her lies and the fact that she had had knowledge of the child's spending the night at Hopewell, her odd and nervous manner took on a new significance, convincing harried and pressured officials that their belief in her complicity in the kidnapping was totally justified. A second and more relentless interrogation undoubtedly brought this fact home to the young woman. On June 10, 1932, a determined Inspector Walsh telephoned the Morrow home and announced that he was coming to interrogate her for yet a third time. After that warning call the hunted, highly-strung young woman suddenly fell apart. Brokenly exclaiming that she was being blamed for the tragedy and could take no more, she rushed up the stairs to her room and snatched up a bottle of silver polish. Violet Sharpe agitatedly mixed a portion of the cyanide-based solvent with water, gulped it down, and died an agonized death within minutes.

Her dramatic suicide brought Colonel Schwarzkopf under considerable censure for having allowed the hapless woman to be hounded to death. What if Violet Sharpe had only lied about her whereabouts on the night of March 1 because she hadn't wanted her fiancé to learn of her involvement, however casual, with another man? or because she feared losing her job due to "immoral" behavior? Officials continued to maintain, however, that her suicide indicated a guilty conscience about her own complicity in the Lindbergh baby's kidnapping.

Months before Violet Sharpe's death, the tense kidnap drama was still being played out. The second ransom note, postmarked March 4, had arrived at the Lindbergh home on March 6. It advised that the ransom had now been raised to $70,000, to take care of additional accessories-after-the-fact who'd had to be called in because the police had been notified.

On March 8, Colonel Lindbergh had received a third ransom note, rejecting the person the Colonel had proposed as intermediary for the negotiations. Coincidentally, on that same date, septuagenarian New Yorker and former educator John F. Condon inserted himself into the seething situation: in a newspaper interview, he let it be known that he'd be willing to serve as go-between in the ransom negotiations. The next day, Condon received the fourth ransom note, accepting Condon's agency and delivering further instructions. Colonel Lindbergh agreed to the setup. Continuing to communicate via newspaper insertions under the alias "Jafsie"—a play on his initials—Condon began negotiations for effecting delivery of the ransom money and the safe recovery of the child. Forced to follow convoluted cloak-and-dagger directions that involved maneuvers like traveling to abstruse addresses and looking under stones for the next set of clandestine directions, he moved toward face-to-face meetings with the kidnappers.

On March 12, a cabdriver named Joseph Perrone delivered the fifth ransom message to Condon, from a sender unknown to the driver. The note sent Condon to another location, where the sixth ransom note was waiting. That note directed Condon to Woodlawn Cemetery at a specified hour, where Condon at last made contact with an unidentified stranger who called himself simply "John." For over an hour, Condon and "John" discussed the terms of the payoff and the restoration of the baby. "John" had consented

## The Case of the Lindbergh Kidnapping

to provide evidence proving the identity of the child, and on March 16, Condon received a seventh ransom note along with a child's sleeping garment. The Lindberghs positively identified the garment as belonging to their son.

The ransom money had meanwhile been prepared for the payoff. The bills had not been marked, but authorities recorded serial numbers of some of the notes. During the ensuing weeks, Condon took delivery of several more wary and evasive messages from the kidnappers, and by April 2, a total of ten ransom notes had been received. On that date, Condon received the eleventh ransom note, which directed him to the twelfth message, found under a stone near a Bronx hothouse. The note led to a thirteenth message—and a rendezvous that same night, where Condon negotiated the ransom price down to its original $50,000. On Condon's handing the money over to him, "John"—by now known as "Cemetery John"—handed Condon in return what he said were instructions on where to locate the Lindbergh baby. The note read that the child was being held on a boat called *Nelly*, which lay in waters near Martha's Vineyard. The next morning, a search for the boat—and the child—proved futile. The kidnappers had betrayed the deal and reneged on their promise to return the child.

But on May 12, 1932, all the desperate hopes and efforts to recover the boy alive and well came to an appallingly sad end. Nearly two months after the kidnapping and the onset of one of the most publicized and sensational crime-enforcement operations in American history, Hopewell truck driver William Allen and a companion, Orville Williams, happened upon the body of the child, in a leaf-covered shallow grave within 5 miles of the Lindberghs' Hopewell home. It fell upon Mrs. Morrow, the child's grandmother, to break the devastating news to his mother: "The baby," Mrs. Morrow told her daughter gently, "is with Daddy" (Douglas and Olshaker 124).

Postmortem evidence found that the boy had died of a fractured skull, and had died some two months earlier—probably killed on the very night of his abduction. With this end to one phase of the ordeal, another one was commenced: the search for a murderer or murderers.

The tracked ransom money was instrumental in leading to an eventual suspect. Following the discovery of the slaying, officials kept an eager but determined and careful watch out for reported passing of any of the traceable ransom bills. Trickles of the tracked gold certificates began surfacing soon after the ransom had been paid, but the biggest break in the case came two years after the crime. A customer had paid a gas station attendant with a gold certificate. The customer's slightly off-key demeanor prompted the attendant to note down the license number of the purchaser's car on the note itself. The certificate was confirmed to be one of the tracked bills, and the license number was traced to the automobile of one Bruno Hauptmann. Officials proceeded with caution as they investigated the background of the man, who proved to be a 32-year-old German carpenter, born in Saxony, Germany in 1902, and a resident in the United States for over a decade. Hauptmann fit Condon's description of "Cemetery John" and the gas station attendant's account of the purchaser who had paid with the telltale gold certificate.

On September 19, 1934, officials decided they had enough evidence to proceed. Bruno Richard Hauptmann was arrested by FBI and local investigative agents as he exited his residence at 1279 East 222nd Street, the Bronx, New York. On September 26, 1934, Hauptmann was indicted in the Bronx on charges of extortion. The following October 8, 1934, he was indicted for the murder of Charles Augustus Lindbergh, Jr.

Hauptmann's monthlong trial for the crime commenced on January 2, 1935, at Flemington, New Jersey. The case against him was dependent on pieces of circumstantial evidence, chief among which were the facts that he was identified by Condon, Colonel Lindbergh, and others as "Cemetery John," and by others as someone seen near the Lindbergh estate at the critical times. Hauptmann had also made several purchases using gold certificates from the tracked ransom monies; $11,000 to $14,000 of the ransom money was found hidden at his home; and part of the ladder used in the kidnapping was made from wood flooring of his attic. In addition, Hauptmann's handwriting was declared to be the same as that in the ransom notes and Condon's telephone number was found written on a closet wall in Hauptmann's home. Hauptmann's defense, led by Ed Reilly, claimed that Hauptmann had been keeping the money found at his home for a friend named Isadore Fisch, who had died in 1933 after returning to Germany. Hauptmann had denied his guilt, and testified that he'd been beaten and forced to alter his handwriting to resemble that of the ransom notes. On February 13, 1935, a jury convicted Hauptmann of first degree murder, which carried the death penalty. His appeal to the New Jersey Supreme Court was denied in October 1935; his appeal to the United States Supreme Court was denied in December 1935. He was scheduled for execution by electrocution on January 17, 1936, but received a 30-day reprieve; in February 1936 his date with death was rescheduled to take place in March. When New Jersey denied a last-ditch request for clemency, he was finally executed on April 3, 1936. He maintained that he was innocent to the last.

The Lindbergh kidnapping case has continued to generate both controversy and speculative alternative solutions to the crime. Was Hauptmann afforded a fair trial? Was evidence manufactured or tampered with? If he was innocent, who was really guilty? If he was guilty, did he also have an accomplice or accomplices? Alternative nominees bruited for committing the crime included such unlikely candidates as Anne Lindbergh's sister and Colonel Lindbergh himself, among many others. Hoax theories abounded, including one maintaining that the body identified as baby Lindbergh was not little Charles at all: the real Lindbergh child was spirited away and raised in some foster abode, never having his true identity revealed to him. Contemporary revisionist works about the still-fascinating case attempt to prove convincing new or re-worked solutions for the lingering doubts and mysteries of the case.

## Murder on the Orient Express

In the novel *Murder on the Orient Express* (1934), Hercule Poirot finds that he has suddenly been recalled to England from a visit to Istanbul. By a series of accidents and contrivances, the little detective manages to latch onto a last-minute berth on the unexpectedly sold-out Simplon Orient Express, which journeyed from Istanbul to London by way of Calais. It seems that fate took a hand in making sure that the dapper little detective was aboard the train on that exceedingly harsh winter night: for, just before the Express is unforeseeably snowbound, someone commits a bold murder in one of its sleeping cars.

It is a strange, ferocious murder, for the victim was stabbed twelve times as he lay in his berth during the night. Circumstances make it plain that the culprit had either departed the train before it was stopped by the snowbanks—or perforce remained among passengers still on the liner, prevented from escape by impassable drifts. The train's immobilization allows Poirot time to investigate before the local authorities arrive; he does so at the fervent entreaty of his excitable friend M. Bouc, a director of the Compagnie Internationale des Wagons Lits. Understandably, M. Bouc urgently desires that the scandalous murder be cleared up without delay, both to mitigate as much as possible the damage to the line's reputation and to avoid the imminent and muddled ministrations of the local police.

The victim is discovered to be a much-hated criminal, an American organized crime figure. He had called himself Ratchett, but his real identity was that of the infamous Cassetti—the monster behind the internationally notorious kidnapping for ransom, and subsequent cold-blooded killing, of a young child from a revered American family. The tragedy had taken place five years earlier. The child was little Daisy Armstrong, daughter of Colonel Armstrong, the famous and beloved war hero. The kidnappers demanded a large, promptly-paid ransom from the wealthy family, but tragically little Daisy's body had been found soon after. Evidence revealed that the child had been killed almost immediately after the abduction, long before the ransom was asked for and received. It had been a heartrending case. Not only had dearly-loved three-year-old Daisy been ruthlessly slain, but the repercussions from the unimaginable tragedy claimed several more innocent lives while irreparably ruining a number of others.

When the kidnapping was first discovered investigators felt pressured to produce an immediate solution to the high-profile case—a case which all the world was following with close and horrified attention. Officials focused initially on organized crime, but soon local authorities had turned their attention to little Daisy's household. Several believed the abduction had all the earmarks of an inside job, and officials came down hard on the servants of the household to prove it. Among the employees targeted for suspicion and relentless questioning were the governess, the cook, the chauffeur, the Colonel's valet, the nurse, and the nursemaid. All of them professed to be deeply devoted to little Daisy or to her parents, but they had all nevertheless been put through the terrors of repeated hostile examination and cross-examination.

In swift, relentless succession horror upon horror had followed the merciless abduction and murder of Daisy Armstrong. The child's mother, Sonia Armstrong, had been pregnant at the time; the shock and grief of the sudden terrible events sent her into premature labor and both baby and mother died. Colonel Armstrong, with all his family snatched from him in an appalling instant, committed suicide in broken despair—as did Daisy's young French nursemaid, Susanne, driven to self-murder by the ceaseless torment of police who were convinced of her complicity in Daisy's abduction.

The inexorable rain of unbearable losses one after another sent surviving relations and friends reeling. They included Sonia Armstrong's mother and her younger sister, the grieving grandmother and aunt of little Daisy, and Sonia's godmother as well. There was also Colonel Armstrong's stalwart best friend. Susanne's death left behind a stricken father and a stunned sweetheart. And there were other allies and adherents who also suffered from the unthinkable turn of events.

To compound the horror, although Cassetti's trial had proven him guilty beyond a doubt of Daisy's kidnap and murder, the killer had escaped conviction on a technicality. An outraged public heaped opprobrium and blame for failure on the district attorney who had charge of the case. The gang which Cassetti masterminded had made a profitable practice of extorting money through abduction and ransom—and of callously killing the victim when that course seemed expedient. With the blood-tainted money gained from these crimes, Cassetti had fled the country after the trial. Now, retribution of one kind or another had apparently caught up with the vicious murderer.

Poirot finds sparse clues in the baffling case. The breakthrough comes when he unearths a telling clue; from there it was a short step to discovering that the dead man was not Ratchett but Cassetti, the undoubted engineer of the kidnapping and murder of the Armstrong child five years before. The clue leads inescapably to the conclusion that someone connected with the Armstrong case is the criminal's assassin. Which passenger on the train had that connection? Poirot determines to find out.

The travelers turn out to be a wildly disparate lot, composed of differing classes and different nationalities. Poirot had first encountered two Britons when he initially approached the train: Colonel John Arbuthnot, a distinctly military type; and Mary Debenham, a coolly correct young woman. The murdered man's valet, Edward Masterman, was also a British subject. The aristocratic Princess Dragomiroff was a naturalized French citizen; Count Andrenyi was Hungarian. His lovely young bride the Countess was discovered to be American, though now traveling on a Hungarian passport. The private detective Cyrus Hardman; Hector Macqueen, the slain man's secretary; and the unabashedly loud and lively housewife Mrs. Hubbard were also American, as was the brash Italian-born car salesman from Chicago, Antonio Foscarelli. Sweden was represented by the meek missionary, Greta Ohlsson, while the Princess's biddable but ungainly maid, Hildegarde Schmidt, was German. Apparently fate had assembled a train full of passengers thrown together by the luck of the draw—people who, in the ordinary course of events, could have had very little to do with or in common with each other. But they were about to be united by a unique and bizarre circumstance: they now had in common the fact that they were all about to be considered equal suspects in a case of murder.

Poirot pursues his investigations, patiently interviewing each traveler and painstakingly unraveling the scenarios they present to him. Then, though each tries at first to sidetrack the little detective, to hide their true identities, and to bluff their way through, Poirot little by little is led to a staggering truth: incredibly, each and every passenger on the Express is somehow linked to the Armstrong case: Mrs. Hubbard is revealed to be the great actress Linda Arden—the mother of Sonia and grandmother of little Daisy. Count Andrenyi is her son-in-law, husband of Helena, Countess Andrenyi: Linda Arden's younger daughter, and therefore the younger sister of Sonia Armstrong and aunt of Daisy Armstrong. The formidable Princess Dragomiroff is Sonia's godmother, and great friend of Linda Arden.

Colonel Arbuthnot is shown to have been Colonel Armstrong's best friend; Mary Debenham was Sonia Armstrong's dedicated secretary and had once been Helena's governess. Ratchett's secretary Hector MacQueen is the son of the district attorney who unsuccessfully tried the Armstrong case; and was besides a great admirer of Sonia Armstrong. Ratchett's valet Masterman was Colonel Armstrong's batman during the war; Hildegarde Schmidt, now masquerading as Princess Dragomiroff's maid, had been the

Armstrong family cook; the missionary Greta Ohlsson had been little Daisy's fond nurse. The ostensible car salesman Antonio Foscarelli turns out to have been the Armstrong family chauffeur. Unbelievably, it also transpires that one of the train's own crew is the father of Susanne, the French nursemaid who committed suicide, while Cyrus Hardman proves to be the man who'd been in love with her. A train full of suspects, all bound to the Armstrong tragedy in one way or another: it seems a foregone conclusion that the murderer of the evil Ratchett had to be among this group, and that revenge was the motive.

But which one of them, among all the likely candidates, actually committed the murder? An astonishing denouement, constituting one of her most ingenious solutions, provides the answer to the question—and once again, Agatha Christie has served up a tour de force that demonstrates why she is the "Queen of Crime."

# The Case of the Lindbergh Kidnapping + *Murder on the Orient Express*

In several of her works of detective fiction Agatha Christie takes the opportunity to comment, via her stories' themes, on topics of social injustice. In *Murder on the Orient Express* (1934), two of those themes are foregrounded: the need to right a terribly "unrighted," real-world criminal wrong, if only vicariously through her fiction; and the need for "saving" publicly persecuted but guiltless bystanders—again, if only through her fictional creations—who, through no fault of their own, have been entrapped and vilified in real-world, sensational crimes. She uses the forum of her novel to "punish" a terrible and tragic injustice: the fictional kidnap and killing of little Daisy Armstrong, whose known murderer has nonetheless escaped justice, and to vindicate innocent individuals whose lives were destroyed by wrongful suspicion of taking part in the crimes.

The background story of Agatha Christie's novel *Murder on the Orient Express* is inspired by the tragic Lindbergh Kidnapping case of 1932. The framework characters of the novel present little difficulty in identification with the real-life individuals involved in the Lindbergh affair: the story's three-year-old "Daisy Armstrong," her father "Colonel John Armstrong," and her mother "Sonia Armstrong" correspond respectively to the true crime's two-year-old victim, Charles Lindbergh, Jr.; his famous father, American aviation hero Charles Lindbergh, Sr.; and little Charlie's gentle, socially and literarily prominent mother, Anne Morrow Lindbergh.

Charles Lindbergh, Jr., was kidnapped from his nursery on the night of March 1, 1932. A note had been left demanding ransom. The crime stirred the nation and large parts of the world as an unprecedented manhunt and all-out effort to recover the child safely was unleashed. Organized crime figures were first suspected of the crime, and Lindbergh as well as law officials focused on negotiating with various gang leaders for return of the child. But that path proved fruitless, and authorities, believing the abduction to be at least partially an inside job, turned fierce attention on the domestic staffs of the Lindbergh and Morrow households. Scandalous details of the frailties and personal lives of the servants were blown up, sensationalized, and blared across newspaper columns everywhere. The alcoholism of a butler, the terminated pregnancy of a maid, a lie about a visit to a movie theatre—all became fodder for voracious purveyors of sensational news, catering to an equally voracious public appetite for any information related to the case. Every smallest aberration was hysterically distorted, taking on ominous significance, and also taking its toll in human suffering: in one case high-strung Violet Sharpe, a maid in the Morrow household, sadly snapped under the strain and committed suicide.

The ransom was duly paid, but the child was never recovered. The heartbreaking end to the search came when the body of little Charlie was found in May 1932; it was determined that he had been killed only hours after the kidnapping that March night. All the intervening days and weeks of grimly determined investigation and desperate hope had therefore been spent on an already-lost cause.

In 1934, one of the bills from the ransom money was passed, leading authorities to Bruno Richard Hauptmann. The German carpenter, who had lived in the United States for over a decade, was arrested and tried for the kidnap and murder of the child. He claimed innocence, but strong circumstantial evidence tied him to the crime. Found guilty after a sensational trial, he went to the electric chair in 1936. Controversy over Hauptmann's guilt or innocence has raged from the time of his execution to the present day.

The storyline of *Murder on the Orient Express* commences years after the kidnapping and murder of Charlie's counterpart, little Daisy Armstrong. Agatha Christie usually focused on members of the higher social classes as principal characters in her fiction accounts, and *Murder on the Orient Express* is not really an exception. Countess Helen Andrenyi, whom we discover in the novel is Sonia Armstrong's sister, seems a composite of Anne Morrow Lindbergh's sisters Constance Morrow and Elisabeth Reeve Morrow. In the imaginary account Mrs. Hubbard is revealed as the great actress Linda Arden, mother of both Helen and Sonia and therefore little Daisy's grandmother, thus equating to real-life matriarch Elisabeth Morrow, the stalwart yet motherly mainstay of the families during the anguish of the kidnapping and its outcome. Colonel Arbuthnot, best friend and war buddy to Colonel Armstrong in the novel, corresponds to Major Thomas Lanphier, real-life best friend, business partner, and flying instructor of Colonel Charles Lindbergh. Yet, reflecting the large number of domestic and estate servants prominently publicized during the Lindbergh investigation, in her novel Christie concentrates more than usual on the personas and concerns of a larger than customary contingent of servants and employees. Social class plays an important part in the story, as it did in the real-life event, and servants have considerable roles to play in both the creation of Christie's mystery and in its unraveling. This approach echoes the sensational role that the Lindbergh and Morrow servants were compelled to play in the true-life kidnapping saga, as several were forced into defensive reactions for self-protection. Agatha Christie seems to have perceived in their dilemmas a prime example of a situation she deplored, and in her novel she exposes and denounces that situation, providing the optimum scope for weaving both the denunciation and the true crime's elements into her own fictional puzzle of detection.

In the Lindbergh case, local authorities and rapacious news media targeted the domestic servants of both the Morrow and the Lindbergh households as viable "inside job" suspects, brutally spotlighting and sensationalizing the flaws in their private lives. The Morrow estate's English butler Septimus Banks, a faithful retainer who was faithfully retained by Mrs. Morrow despite his alcoholism, and Lindbergh butler/factotum, the Englishman Aloysius (Olly) Whateley, are both reflected in *Murder on the Orient Express* as composite character Edward Masterman, Ratchett/Cassetti's supposed English valet. The fictional Masterman (whose name plays on the relationship of "master" and "man," or valet), had begun his relationship with Colonel Armstrong as his batman during the war. He continued the relationship later as Armstrong's loyal valet while also serving as butler to the Armstrong household.

Several other domestic characters in *Murder on the Orient Express* also formed close relationships with the Armstrong family: they had either adored little Daisy, revered her parents, or were strongly attached to associates of the Armstrongs. Their knowledge of household routines and access to the child—or to individuals who had that access—made it inevitable that officials would severely scrutinize their possible complicity in the abduction. Conversely, these same circumstances help to make understandable their dramatic roles as revealed near the conclusion of the novel.

During the drastic inquiries into the Lindbergh child's kidnapping, the Morrow family chauffeur, American Henry Ellerson came under heavy suspicion. He is reincarnated in *Murder on the Orient Express* in part as Italian Antonio Foscarelli, the Armstrong family chauffeur. Betty Gow, the capable, efficient yet loving Scottish nanny to little Charlie Lindbergh, is reborn in Christie's tale partly as Mary Debenham, the Scottish governess to the

Armstrong family and secretary to Sonia Armstrong. Also, Gow is reborn partly as supposed Swedish "missionary" Greta Ohlsson, who had been, in the novel, the Armstrong child's nurse. Investigators had grimly latched on to Gow as of major interest in the crime because of her position as primary caregiver to little Lindbergh. Hector MacQueen, Cassetti's ostensible secretary in the story, turns out in truth to be a devotee of Sonia Armstrong. Hector's major domo role reflects that of Arthur Springer, the chief of the Morrow estate employees as its manager and head of staff. In addition, Hector's references to the attacks on his District Attorney father's handling of the fictional Armstrong case brings to mind the real-life strictures on the performance of police superintendent H. Norman Schwarzkopf Sr., in the Lindbergh case.

Christie also evokes the differing nationalities of employees in the Lindbergh and Morrow homes, by her use of differing nationalities for characters in the novel. The Swedish nationality of Greta Ohlsson recalls the corresponding Scandinavian background of Red Johnsen. Johnsen's girlfriend Betty Gow's own Scottish ethnicity, as well as her charge of the Lindbergh child, is in turn invoked by Mary Debenham's Scots nationality and by her former charge of the Armstrong family children; Fräulein Hildegarde Schmidt, Armstrong family cook masquerading as lady's maid to the redoubtable Princess Dragomiroff, seems a German counterpart to Englishwoman Elsie Whateley, the Lindbergh family cook.

The author also forges connections among the nationalities with interpersonal or occupational roles that overlap or correspond, sometimes arbitrarily, with those roles in the Lindbergh case. For example, Septimus Banks' fiancée, Mrs. Morrow's English house-parlormaid Violet Sharpe, is comparable to the young French nursemaid to Daisy Armstrong in the novel who is sweetheart of American Cyrus Hardman. Their fictional romantic relationship echoes the real-life pairing, in the Lindbergh saga, of Norwegian Henry "Red" Johnsen and Betty Gow; and also reminds of the affair between Banks and Sharpe. The true-life situations of the persecuted Lindbergh and Morrow domestics seemed perfectly matched to the type of situation which Christie at times took pains to decry in her fictional works. The servants' stories would have provided a rich lode for the author's commentary on a favorite theme: the effect on the lives of the guiltless who, suspected of a sensational crime, are helplessly caught up in the inescapable juggernaut of that suspicion. The cases afford a forum for the author's commentary, via her fiction, on the terrible individual and social fallout from that kind of injustice.

There is a primary, and overriding, moral theme pervading the narrative of *Murder on the Orient Express*. Agatha Christie, in her works of mystery fiction, aims high, seeking to provide refined, quality, and pleasurable entertainment through her detective-story puzzles, and *Murder on the Orient Express* duly accomplishes this goal. The novel's storyline and the solution, however, are problematic as well as ingenious. *Murder on the Orient Express* is in company with several other Christie tales, such as "Three Blind Mice" and *The Mirror Crack'd*, where characters take the law into their own hands to punish tragic wrongs which escape societal mechanisms for sufficiently redressing those wrongs.

Christie appears to assert the moral right of surviving victims to feel rebellious against the fact that justice, in their eyes, has been denied them. But though their desire to avenge injustice is understandable, even inevitable, just how far they may forgivably go to act out their revenge becomes the moral question of the tale. Therefore the denouement and outcome of *Murder on the Orient Express* may cause even the least philosophical of readers to pause a moment to take in their import. The invitation to meditate on the nature of justice is present in greater or subtler degree in many of Agatha Christie's narratives. However, that encouragement becomes almost an imperative in *Murder on the Orient Express*. Beneath the surface of the story, Christie embeds challenging ethical questions within the tale's premises. Readers are left, if they so desire, to make choices, as did the characters within the pages of the novel—including Hercule Poirot.

## Chapter 5

# "The Kidwelly Mystery"
## Harold Greenwood and "The Lernean Hydra"

The short story "The Lernean Hydra" makes up one of Hercule Poirot's twelve *Labors of Hercules*, first published in a book collection in 1947. It was much earlier, however, that "The Lernean Hydra" made its very first appearances. The work was published in 1939 in London's *Strand Magazine* and in the American periodical *This Week*, under the title of *Invisible Enemy*. The short story's original publication, therefore, came 19 years after Harold Greenwood's notorious trial, and mirrors in a number of components the features of that sensational affair.

## Harold Greenwood

The almost incredibly insouciant behavior of Harold Greenwood, Mabel Bowater Greenwood's husband, just before, during, and after her passing, gave rise to the town gossip that led him to the dock. His conduct had marked him as a man of little insight, who had little care for anything beyond his own self-interested desires—but did that also mark him a cold-blooded uxoricide? The people of Kidwelly thought so. Just after World War I, the philandering solicitor was charged in Wales with the willful murder of his wife by arsenic poisoning.

Even among accounts of true crime, which by their very natures are dark, the story of Mabel Greenwood's death and its repercussions is particularly unpleasant. The mystery of the death of this quiet, reserved wife and mother still remains unresolved a hundred years afterwards. Her poignant claim on justice seems to have been lost in the clamor of individual survivors and bystanders as they struggled for survival or gain in the aftermath of her demise.

Though there was true tragedy in her death, and later, real dignity in the conduct of the ensuing murder trial's prosecutors, judge, and jury, the clumsy insensitive infighting of associates and "friends" throughout the process threatened to undermine the deadly gravity of the situation.

The mystery of the estimable woman's death is accompanied by a bizarre subtext displaying nearly all the ingredients of a Restoration play—one almost worthy of a Wycherley or a Vanbrugh—save for the missing wit and sense of purpose. Something approaching cynicism toward social convention abounds. Rampant vicious rumor, in the guise of social concern, masks complicated motives and hidden agendas; and desperate, inept, near-farcical sexual politics taint and distort the true tragedy of a woman's problematic death. As noted, this subtext lacked the sharp and edifying sting of deliberate satirical wit—but satire it turns out to be all the same, and nonetheless mordant for its accidental manifestation as byproduct of a tragic occurrence that deserved more respect than many were equipped to give it.

Greenwood himself seemed to exhibit the behavior of a moral slob, while several of the other main characters, including Greenwood's famous defense attorney—succumb, too often for comfort, to the lures of opportunism, in pursuit of what should have been more laudable goals.

Harold Greenwood went on trial for the murder of his wife, Mabel, in November 1920. The strange path leading to this strange circumstance had begun mundanely enough some 24 years earlier. Greenwood, a Yorkshire solicitor, and Mabel Bowater were married in 1896, and two years later Greenwood relocated his practice to the Welsh town of Llanelly. The couple set up household in nearby Kidwelly, in Carmarthenshire, Wales. In time, they became parents of four children: Irene, the eldest; Eileen, Ivor, and Kenneth. The family resided in a fine mansion called Rumsey House where they lived a comfortable middle-class life, complete with servants such as young parlormaid Hannah Williams and middle-aged cook Margaret Morris.

Mrs. Greenwood was the spouse with the money, a private fortune of her own, and it was she who had purchased their home. She came of a politically and socially prominent Middlesex family and could boast that her brother, Sir Thomas Vansittart Bowater, had been Lord Mayor of London from 1913 to 1914; he would later serve as Member of Parliament for the City of London from 1924 to 1938. Mrs. Greenwood's husband seemed less successful all around. Greenwood's income from his profession was erratic at best—his practice failed to flourish, and what clientele he had seemed to be of a rather shady nature—"moneylenders and their ilk" ("Mystery"). He had also contracted a reputation as a womanizer in that part of the world, and in so doing became fair game for whispered local gossip. There had reputedly been specific rumors about Greenwood and his relations with May Griffiths, the local doctor's sister; but though there were reports of jealousy on Mabel's part, it didn't seem to interfere to any serious degree with the Greenwood marriage.

The couple seemed to be on good terms with one another, despite the town gossip about Harold Greenwood's extramarital escapades, which provided the ongoing and incessant murmur underlining the tenor of their marriage. The Greenwoods were of course prominent in their local community, where Mrs. Greenwood was well thought of by the townsfolk: she comported herself like a lady, attended church at St. Mary's, and took part in local social functions, although she was not always in the best of health. It was known that she suffered from a heart complaint, and had been subject at infrequent times throughout the years to fainting spells that would last from a few minutes to an hour. She also endured fears that she had cancer, but never followed through on a medical examination to find out for certain if it were so. Her husband seemed to like a good time and a good joke, but was considered unrefined and somewhat of a deliberate troublemaker. He had few local friends, and fewer still who were male.

On the Sunday afternoon of June 15, 1919, 47-year-old Mabel felt unwell after the one o'clock luncheon meal of vegetables, lamb roast, burgundy wine, and gooseberry tart which she had just shared with her family: her husband, 21-year-old daughter Irene, and nine-year-old son Kenneth. The pain in her abdomen, she thought, was caused by a complaint she'd had before, and she ruefully blamed it on the dessert she had eaten, stating, "gooseberry tart always [disagreed] with her" ("Poison-Tongue" 4). She felt well enough to try going on with her Sunday routine, especially when longtime friend Florence Phillips stopped by that afternoon. Mabel managed to greet and to visit with her awhile, inviting her to return for supper later that evening.

When Mabel Greenwood's complaint progressed to vomiting and diarrhea, her physician of longstanding, Dr. Thomas Griffiths, was called in at about six that evening. Doctor Griffiths lived with his sister May across from Rumsey House. He was not only a very near neighbor to the Greenwoods but a family friend as well, despite rumors about his sister and the master of Rumsey House. The medicines he provided Mabel that day were familiar to her: bismuth, sent over after the doctor's later seven o'clock visit, was a stomach medication she had taken before.

More vomiting and purging ensued throughout the remainder of the day as her condition steadily deteriorated. By the time Miss Phillips returned that night, at about seven-thirty, Mabel had already been twice seen by Dr. Griffiths, and had retired to her room, racked by bouts of sickness. On learning of her friend's illness, Miss Phillips went quickly to fetch the district nurse, Elizabeth Jones, who arrived at the Greenwood home at about eight that night. She found Mabel Greenwood in what she described as a state of cold and collapse. Later that night the doctor sent over a dose of sedative pills by Greenwood, but they were administered to no avail. The patient showed no improvement but fell into a comatose state. Nurse Jones later deposed at the inquest to have become suspicious about the state of affairs at about one in the morning, as the patient had throughout exhibited symptoms which the nurse considered strange for Mrs. Greenwood's assumed gastric condition.

At about three-thirty in the morning of June 16, Mabel Greenwood suddenly died. The doctor reportedly expressed no surprise at her death, since she had been ailing for a long while, and had even seemed worse in the past few months. He certified her death as due to valvular heart disease. This attestation did not satisfy some of her acquaintances. The fact that it had already been generally "known" even before Mabel's death that her middle-aged husband had been "carrying on" seemed to give license to local gossipers to ratchet up their output. Greenwood's name had been coupled not only with that of Dr. Griffiths' sister, but also with that of one Gladys Jones, among others, and now more and more gossip began to rise and circulate, becoming louder and more insistent now that the wife of the philanderer was no longer alive to suffer from it. And now her very death was about to add a new and darker facet to their conjectures.

The new widower's demeanor and his womanizing behavior were scarcely discreet. Greenwood's heedlessly scandalous behavior escalated, and the scandalized talk kept pace with it, driven now by the added spur of agitated speculation that there was something extremely suspicious about Mabel's sudden death.

On July 12, not even a month after his wife's demise, Greenwood became more or less secretly engaged, presenting the selected lady with an engagement ring which he'd bought the day before. Surely he should have known how dangerously fatuous a move this was, since he could not have been unaware of the talk swirling around the village both before and after Mabel Greenwood's death. Such a provocative step was too momentous to have had any real hope of being kept secret, or of spiking the guns of the gossipmongers, if such had been his misguided intention—not in an environment of roiling village intrigue like the Kidwelly of the time.

And then, on October 1, 1919, a scant four months after the death of Mabel Greenwood, Harold Greenwood officially took unto himself a second wife. His chosen bride, the Gladys Jones whose name had previously been linked with his, was daughter of the owner of a local newspaper, the *Llanelly Mercury*, and the lady was nearly 20 years younger than her 48-year-old bridegroom. The apparent callousness of this further piece of social folly had obviously never penetrated the solicitor's consciousness before he did the deed—but its consequences were certainly brought home to him in no uncertain terms immediately afterwards.

Town gossip exploded.

Mabel Greenwood had been popular with Kidwelly's townspeople and her widower's abrupt remarriage was in disgracefully unseemly haste after her very recent death. It was the last straw: many now did not hesitate to state freely, flatly, and openly their belief that Harold Greenwood, "undoubtedly what is known as a 'ladies man'" (Duke 8), had murdered his wife—had poisoned her to take a younger bride.

Yet it was particularly puzzling to pinpoint the origins of the rampant rumors alleging that murder had been committed—the rumors that triggered the authorities' reaction and set the wheels of official investigation in motion. But when the smoke of subsequent official inquiry cleared, four Kidwelly villagers stood out from the rest—four whose gossip-mongering zeal appeared to be at the core of circumstances which plunged Harold Greenwood into a trial for his life. The town vicar—the Reverend D. Ambrose Jones—was one of this quartet. The other three were women who were closely involved with the Greenwood family or with the events of Mabel Greenwood's last hours on earth: the district nurse, Elizabeth Jones; the doctor's sister, May Griffiths; and Mrs. Greenwood's longtime friend, Miss Florence Phillips. The latter came to be bitterly characterized by Greenwood as the "Kidwelly Postman" for her tale-bearing propensities. The vicar seemed to have been truly motivated by concern for the dead Mabel Greenwood, and for justice on her behalf; however, each lady was believed to be motivated at least partially by a desire to snaffle the widower for herself—or so other village gossip inevitably had it.

At about eight in the morning on June 16, the morning of Mabel Greenwood's death, a very upset Nurse Jones had brought the news of Mrs. Greenwood's demise to the vicar, the Rev. Ambrose Jones. The surname Jones was a very common one in Wales; the various Joneses named in Greenwood's story were apparently unrelated to each other. The vicar, too, was startled and shaken, particularly at the suddenness of the lady's decease, having seen her only the Saturday before in her usual consistent-if-not-blooming health. Nurse Jones hinted at her growing conviction that something wasn't right with the death; the vicar apparently concurred. Later, when Greenwood neglected the routine of sending the death certificate to him, the cleric's reaction was to interpret the omission as ominously suspicious.

Meanwhile, Nurse Jones was confiding her own apprehensions about Mabel Greenwood's death to more and more people. She continued highly vocal in her suspicions of her patient's husband both at the time of Mabel's illness and just after her death.

But a curious circumstance began to manifest itself in the weeks after Mrs. Greenwood's passing. By the time of the inquest, the nurse seemed to reverse directions. She denied making many of the remarks attributed to her about the suspicious nature of Mabel Greenwood's sudden passing, and now testified that she had seen nothing untoward in the death. Some time before the inquest, the nurse had begun visiting Greenwood at Rumsey House; she later hastily explained that the solicitor was attending to some personal legal business of hers. But was that the truth— or at any rate all of the truth? Was it nearer truth that "She now saw in Harold Greenwood a possibly worthwhile suitor"? ("Mystery"). Had she begun to reconsider her own attitude toward the now available solicitor and was throwing her own hat into the matrimonial ring, alongside those of other local ladies—having somewhere along the way begun to cherish hopes of wedding the new widower herself? Even after Greenwood's stated intention to wed Gladys Jones became known, the nurse continued her visits to Greenwood almost up to the day of his second marriage, staying late alone with him at Rumsey House the night before—and telling his fortune.

And at the November trial, Miss Griffiths testified that, while Mabel Greenwood lay on her way to death on the night of June 15, a hardly grief-stricken Harold Greenwood was at the Griffiths home, jocularly telling May that Mabel probably wouldn't recover—and further intimating that perhaps he and May would soon be away on their honeymoon. Greenwood denied that any such conversation had taken place, but couldn't bluster away a letter he had actually written to May Griffiths on the eve of his wedding to another woman—proposing marriage to the doctor's sister!

*"My dearest May,"* the compromising letter ran, *"I have been trying hard to get you this last fortnight, but no luck, always someone going in or you were out. Now I want you to think very carefully and to send me over a reply tonight. There are very many rumours about, but between you and I this letter reveals the true position.*

*"Well, it is only right that you should know that Miss Bowater* [Mabel Greenwood's sister] *and Miss Phillips between them have turned my children against you very bitterly, why I don't know. It is only right that you should know this, as you are the one I love most in this world and I would be the last one to make you unhappy.*

*"Under the circumstances, are you prepared to face the music? I am going to do something quickly as I must get rid of Miss Bowater at once as I am simply fed up with her.*

*"Let me have something from you tonight.*

*"Yours as ever, Harold"* (Duke 25).

Whatever may have been the hopes of May Griffiths involving Greenwood, or those of Nurse Jones, Miss Phillips, or any others, it was undoubtedly Gladys Jones whom the solicitor finally wed. Tongues continued to wag incessantly about the suspicious circumstances of the first wife's death, spewing speculation now refueled by this marriage, this new affront to decency. And eventually they wagged to official effect. Outraged tittle-tattle reached such a crescendo of scandal by December 1919 that local authorities determined to exhume Mabel Greenwood's body. The Home Secretary issued the necessary order, and when officially apprised of the intended exhumation a few days before the event, Greenwood's somewhat unusual response was "Just the very thing; I am quite agreeable!" (30).

Mrs. Greenwood's grave in St. Mary's churchyard was quietly—almost furtively—opened in the hushed nighttime hours of April 16, 1920, avoiding the sensationalism that would surely have accompanied a more publicized procedure. Ensuing analysis of Mabel Greenwood's mortal remains yielded stunning news: she had *not* perished from a heart condition; that organ was found to be free of disease. A tumorous growth was also found, though not cancerous.

But throughout her body, in every organ, traces of arsenic were found which amounted to about a quarter to a half grain. Nurse Jones fainted when this was revealed at the inquest.

The town gossips thus felt themselves vindicated, and free to express even more hostility toward Greenwood. Community rumors redoubled in both spite and vehemence, this time aided and abetted by mushrooming newspaper coverage of what had suddenly metamorphosed from a local "village" scandal to a widespread *cause célèbre*.

A coroner's inquest was begun on June 20, 1920, at Kidwelly's Old Town Hall. Harold Greenwood failed to appear. But the jury and the avid capacity crowd heard testimony that he had purchased Cooper's Weedicide in June 1917, and more weed-killer containing arsenic in February 1919 and April 1919. They also heard testimony that he had been having an affair with Gladys Jones before his wife died. The Greenwoods' parlormaid, Hannah Williams, testified that she had observed Greenwood alone in the pantry where the wine was kept, for about 15 minutes on June 15, 1919, the day of Mrs. Greenwood's death, before the luncheon was served and the wine drunk that day. The hearing resulted in a unanimous and unsurprising verdict of "murder by arsenical poisoning" which was "administered by Harold Greenwood" (32) to the sanctimonious and open delight of the inquest attendees, who clapped loudly when the verdict was announced. When he heard the news, "Oh, dear!" was reportedly Greenwood's immediate reaction to the verdict (33).

After Greenwood's arrest on the charge, he spent four months in prison awaiting trial. Then, on November 2, 1920, Greenwood's trial for the willful murder of Mabel Bowater Greenwood commenced at the Carmarthen Assizes. The public thronged the courthouse, eager to witness this most exciting scandal as it continued to play out in their midst. The newspapers' feeding frenzy pumped up the alleged crime's components to the level of a national, and even international, media sensation: not only was this a juicily shocking domestic murder involving flagrant adultery among professional and moneyed segments of society, but it also involved a lawyer's being placed on trial for his life in a sordidly scandalous case. To top it all off, it was also the first arsenic-poisoning murder trial held in Britain outside of England proper.

Mr. Justice Montague Shearman presided at the proceedings, while Sir Edward Marlay Samson, K.C., led for the prosecution. Greenwood had retained the celebrated Edward Marshall Hall, K.C., to lead for his defense. The prosecution based its case on the bottle of burgundy served at Mabel Greenwood's last luncheon, asserting that Greenwood had placed poisonous weedkiller in the bottle to murder his wife. The original wine bottle had long since disappeared; and almost immediately after Mabel's death, her store of medicine and other bottles had been jettisoned wholesale. But the maid Hannah Williams repeated her inquest statement that before the luncheon on June 15, 1919, she had seen her master closeted alone for a quarter-hour in the pantry in which the burgundy had been stored, the inference being that he had had plenty of time to lace it with weedkiller.

Marshall Hall was at the height of his fame at the time; a barrister who knew how to use his dynamic physical presence and his intimidating eloquence to influence a jury—and to disconcert an opposing witness. The famed lawyer verbally attacked both the forensic evidence and the testimony of the main prosecution witnesses in his characteristically theatrical style. It was mere scurrilous rumor and vicious gossip, fomented by Kidwelly busybodies, he maintained, that had brought the innocent Harold Greenwood to this dangerous pass: the whole ridiculous cause for the trial was based on the unfounded tittle-tattle of meddlers and troublemakers. In his opening for the defense, he characterized such tittle-tattle with the same contempt that he hoped to instill in the minds of the jurors (Duke 230). With his strikingly emotive approach and commanding personality, he set about driving these points home, while impressing jurors' minds with other viable alternatives to the proposition of Harold Greenwood as poisoner. Marshall Hall's major strategy included tearing down the testimony of the two key witnesses against Greenwood: the doctor and the parlormaid. The timeline and content of the doctor's ministrations to the patient on June 15 and 16, 1919 were of great importance, and Dr. Griffiths testified at the inquest that, though other witnesses put the number of his visits at five, he saw Mrs. Greenwood on only four occasions in that time span: first at about six or six-thirty that evening, next at seven or seven-thirty, and then at ten or ten-thirty on the night of the 15th; and finally at about three or three-thirty on the morning of the 16th, at the time of the unfortunate woman's death. His inquest declaration also asserted that after his ten o'clock or so visit, he had sent over, by Greenwood, two sedative tablets to be given the sick woman; and further that the pills were morphia, or morphine, tablets. Nurse Jones and Greenwood, on the other hand, declared that (a) the doctor also had made a visit at one in the morning of the 16th, and (b) it was after that visit that Greenwood brought the pills over, and the nurse had subsequently administered them; and (c) Mrs. Greenwood soon thereafter lapsed into a coma from which she never awakened. The nurse and Greenwood had immediately blamed Mrs. Greenwood's death on the pills.

At the trial, the good Dr. Griffiths continued to maintain on oath that he did not recall making the one o'clock visit that Greenwood, Nurse Jones, and even Miss Phillips seemed to recall so vividly. And a further surprise in his testimony was awaiting the witnesses, the spectators, and the court: Dr. Griffiths nervously recanted a vital part of his inquest testimony, now deposing that he had made a mistake at the inquest about naming the pills he'd dispensed. He had said they were morphine pills; but they had actually been opium tablets instead.

His flip-flopping on the type of pill he had sent by Greenwood represented a serious change of front: Marshall Hall's defense had been poised to show that administration of the high dosage of morphine originally mentioned was in itself enough to have caused Mrs. Greenwood's death, but the opium medication would have been much weaker in effect than the morphine. The barrister exploded in anger at the surprise alteration, earning a reprimand from the judge for his behavior. Marshall Hall went on, however, to turn the doctor's seeming vacillations to account. The physician made a poor witness, showing himself clearly unsure in much of his testimony. He was easy prey for a scoffing Marshall Hall, who advanced the further theory that the doctor himself may have unintentionally killed his patient by an accidental route: inadvertent switching of medicine bottles when he had prepared and administered the bismuth medication.

The lawyer had learned beforehand that the doctor kept bottles of bismuth and of Fowler's solution—which contained arsenic—near to each other on his cupboard shelves, and that these bottles were very similar in appearance. Marshall Hall used this circumstance to inject a bit of hocus-pocus showmanship into the trial at the further expense of Dr. Griffiths' shriveling credibility. The barrister had himself purchased bottles of the two medications from a druggist, and subsequently showed them in court. Did they not look almost exactly alike, he insinuated? Might not it have been easy for Dr. Griffiths, in a state at the time of natural perturbation at the condition of his patient, to have confused the two? Then erroneously to have administered to Mabel Greenwood the arsenical Fowler's solution instead of the intended bismuth?

The legality, not to mention the ethics, of this ploy were questionable, since the containers he displayed to the jury were not at all the original bottles that figured in the case, and had certainly not been admitted into evidence. But Marshall Hall got away with it: the point was indelibly made in the minds of the jurors, and it told against the doctor's believability. Star witness Hannah Williams's statements fared no better. The barrister, with polished facility, tied the maid and her testimony into figurative knots, bringing out the probability that the several conversations she had had with police prior to her testimony had heavily influenced and biased her statements. He also exploited the fact that she had altered her story on more than one occasion.

But the *coup-de-grâce* to the prosecution's case arrived on the testimony of Irene Greenwood, the 22-year-old daughter of Mabel Greenwood and the prisoner in the dock. She testified that she too had shared the luncheon of June 16 a year earlier, and had actually drunk wine from the same bottle as had her mother. Miss Greenwood asserted that no arsenic could possibly have been in the burgundy which was named by the prosecution as the means of murder, and which was served at that meal, for she herself had suffered no ill effects at all from imbibing it.

Edward Marshall Hall went on to cap a stellar performance with a stunning closing defense speech to the jury. Dramatically drawing himself into his tallest stature, flinging out his arms to represent the scales of justice, he quoted from the "put out the light" sequence from Shakespeare's *Othello* (230), then thundered "are you by your verdict going to put out that light?" He then tipped one arm of the "scale" slightly to represent the justice that would result from freeing the accused man before them.

Mr. Justice Shearman's summing up seemed to lean toward acquittal. The importance of Irene Greenwood's statement was enormous—if the jury believed it. As the case went to the jury on November 10, 1920, Mr. Justice Shearman directed that "if [Irene Greenwood] also drank from the bottle, there is an end of the case" (262). The jury apparently agreed with this view: after deliberating for a little more than 2½ hours, the panel returned a verdict of "Not Guilty."

But the jury had also delivered at the same time a written statement to the judge which asserted, "We are satisfied on the evidence in this case that a dangerous dose of arsenic was administered to Mabel Greenwood on Sunday, 15th June, 1919, but we are not satisfied that this was the immediate cause of death. The evidence before us is insufficient, and does not conclusively satisfy us as to how or by whom the arsenic was administered. We therefore return a verdict of 'Not Guilty'" (50). If this temporizing addendum had been read out in court at the rendering of the verdict—as the jury had meant it to be—the whole complexion of the trial's outcome would have changed. Immediately after the trial, the press and legal pundits criticized the prosecution for bringing such a flimsy case, and certainly for failing to have questioned Irene Greenwood in a much more timely and thorough manner before doing so. Had the entire verdict been read at the trial, the implications would have gone quite a way toward vindicating the prosecution's premise for the case, if not its handling of it. The world didn't learn of the extended version of the verdict, however, until much later.

As it was, Edward Marshall Hall had done his work well, even though he had himself been seriously ill during the whole process. Harold Greenwood departed the courtroom on November 10 a free man. But the community did not welcome him back. The indignant townsfolk held fast to the belief that, despite the verdict, Harold Greenwood had indeed poisoned his wife to wed a younger woman. Gossip and rumor never flagged, and this time it was tinged with the sullen vindictive bitterness of those balked of their prey. Greenwood had been ruined by his ordeal: his practice was defunct, his social standing erased, his finances uncertain, though presumably he earned what he could from selling versions of his story to several publications ("Not Guilty" 12). When life became at last completely unbearable in Kidwelly, Greenwood, with his second wife, removed himself to Herefordshire and took up residence thereafter changing his name to Pilkington. Perhaps in the new locale, under the new pseudonym, he regained some of his lost ground and equilibrium. Some reports portray the solicitor as having succeeded despite his notoriety: in 1924, *The Auckland Star* stated, "Greenwood is now a partner in a firm of solicitors, his identity hidden under a new name" ("Prison" 24). Other news accounts described him at the time of his death as "aged with extraordinary rapidity ... he ... seemed a broken man. At times he would brood sorrowfully ... he seemed like a man in a daze, very sad and worried'" ("Hermit" 12).

Harold Greenwood's name briefly resurfaced in the news a few more times. In 1921, he penned an editorial letter, first printed in the periodical *John Bull*, entitled "Armstrong's Fight for Life" (Young, *Greenwood* 363). The communication sympathized with the amazingly similar ordeal of fellow legal man Herbert Rowse Armstrong, who had also gone to trial for the arsenic poisoning of his wife. In 1922, Greenwood's name again cropped up in the news when he sued a wax museum for displaying his image in company with those of convicted criminals; he won that case. When next Harold Greenwood's name appeared prominently in newsprint, it was to announce his death at the age of 57, on January 17, 1929, in Ross-on-Wye, Herefordshire.

Yet the melody lingered on. In 1949, his widow brought legal action against authors Edward Percy (pseudonym of E. P. Smith) and Reginald Denham, who wrote and planned to stage a play called *The Man They Acquitted*. The action alleged that the work was based on Harold Greenwood's life. The writers responded that the work was inspired by Greenwood's case, but not based on it ("Producers" 1).

## "The Lernean Hydra"

Charles Oldfield had lost his wife to a chronic disease a year earlier. She had been older than he, and the rich partner in the marriage. Her customarily irritable behavior and habit of life had been exacerbated by long martyrdom to painful battles against the gastric disease that had finally killed her. But immediately after his wife's death, a whispering campaign sprang up against Dr. Oldfield in his home town, the village of Market Loughborough; a campaign that seemed to intensify rather than abate as time passed. The physician fears that the frustratingly nebulous menace was about to explode into full-blown, open accusations to the authorities: accusations that he poisoned his wife for her money—and in order to wed another, younger woman. In desperation, the doctor goes to Poirot for help.

Gossip continues rife, and the hagridden Oldfield expects at any minute that the police will arrive at his door to charge him with murder. Poirot senses that the doctor is holding something back, and rightly surmises that there is another woman involved in the case. "The village gossip," he tells Oldfield, "it is based always, always on the relations of the sexes.... It is because [the villagers] are convinced that the murder has been committed in order that the man may marry another woman that the talk grows and spreads" (Christie, "Lernean" 43). With evident reluctance Oldfield feels forced to reveal to Poirot a detail of his personal life that he would clearly have preferred to keep to himself: he is in love with his dispenser, Jean Moncrieffe, and the most damaging brunt of the gossip spitefully couples her name with his. Jean reciprocates the doctor's affections, but the hate campaign has forced them to a bitter acknowledgment: they dare not go ahead with plans to wed, lest the marriage give their enemies an opening for jeopardizing their happiness—and their lives.

Poirot senses two significant points in the situation the doctor describes to him: an opportunity to perform one of the "twelve Labors of Hercules" that he has set for himself—and a real and purposeful malevolence toward Dr. Oldfield behind the crusade of rumors against him. Someone was deliberately and relentlessly trying not only to destroy the unfortunate doctor's happiness, but the doctor himself as well.

Poirot accepts the troubling case. Like the terrifying, many-headed Hydra of Lake Lerna that Heracles (Roman equivalent *Hercules*) of Greek myth was commanded to destroy, the many-tongued monster of malicious gossip which Hercule Poirot had engaged himself to hunt down and demolish was nearly impossible to kill. The Hydra had been possessed of many heads; only one was the monster's master engine. To strike it off was the only way to slay the beast; cutting off any but that one vulnerable head would only spawn two more writhing and venomous replacements in its stead.

When Poirot travels to Dr. Oldfield's village to investigate, he finds a symbolically similar situation. The physician's hidden nemesis had artfully bred a network of venom with as many heads as the mythological Hydra. The venom had been spread from person to person, and by person to person, until its origin was lost in repetition and subtly increased embellishment. The little detective decides to fight fire with fire, and in order to gain his own ends embarks on a campaign of guile just as artful as that of his unknown quarry. He adopts the ploy of professing to be on clandestine embassy from the Home Office, covertly testing whether the rumors about Mrs. Oldfield's demise merited an exhumation of her body. He first interviews the intelligent but warily reticent Jean Moncrieffe, gaining from her an additional understanding of the murky situation. But Moncrieffe shrinks in horror from the idea of an exhumation. When Poirot quietly presses for her reasons, the dispenser declares that since no arsenic would be found in an autopsy (the doctor being of course innocent of poisoning his wife), the danger was that analysts might label their findings as inconclusive. Charles Oldfield would then be worse off than before: the very vagueness of the outcome would only fix the idea of the doctor's guilt more firmly in the minds of the locals. But, Poirot wonders, is that reason the true explanation for the lady's adamant opposition? Was she afraid that an autopsy would indeed unearth proof of poisoning, and would therefore definitely incriminate the doctor—or perhaps herself?

As Poirot ruminates on the dispenser's possibly disingenuous logic, he is introduced to Miss Leatheran, Market Loughborough's most confirmed gossip. Once more pretending to have been sent secretly from the Home Office, Poirot notes well the lady's responses to his hints about a possible exhumation of Mrs. Oldfield's remains. The avid Miss Leatheran is predictably thrilled by the prospect, though outwardly registering horror at the very idea. Poirot skillfully gleans possible leads from the gossipy spinster's subsequent disclosures. One of the most promising of her insinuations points to the Oldfields' dismissed and resentful servant girl, Beatrice, as the probable instigator of the gossip. Poirot decides to investigate fully this suspicion, but before tackling Beatrice, he speaks to Nurse Harrison, the former nurse-companion of ill-starred Mrs. Oldfield. He senses that the nurse, too, had been disturbed about the circumstances of her client's death. Despite the liking she'd had for her patient, and despite the sudden dislike she'd shown toward Dr. Oldfield after Mrs. Oldfield's death, Nurse Harrison strove to discuss the affair with noncommittal fairness. Poirot perceived nonetheless that the thoroughly professional woman had her own ideas about the cause of Mrs. Oldfield's demise—and they weren't favorable to the dead woman's husband. Poirot also discerns that Nurse Harrison, like Miss Leatheran, believes that Beatrice knows more about the gossip—and the circumstances related to Mrs. Oldfield's demise—than the servant girl had been willing to divulge. Since all her misgivings were more or less unsubstantial or unsubstantiated, the nurse had never voiced explicit suspicions to anyone. To the astute Poirot however her very unwillingness to speak out told its own story. Continuing his policy of testing the villagers' responses to the notion, Poirot ends his inquiries of the nurse with the repeated mendacious assertion that the Home Office was considering disinterment. The nurse is initially horrified and distressed, but after thinking it over and digesting the implications, in the end agrees with Poirot's smoothly declared contention: an exhumation would be a sure way of exonerating the doctor—or of proving his guilt.

Poirot follows up with a visit to the sly Beatrice, who isn't sly enough to keep from letting slip some extremely suggestive information. Poirot feels it is time to act. The hero Hercules had known that his only chance of killing the monstrous Hydra was to find, quickly, the one true head and to strike it off before the beast could kill him. Likewise Poirot also realizes that, before it was too late, he must just as speedily reveal the secret fomenter of the spate of spite aimed at destroying Dr. Oldfield.

He elects to force an autopsy. The body of the doctor's wife is duly exhumed—and the outcome sets the village agog with both scandal and vindication: the unfortunate Mrs. Oldfield had in fact been callously murdered by poison, just as their whisperings and rumors had asserted—and undoubtedly by her husband. Even worse for Charles Oldfield, the stunned Nurse Harrison, with the irrefutable truth now publicly known about the cause of her former patient's death, feels free to reveal information to Poirot that she'd held back before. Her revelations constitute incriminating evidence against two individuals—and, unwittingly, even more so against one other person. Poirot, with all the threads now in, applies his little grey cells to the problem; the wily sleuth gauges all the evidence, assesses all the people involved, and sees through all the feints and falsities thrown at him to derail his discovery of the truth. Triumphing spectacularly in the end, he sets a cunning trap, and outwits a subtly calculating killer before other victims can be claimed.

## Harold Greenwood + "The Lernean Hydra"

In "The Lernean Hydra" Agatha Christie's art beautifully incorporates the analogy between the many-headed mythical Hydra and the "many-headed" gossipers of a Berkshire village, whose hostile whispers accuse Dr. Oldfield of poisoning his wife to death. Even more artistically, Christie captures in this tale the very nature of the true crime case of solicitor Harold Greenwood, who was brought to trial for the arsenic murder of his wife Mabel in 1920. It was a trial that might never have taken place but for the groundswell of angry and accusatory rumors against the solicitor. When subsequent exhumation and analysis of Mrs. Greenwood's remains revealed that she had indeed died of arsenic poisoning, the stage was set for one of the most notorious trials in British crime history.

"The Lernean Hydra" appeared in Agatha Christie's 1947 short story collection *The Labors of Hercules*, but was first published in the December 1939 issue of *The Strand Magazine*.

In fear and frustration the fictional Dr. Oldfield, hammered by gossip in much the same way as had been the factual Harold Greenwood, takes steps to counter his danger before the inevitable blow of arrest and trial actually falls: he consults that eminent sleuth, Hercule Poirot. In order to annihilate the Hydra, the Hercules of classical myth had to identify quickly which, among its many false ones, was the beast's true governing head, and destroy it before the monster could destroy him. In order to save his presumed-innocent client, just so must Hercule Poirot quickly identify the shadowy true instigator hidden among many other gossipers in the village of Market Loughborough—and must do so before Dr. Oldfield falls victim to his unknown enemy's deadly machinations.

Dangerous gossip is the central motif in both the true-crime and the fictional scenarios. The real-life drama surrounding the mysterious poisoning of Mrs. Greenwood and the fictional story of the murder of Mrs. Oldfield were driven by the force of scandalized rumor and talk. Harold Greenwood, like Dr. Oldfield, was a professional man who'd been put in jeopardy by an unprecedented rumor crusade when his sickly wife died suspiciously and suddenly. Historically, vigorous tittle-tattle campaigns had prodded or accompanied many an official inquiry into many a true crime, both before and since the Greenwood drama. Not one of the investigations, however, was so thoroughly a result of full-out rumor as the 1920 investigation into the death of Mabel Greenwood. The scale of innuendo and pointed accusation was so massive that it overflowed the Welsh borders of Kidwelly, where the Greenwoods resided; it grew into a rancorous wave so insistent that the Home Office ultimately had little choice but to act, resulting in Greenwood's arrest and trial for murder. The outcome—the solicitor's acquittal—constituted a slap in the face to Kidwelly's tongue-wagging inhabitants, but Greenwood never thereafter regained his former social or professional status with his still-hostile neighbors.

Both protagonists, fictional and factual, had "secret" lady friends in the offing. Dr. Oldfield being modestly limited to only one, while Greenwood seemed to have played the field with a vengeance. In both instances, the unbridled spread of rumors gave officials no choice but to delve into matters—and in both instances poisoning by arsenic was found to be the true cause of death. Both Mrs. Oldfield and Mrs. Greenwood had had personal medical attendants—Nurse Jones for Mrs. Greenwood, "Nurse Harrison" for Mrs. Oldfield—whose opinions not only gave weight to the way the cases were interpreted, but who also featured dramatically in the life-and-death conflicts permeating events.

Similarities between the factual and fictional cases did not stop there. As with Greenwood's situation, the principal purveyors of the gossip that imperiled Christie's Dr. Oldfield were disgruntled ladies who didn't hesitate to express their dissatisfaction in various ways. The Greenwood case was also overrun by women with a spite or suspicion of one sort or another against the solicitor: women to whom he had promised matrimony or who had been led on in some way by the philanderer; or others who cherished a militant allegiance to Mabel Greenwood and resented her sufferings. Their counterparts exist in Christie's tale, represented sparingly in three or so characters. Both the true-life and the imaginary cases boasted maids (Hannah Williams in the true-crime incident and "Beatrice King" in the short story) who witnessed tamperings with suspected bottles or containers, and from which the victim purportedly drank. Both scenarios also featured busybody neighbors all too willing to keep the cauldron of controversy boiling around the strangely mysterious deaths.

The two histories also featured gossipers engaged in spiteful personal sniping attacks of a stereotype attributed to vengeful female mentality. In both scenarios, too, the venom of the attacks had spiked and peaked when it came to be known that "outsider" women—Gladys Jones of Llanelly in the case of Greenwood; "Jean Moncrieffe," the "bit standoffish" dispenser in the detective story—had carried off the prize of the matrimonial sweepstakes in the very teeth of the hometown competition: the local womenfolk who so coveted it. The trespassing victors were somehow not considered part or parcel of the true Kidwelly or Market Loughborough scenes—nor had they done what some had done to earn the right of succeeding the conveniently defunct first wives. The new widowers nevertheless had basely preferred the charms of interlopers over those of more deserving local candidates, leaving miffed ladies in their wake who had, or who felt they had, reason to take Greenwood's or Oldfield's marital defection very personally.

The Greenwood occurrence has often been compared to an even more notorious case which took place some years later: that of Major Herbert Rowse Armstrong. He too had been a solicitor practicing in Wales, and in 1923 the Major, very like Greenwood, was also tried for the arsenic-poison murder of his own wife, Katherine. But the outcome for Armstrong was far different from that for Greenwood. After a sensational trial, the little Major was found guilty, and was subsequently hanged.

# Postscript

*Gossip* is almost a palpable entity in "The Lernean Hydra"—Hercule Poirot's third Labor of Hercules. Within the story, ultimately even Poirot himself craftily engages in an ersatz bout of rumor-spreading to lure the story's killer away from the veil of anonymity. Later, while pursuing his sixth Labor in "The Augean Stables," the detective revives that ploy once again—but this time on a much grander scale. Poirot determines to outsmart a sleazy blackmailer who's threatening the country's interests at a particularly sensitive time. To bite the biter, the detective takes a risky gamble as he splashes a sensational story across the pages of a national publication (Christie, "Augean" 732).

Gossip, rumor, and tittle tattle show up as significant factors in other Christie storylines as well, evincing themselves often as important plot devices. The novel *Murder in Mesopotamia* tells the tale of murder at an archaeological site in the Mideast. Chapter 3 of the work is not only baldly entitled "Gossip," but goes on to reveal spiteful speculation about motives and actions of "Lovely Louise" Leidner—the troubled, and trouble-making, wife of the revered expedition director. Mrs. Leidner is the brand new patient of partial narrator Nurse Amy Leatheran, who gives readers brisk, no-nonsense but sympathetic interpretations of the mystery as it unfolds. Though she fastidiously decries gossip as it swirls around the personality of her attractive charge, the gossip she hears as well as her own observations inevitably color the nurse's perceptions of tense situations at the dig—even before that tension explodes into murder.

In several Christie tales, rumor and gossip come in for their share of high-minded detractors, as exemplified by Nurse Leatheran; they also come in for their share of spirited defenders as well. The foremost proponent of the latter point of view is, unsurprisingly, St. Mary Mead's Miss Jane Marple, the detective-story genre's very emblem of sleuthing-by-gossip.

The work *The Murder at the Vicarage* features both pro and con philosophies regarding gossip and tittle-tattle. A personage in the novel has reason to comment explosively on "what an absolutely rotten thing gossip is!" (35), and in another instance the vicar gently warns Miss Marple that "inestimable harm" could result from "foolish wagging of tongues in ill-natured gossip." But Miss Marple merely reminds the vicar unanswerably that although "idle tittle-tattle is very wrong and unkind," it was, in addition, "so often true" (19).

For its genteel elderly ladies, gossip seems to be the very raison d'être of St. Mary Mead's social gatherings. Nowhere in Christie's works is this more picturesquely proclaimed than in the words of the vicar's young wife, Griselda, as she comments to her husband that her afternoon would be spent presiding over "tea and scandal at four-thirty" (5) with the parish ladies.

Griselda's concept is further endorsed in the novel *A Murder Is Announced*. Elderly Miss Blacklock, victim of an attempted murder in the village of Chipping Cleghorn, echoes the sentiment when she finds her friend Dora "Bunny" Bunner at the local tea shop, engaging in "tittle-tattle" about the attempt with Miss Marple: "Coffee and gossip, Bunny?" (122) asks Miss Blacklock, in exasperated reproof.

It is in the story "A Christmas Tragedy" (156) that Miss Marple most forcefully delivers her own manifesto on the subject. After Colonel Bantry has grumbled about the practice of a "lot of old women sitting round talking scandal," Miss Marple has the last word, repeating the stance she took in *The Murder at the Vicarage*. People who condemn gossiping out of hand, she declares, don't consider that "the whole crux of the matter is this: How often is tittle-tattle, as you call it, true!" (Christie, "Christmas" 156).

## Chapter 6

# "An Outbreak of Sadism"
## The Case of Dennis O'Neill and "Three Blind Mice"

The short story/novella "Three Blind Mice" by Agatha Christie was first published in 1948, but the tale had its original incarnation a year earlier in the form of a radio play, written to celebrate the 80th birthday of Queen Mary, consort of George V. The play was broadcast May 30, 1947, and Christie afterwards adapted the offering into a story appearing in the May 1948 issue of *Cosmopolitan* magazine. In 1948 and 1950, the tale was published in the United States by Dodd, Mead in the book collection *Three Blind Mice and Other Stories*. Without going into undue depth, Agatha Christie allows readers to glimpse the psychological workings of major characters' minds, showing their humanity and frailty.

All of Christie's versions of the tale, first created in 1947, hark back to the tragedy of young Dennis O'Neill just two years earlier in 1945, and contain many elements that echo the circumstances of that affair.

### The Case of Denise O'Neill

In 1940, John Thomas O'Neill and his wife Mabel Blonwyn O'Neill resided in the venerable market town of Newport in Shropshire. They were by then parents of several children, among them three young boys: Dennis, Terence, and Frederick. Mr. and Mrs. O'Neill, due to criminal convictions for child neglect and other offenses against the law, had been deemed unfit to care for the children, who were then placed in a succession of foster homes.

By May 1944 the boys had come under the care of Newport County Council. The youngest of the three brothers, Frederick, then 8 years old, was sent to reside with the family of Harry and Doris Pickering of Shropshire. Dennis and Terence had also been slated to go to the Pickerings, but

## Chapter 6. "An Outbreak of Sadism"

the family was unable to accommodate the elder two boys. In July 1944 the Newport Education Authorities arranged for 12-year-old Dennis and ten-year-old Terence to be placed under the foster care of a farmer and his wife, Reginald and Esther Gough, who lived at Bank Farm in the Hope Valley area of Shropshire. Jurisdiction for oversight of the O'Neill brothers' placement then became a shared matter between two Council districts, Newport Education Authority and Shropshire Council. Some months later, on December 20, 1944, Eirlys Edwards of the Newport Education Committee, a relatively inexperienced clerical assistant, paid a routine call on the Goughs to check on the wellbeing of the two children. Normally, visits would have been made much sooner: the overlong 6-months gap of time between the boys' placement and this official visit was an anomaly due to wartime conditions. There existed at the time a pervasive shortage of staff—especially well-trained and experienced staff; a lack of coordination of efforts; a confusion over jurisdiction of oversight—and they were all clearly to play a more than usually devastating part in shaping the tragedy to come. At the time of Miss Edwards' visit she perceived that the children appeared uncared for and apprehensive, despite their nervous verbal assurances to her that they were happy in their situation. Miss Edwards also thought that Dennis appeared to be in need of medical attention. She had secured an agreement from Mrs. Gough that a doctor would be called in to attend the child. Subsequent to her visit, Miss Edwards wrote both the Shropshire and the Newport administrators, urging that the O'Neill children be immediately removed from the care of the Goughs (Sly). After some delay, her director requested that the Shropshire Education Committee should take the children away from the Gough farm, but the request was never followed up ("Foster-Parents" 2). The timelines of the harrowing events to follow were revealed through testimony subsequent to those events.

On January 6, 1945, Dennis was sent out to collect branches and sticks. He returned with few branches, shaking from the cold, but was again ejected out into the chill by his foster father. When he stood weeping outside, Esther Gough emerged from the farmhouse, chased him with a branch, and forcibly dragged him by the hair into a wooded area. Later that night he was severely beaten for trying to appease his hunger by taking a bite from a stolen rutabaga. The next day, January 7, Gough stripped the boy and again beat him with such force that he broke the branch. On the day after that, January 8, Dennis was locked in a 3' × 6' kitchen cabinet, where his brother Terence found him when he himself returned from school (Underwood 101).

At one o'clock in the afternoon of January 9, 1945, Shropshire physician Dr. Holloway Davies received a telephone call from Esther Gough. Mrs. Gough was calling from the home of a neighbor, urging that the doctor should come as soon as possible, as one of her foster children was "having a fit." The doctor arrived at Bank Farm around three-thirty—to find no ailing child, but the emaciated and bruised corpse of a 12-year-old boy. The doctor concluded that the child had expired from three to four hours before his arrival, and had therefore already been dead when Mrs. Gough had called him in. Doctor Davies refused to sign a death certificate and immediately alerted police to the situation.

The later inquest on the remains of Dennis O'Neill would determine that he had died of cardiac failure after previously sustaining a ferocious rain of blows to his chest and a brutal beating on his back. The child was also found to be much below weight-level for his age; his legs and feet were covered with sores and abrasions; all of which conditions attested to abuse and neglect of long standing.

On February 3, 1945, 31-year-old Gough was arrested and charged with manslaughter. A scant few days later, on February 8, Parliament raised the first of what were to be many questions regarding the case and its ramifications, and the part played by the nation's system of care for foster children. For the accused perpetrators of the crimes leading to the death of Dennis O'Neill, committal proceedings began on February 13, a day after Esther Gough had also been detained. Terence O'Neill testified to the brutal ill-treatment that he and his brother suffered at the hands of the Goughs, revealing that the boys had been forced to subsist on three slices of bread each per day; that they had resorted to trying to steal food from the Gough pantry to keep from starving; that Dennis had even resorted to sucking the udders of the farm's cows in a desperate try for sustenance; that each night they were forced to "confess" to whatever "bad things" they had done that day, for which Gough would then beat them on legs or hands, up to 100 strokes each; and that the night before he had died, Gough had tied Dennis naked to a "pig bench"— one used to dissect slaughtered hogs—and beaten him on his back.

In the war-ravaged England of the time, the case excited such a storm of public horror and outrage that it eclipsed even the wearisome perils of World War II as primary topic in homes and public gatherings. Newspaper headlines and media reports kept the story constantly at the forefront. The fact that investigations revealed Reginald Gough to be a known criminal rankled greatly in the public mind. He had years earlier been convicted on a charge of violence—a circumstance that surely would have precluded placement of children in his care, had responsible officials investigated with due diligence his background before the tragedy. Although the Goughs themselves came in for their share of thoroughly impassioned hatred and repulsion, "the authorities" were freely condemned by all segments of society and ultimately held responsible for the sad death of Dennis O'Neill. The welfare, the very life, of a child entrusted to the governing bodies had fallen devastatingly, tragically, and irreversibly through cracks in the system, and ensuing examinations of the case made no bones about the fact. Authorities felt the sting, and acted on the imperative behind it. "The death of Dennis O'Neill, or rather the general reaction to it, underlined a change in public attitudes to children and family life, and signalled the way to the next half-century of public policy" (Abrams), as one report put it. "What set this death apart from the countless other deaths of neglected and abused children was that the central failure, in the eyes of the world, was not that of the individuals involved—though that had indeed been grievous—but of the state."

Some of the reasons for the system's failures were bared in the committal proceedings and the subsequent trial of the Goughs. Months before Dennis's death, due to a difference in the rate of pay for foster care, the Newport Council had requested the Shropshire Council to take over supervision of the O'Neill boys' case as soon as practicable. After a dilatory interval, the Shropshire Council had finally declared, in writing to the Newport Council, that they could not oversee the Newport cases. The resultant ambiguity over which authority had actual jurisdiction led each council to believe that the other had responsibility for oversight.

Clerical worker Eirlys Edwards of the Newport Education Committee testified at the committal hearing, repeating the facts that she had visited the Goughs on December 20, 1944; had seen even then that Dennis appeared to be in need of medical attention; and had secured an agreement from Mrs. Gough that a doctor would be called in to attend the child. Miss Edwards had subsequently written both the Shropshire and the Newport administrators urging that the O'Neill children be immediately taken away from the care of the Goughs (Sly). After some delay, her director requested the Shropshire Education Committee to remove the children from the Gough farm, but the request was never followed up ("Foster-Parents" 2). The regrettable lapses and breakdowns in communication between the two authorities were later attributed in large part to the overloaded, undertrained and understaffed status of both councils in the war-straitened England of the time.

The trial of Reginald and Esther Gough began at Stafford Assizes on March 15, 1945. The presiding judge was Mr. Justice Frederick J. Wrottesley, with the prosecution lead by W. H. Cartwright Sharp, K.C. The Goughs were represented by separate counsel: Gough was defended on the charge of manslaughter by J. F. Bourke, while Esther Gough was defended on the lesser charge of neglect by A. J. Long, K.C. The two councils connected to the case, coming under both heavy public censure and official scrutiny for slipshod administration, made sure of representation: Mr. Norman Carr acted for the Shropshire County Council while the Newport Corporation was represented by Mr. W. F. Hunt. Gough, testifying in his own defense, blustered his denials of the charges and declared that he had been indeed quite kind to the boys, who were disciplinary problems; he had fed them good meals up to even 5 times a day ("Farmer Gough" 3); the pig bench had been a "joke" ("Gough" 3); and he had never beaten Dennis. Since other witnesses and much evidence spoke irrefutably to the contrary, when the case went to the jury on March 19, 1945, that body took only 20 minutes to convict Gough of manslaughter. Esther Gough—who had testified as to her fear of and brutal coercion by her husband ("Mrs. Gough" 2), as well as to Gough's cruel and sadistic mistreatment of the O'Neill brothers—was also convicted of neglect. She was ultimately sentenced to six months imprisonment for that crime. Another public outcry rose up at Gough's six-year sentence for manslaughter, which prompted a later revision of the sentence to ten years for murder.

The system for boarding children out and following up on their welfare continued to come under heavy social and political fire. A public inquiry into the case was instituted on March 22, 1945. The Home Secretary, Herbert Morrison, had appointed Sir Walter Monckton to spearhead the investigation, which opened officially on April 10. By May 28, the inquiry had been completed and a report filed, which found that both councils having jurisdiction over Dennis O'Neill's care had made crucial errors at one time or another, but that those errors had not been intentional: "the two authorities failed separately in their duty to take adequate care of these two children ... [but] ... no one was deliberately callous" (Report 16–17). The administrative bodies involved, Newport and Shropshire County Councils, not only admitted to faults uncovered by the Monckton Report, but had also conducted private investigations into the case on their own.

The harrowing and haunting fate of Dennis O'Neill has been credited historically with galvanizing child-care reform and its legislations in modern Britain. The Monckton Report of 1945 called for stricter adherence to and monitoring of the boarding-out rules then in place for the care of children entrusted to the public protection; by January 1, 1947, new rules and regulations regarding such care had come into effect. These revisions were in turn succeeded by the benchmark Children Act of 1948.

## "Three Blind Mice"

In spite of a total lack of experience as landlords, or in business of any sort, young and impecunious newlyweds Molly and Giles Davis decided not to sell their recently-inherited and enormous Victorian house in Berkshire, but to turn it instead into a guesthouse. It would solve for them not only an income problem but a lodging problem as well, difficulties which otherwise would have taken the struggling couple years to overcome in the postwar economy of the times.

## Chapter 6. "An Outbreak of Sadism"

It was a cold and depressing English winter in 1948. The Davises hadn't known each other very long before they married, and so a settled life was far from an assured routine. In gratifying response to newspaper advertising, their exciting and optimistic new business venture had attracted reservations from several respectable-sounding potential guests. On the eve of welcoming this vanguard, Molly and Giles nervously awaited their advent because, on top of everything else, the weather was a real worry. The bitter cold was bad enough, but the threat of heavy snowfall due to arrive any minute added an unwelcome menace to their other apprehensions. Would the roads be passable enough for their clients to find them? Would their stores of provisions hold out in case of emergency?

The weather's ominous mood seemed to communicate itself to the mood of the capacious old domicile as Molly, in the house alone, prepared for the first guest. She felt vulnerable and uneasy. Not only were the coming guests going to be strangers to the couple, but she and Giles, despite their mutual devotion and the exciting fact that they were just about to celebrate their first anniversary, were practically strangers to each other too. Giles' entrance broke the spell of her misgivings, and as she prepared their teatime meal, they speculated about their upcoming guests. The first, Christopher Wren, was going to show up that night; a Mrs. Boyle and a Major Metcalf were due come in the next day. The young couple listened to the wireless, which conveyed the usual government reports, along with an account of the London murder of a Mrs. Lyon—and ever more disquieting details about the coming snowstorm.

To the relief of Molly and Giles, the huge snowstorm had held off just long enough, and all clients scheduled to arrive at Monkswell Manor were duly in place before the storm finally broke. Christopher Wren proved to be a highly-strung young man. Next had come the demanding Mrs. Boyle; predictably, the two did not take to each other at all. Mr. Wren promptly took the occasion of the day's front-page newspaper story, the murder of Mrs. Lyon, to tease and ruffle the ponderously dignified feathers of a highly displeased Mrs. Boyle. Both Molly and Christopher agreed that the police description of a man wanted for questioning in the murder seemed to fit almost anyone. When Major Metcalf, a middle-aged ex-military man, arrived just in time for dinner, things had settled down to as normal a scenario as could be expected. Molly and Giles's venture into guesthouse proprietorship and management was officially under way, and seemed off to a promising start, despite personalities and uncooperative weather. But the murder of Mrs. Lyon and its ramifications were about to break terrifyingly into the slightly tentative peace at unsuspecting Monkswell Manor....

London police investigating Mrs. Lyon's murder learned from the victim's landlady that as the murderer climbed the stairs to Mrs. Lyon's room, "when [he] got round the bend of the staircase he began to whistle softly. The tune he whistled was Three Blind Mice..." (Christie, "Three" 1). This somehow tied in with the two compelling pieces of evidence that the investigation had so far managed to garner: a note and a notebook. The murderer had pinned the note on the victim, and it contained a terse but chilling message: "This is the first" (22). He had also inscribed on the note a childish drawing of three mice and a bar of music for the nursery tune "Three Blind Mice." The killer had accidentally dropped the notebook, and in it police found two items of interest: one was the address of Mrs. Lyon, and the second was the name of Monkswell Manor.

"This is the first," the killer had written. Superintendent Parminter of Scotland Yard thought it imperative to get a policeman to Monkswell Manor as soon as possible to investigate, in spite of the horrific weather conditions. He therefore telephoned the Berkshire police to alert them to the situation.

An unexpected guest whose car had overturned in the snowbanks arrived in the middle of the night at Monkswell Manor, seeking shelter. Mr. Paravicini was an elderly foreigner, a spritely little satyr of a man who, despite his obvious age, disconcerted Molly with his darting movements and satirical comments.

Unsettling as he was, there was an even more unsettling event to come. The next morning, the Davis telephone rang; a cheerful voice with a message incongruous to that cheerfulness announced that he was Superintendent Hogben of the Berkshire Police, and due to a matter of some urgency he was sending a Detective Sergeant Trotter out to Monkswell Manor.

Despite the fact that Monkswell Manor was snowed in and the roads now definitely impassable, the apparently resourceful Sergeant Trotter managed to ski in to reach the guesthouse. The unexpected arrival of the fresh-faced young policeman at a French window caused gasps of alarm, but the message he brought was even more frightening. His visit, he explained, was because of the murder of Mrs. Lyon, and the fact that Monkswell Manor's name appeared in a notebook the murderer dropped near the murder scene. The police thought that the occupants might be in danger; the Sergeant had been sent as both investigator and protection.

It transpired that Mrs. Lyon had been in reality a woman named Maureen Gregg just recently released from prison. The note pinned on her body had made reference to the nursery rhyme "Three Blind Mice," and police had discovered that in 1940, Maureen Gregg and her farmer husband had taken in three war evacuee children—two brothers and their sister—at their place, Longridge Farm. One of the brothers had subsequently died of abuse and maltreatment at the couple's hands, and the Greggs had been sentenced to prison terms for their crimes. The incident had been a particularly distressing *cause célèbre* of the day, and now reference to it had cropped up in connection with the murder of the "farmer's wife," a brutal strangulation slaying. The very words of the cruel little rhyme now had frightening new meaning for Monkswell Manor's inmates as the refrain ran incessantly through their minds: "*Three blind mice, See how they run! They all ran after the farmer's wife, She cut off their tails with a carving knife! Did you ever see such a sight in your life? Three blind mice—*"

The principal suspect was the elder of the surviving children in the case, a young man who'd be nearly in his mid-twenties by then, who had "always been a bit queer." Authorities had no idea of his present whereabouts, nor that of his sister. Though there was a distinct likelihood that it had been the brother who in revenge had killed Mrs. Lyon, he wasn't the only possibility. There were others who had figured in the Longridge Farm case. The young sister, for example, who had been subsequently adopted, or the children's absent father—either could also be out for revenge. Outsiders had also been concerned: the billeting officers who had assigned the children to the farm; the teachers at the children's school; the council officials whose lax, incompetent monitoring had kept the children in an abusive home—they had all come in for their share of public or official censure. Any one of them, feeling somehow aggrieved and injured by the Longridge Farm tragedy, could somehow figure in the present-day mystery. Did anyone at Monkswell Manor, asked Trotter of its current inhabitants, have any connection at all to the case?

Uneasy denial from each inhabitant met his query. No one there, it seemed, had any tie to that distressing long-ago incident. It soon becomes apparent, however, that despite the denials, everyone at Monkswell Manor was indeed hiding something—from mere personal irrelevancies to dangerous, menacing secrets that threatened the lives of the Manor's occupants. The denials—extremely significant ones in several instances—were soon exposed for the evasions they were, but before a killer is finally caught, murder stalks the residents of Monkswell Manor, and startling revelations as to true identities and true motivations are the order of the day. A most surprising denouement ensues, in which a cunning killer is exposed in great Agatha Christie style.

## The Case of Dennis O'Neill + "Three Blind Mice"

The story "Three Blind Mice" is one of Christie's famous "nursery rhyme murders," wherein she uses the framework of a familiar little ditty to great effect. Other examples of this genre include *A Pocket Full of Rye*, and—arguably her most famous work of all—*And Then There Were None*.

## The Case of Dennis O'Neill + "Three Blind Mice"

"Three Blind Mice" loosely reprises the true story of Dennis O'Neill, the child whose cruel fate at the hands of his caretaker in World War II–era England not only touched and outraged a nation, but galvanized that nation into enacting much-needed social reform. Christie explains her point of view on the event in *An Autobiography*: "There was a case once where three children were neglected and abused, after they had been placed by the Council on a farm. One child did die, and there had been a feeling that a slightly delinquent boy might grow up full of the desire for revenge" (499). The tragic event is a taking-off point for the events of Christie's own original creation, which is essentially a compact tale of revenge.

Agatha Christie lengthened the radio-play version of her tale to a full-fledged stage production, changing its name to *The Mousetrap* (another unrelated theatre production had already taken the title "Three Blind Mice"), and premiering it at London's Ambassador Theatre in 1952. At the time of its opening Agatha Christie requested that the story "Three Blind Mice" not be published in Britain as long as *The Mousetrap* continued to play, little dreaming what the length of its actual tenure would turn out to be. The piece has been playing ever since 1952, staged for 21 years at the Ambassador before moving to other London venues. *The Mousetrap* is today a legend, having the longest continuous run of any play in theatre history.

Both the play and the short story essentially deal with an imagined aftermath to the death of young Dennis O'Neill, who died on January 9, 1945, from injuries sustained in brutal beatings by farmer Reginald Gough, his foster father. The child had been one of three brothers taken years earlier from the neglectful home of their parents in Newport, Shropshire. By 1944 Dennis and ten-year-old Terence had both been sent to live with Gough and his wife Esther at Bank Farm in Shropshire, while Frederick, at eight years of age the youngest, was sent to another family.

When a doctor was called to Bank Farm to attend an already-deceased Dennis, the physician quickly alerted police. The resulting mushrooming of sensational publicity about the boy's sadistic killing generated a firestorm of horrified public, political, and judicial reaction.

The two older boys' billeting had been a matter of joint jurisdiction between two districts, the Shropshire Council and the Newport Education Authority. In the difficult national circumstances and staff shortages of the wartime environment, oversight for the welfare of the O'Neill boys fell through the cracks. Six months after the O'Neill boys' placements with the Goughs, Eirlys Edwards, a young and inexperienced clerk of the Newport Education Authority, was finally dispatched to Bank Farm to look into the welfare of the boys. On returning to her offices, Miss Edwards wrote to her superiors that the O'Neill children should immediately be taken from the foster care of the Goughs. The Councils agreed, but somehow never followed up on the recommendation, for which subsequent official reports blamed a "lack of liaison" between the Councils. The school system was no better at detecting or acting on the boys' plight: Dennis was frequently absent from school—having been all too often locked in a closet all day by Gough, as punishment—but apparently no one made an effort to inquire into his absences.

At the beginning of the story "Three Blind Mice," two worlds are about to collide in Agatha Christie's fictional consequence of the true-crime demise of Dennis O'Neill. The year is 1948 instead of 1945; and the death of "Georgie," Dennis O'Neill's imagined counterpart, had occurred eight years prior in 1940. On a cold winter's evening, a muffled figure makes its way to a Culver Street abode in London's Paddington area, seeking a Mrs. Lyon who has recently moved to that address. The individual locates the woman—and leaves her dead, murdered by strangulation. There is a note pinned on the victim. It contains a child's drawing of three mice and a bar of music to the nursery tune "Three Blind Mice." The killer accidentally drops a notebook near the crime scene. Its pages contain two suggestive notations: the Culver Street address of Mrs. Lyon, and the words "Monkswell Manor."

Scotland Yard prepares an investigation, sending a man out to Monkswell Manor to do the job—hoping to out-race an imminent snowstorm that could prevent his reaching the Manor at all. Meanwhile, in Berkshire, young newlyweds Giles and Molly Davis have opened and advertised a new guesthouse—calling it Monkswell Manor. Neither Giles nor Molly had had any prior business experience, and on a bitterly cold winter's day the two nervously await the arrival of their first three patrons. As they neared their first wedding anniversary, they were still learning as much about each other as they were learning about running a going concern, but with the optimism of youth Molly and her husband were entering wholeheartedly into both adventures.

Happily—or so it seems at the time—the three guests have all safely arrived at the Manor by the time the fierce wild storm roars in. The hardy clients are a curiously mixed lot: there is the erratic, disconcerting and slightly puckish young Christopher Wren; followed by the daunting Mrs. Boyle, an exacting and domineering matron. The last guest to arrive is the solid, stolid, middle-aged ex-military man, Major Metcalf. Unexpectedly, a refugee stranded by the storm also joins the group—the dubious, somehow sinister Mr. Paravicini. A little later, despite the snowburst, the police representative does indeed manage to reach the guesthouse—on skis. In the person of this earnest, slightly officious, very young man who announces himself importantly as Sergeant Trotter, officialdom takes over the newly-launched guesthouse routine of Monkswell Manor.

Trotter elaborates on the reason for his presence, to the incredulous dismay of the Manor's occupants: Mrs. Lyon's murder, and the fact that Monkswell Manor had been linked to that murder. The young officer explains the significance of the mice sketch and nursery tune, and the notebook entries found near the murder scene. The slain woman was not Mrs. "Lyon"—a name Christie plays upon to suggest a particularly large, ferocious, and deadly "cat"—but a criminal named Maureen Gregg, recently released from prison. She had served a term for her part, 8 years earlier, in a notorious case involving the neglect and killing of a child left to her foster care and that of her husband. Three siblings—12-year-old Georgie, his 15-year-old brother Jim, and his 14-year-old sister—had been billeted on the Greggs at their home, Longridge Farm. The children had all suffered ill-usage at the hands of the farmer and his wife; and the 12-year-old had died.

The Longridge Farm of the story corresponds to Bank Farm in the true-life occurrence. Reginald Gough, as Dennis's actual killer, was undoubtedly the principal malefactor in the O'Neill case; however, Christie seems to give Mrs. Gregg, the fictional farmer's wife, the more villainous role in young Georgie's death, thus adhering more closely to the nursery rhyme's implications. Her eight-year incarceration also argues a severe degree of involvement in Georgie's death. In the true crime case, the farmer's wife Esther Gough was depicted by her defense attorneys as a victim herself, an abused wife living in fear of her brutal husband, coerced into countenancing her husband's cruelty against their wards for her own survival.

At Stafford Assizes on March 15, 1945, Reginald Gough and Esther Gough were brought to trial for the death of Dennis O'Neill. The sensational case generated huge public interest. The court and the nation heard and read poignant testimony from young Terence O'Neill on the inhuman treatment that he and his brother suffered at the Goughs' hands. The trial ended, ultimately, in a ten-year murder sentence for the farmer; the lot of Esther Gough, the farmer's wife, was conviction on a lesser charge of neglect, and sentence to a six-month prison term.

Within the novella the prime suspect in Mrs. Gregg's murder is Georgie's brother, army deserter Jim, a mentally unstable lad presumed to be bent on revenge. He has disappeared from sight and officials fear that Monkswell Manor is his next destination. Authorities have also lost track of Georgie's sister, by now in her early 20s. Though Jim is first on the list of possible killers, the sister could also figure as a prospect, as well as the father who'd been on military duty at the time of Georgie's death.

Like the O'Neill case, Christie's novella features three maltreated foster children. Although Frederick, Terence and Dennis O'Neill entered foster care in 1940 due to parental neglect, the author's fictional "Jim," "Georgie," and their sister were depicted as wartime evacuee children of 1940. The

## Chapter 6. "An Outbreak of Sadism"

O'Neill boys, at 8, 10, and 12, were younger than two of their fictional counterparts who were, at 15 and 14, thus able to figure eight years onward as adult possibilities in the story. The three O'Neill children had all been boys; Christie's substitution of a girl in the mix allows a widened field of viable candidates in the tale as either possible victims or possible perpetrators, as does the inclusion of the children's father, who would now be middle-aged.

At Monkswell Manor, Trotter questions its inhabitants, asking which of them has a connection—any connection whatever—to the sensational Longridge Farm case of so many years before. Blank, and blanket, denial greets his query: each one disavows any association with those terrible past events.

But only hours later, Mrs. Boyle is found strangled to death—killed in the same way as had been the farmer's wife, Maureen Gregg, just days before in London.

And so Monkswell Manor's frightened residents learn that a wily unidentified killer is actually and terrifyingly among them. It transpires that Mrs. Boyle had deliberately lied about not being associated with the Longridge Farm tragedy. She had been the careless billeting officer who had sent the three unfortunate children to the Greggs in the first place. After Georgie's death she had been blamed for her negligence, but her carelessness had not been a thing punishable by law. She had always refused to admit any responsibility for any part of the subsequent tragedy; but nevertheless it now appeared that she had paid for that responsibility with her life. And who, among the remaining individuals at Monkswell Manor, had been her executioner?

A grim Sergeant Trotter now confronts the guesthouse's surviving tenants. Someone there among them at Monkswell Manor was a murderer—a murderer who was enjoying himself. They are all relative strangers to each other, and as trapped as any mice. Trotter stubbornly continues to insist that someone else among them must also have been connected with the Longridge Farm case, and in just as much jeopardy as Mrs. Boyle had been. Which of them is hiding that association? After all, there had been three little mice, three children who had suffered; and presumably the murderer was bent on avenging the treatment that all three had undergone—especially the treatment of little Georgie, the boy who had died. Therefore, a third murder was clearly indicated. But each of the Manor's occupants continues nervously silent. In spite of their reticence the determined sergeant devises a stratagem to ensnare the murderer, a scheme to catch one more mouse in a trap. When that crafty stratagem is duly deployed, a cunning and surprising killer is unmasked just in time, in a tour-de-force climax and denouement from the ingenious pen of Agatha Christie.

In "Three Blind Mice" Christie paints a revealing, empathetic picture of surviving victims' psychological situations, in place of penning a sermon or diatribe on the subject. In several of her tales, of which "Three Blind Mice" is one, psychologically wounded individuals snap under the burden of intolerable loss of a loved one, especially when that loss is through a deliberate wrongdoing that's been insufficiently punished, or not punished at all. These embittered survivors feel driven toward providing themselves, at almost any cost, some measure of the healing and closure denied them by inadequate societal conventions. They act to inflict a dark and dire revenge, punishing culprits who are, in the eyes of the law, unpunishable, or not punishable enough. In this way Christie manages to effect a kind of wish-fulfillment means of retribution.

Before, during, and after their trial for Dennis O'Neill's death, the Goughs had come in for their full share of execration from the populace, the authorities, and the press. But by far the most virulent public blame and the severest official indictment fell on the country's lax childcare system, and its woefully undertrained and disconnected employees. During the investigation into the O'Neill affair many from the Shropshire area associations were taken to task. Although their inchoate performances were deemed inadvertent and not criminally liable, the chastened employees of the Shropshire Council and Newport Authority conducted their own inquiries and readily admitted their faults, vowing to ensure that a fate such as Dennis O'Neill's would never befall another child entrusted to their care. The horrified national reaction to the fiasco resulted in passage of an Act of Parliament: The Children Act 1948, which mandated accountable, reformed childcare services for unprotected children who, for any reason, came under the safeguarding of the state.

In "Three Blind Mice," the story's strictures on Mrs. Boyle's performance of her duties mirror the blame heaped on individuals of the Shropshire Council and the Newport Authority. Christie also makes it plain that though the character Mrs. Boyle, like the real-world billeting bodies in the O'Neill case, was not legally accountable for the tragic outcome at Longridge Farm, she nonetheless bears a certain moral blame for her mishandling of her responsibilities. In fact, the personage of Mrs. Boyle represents an aggregate of the ineffectual agents whose slipshod handling of the true-life O'Neill affair resulted in tragedy—but it is a representation with a difference. In just a few telling lines from her descriptive pen, Christie reveals both Mrs. Boyle's culpable role in the tale's background tragedy, and the lady's head-in-the-sand attitude toward it thereafter. With accuracy and economy Christie deftly distills the deficiencies of the ineffective true-life agents into one masterly fictive rendering, while at one and the same time she tightens and focuses the brief fiction tale with that same artistically composite portrayal. In contrast to the contrite "mea culpa" attitude of the real-life Shropshire associations, Christie's depiction of Mrs. Boyle's selfish and impervious attitude adds another facet to the detective story's dramatic impact: her recalcitrance thus makes her equally viable as potential victim or potential villain in the story.

The unproductive intervention of agents in the true-crime O'Neill case is also echoed in the tale, partially reflected in the composite character of Mrs. Boyle; however, the distress and self-blame that well-meaning agents may well have felt after Dennis O'Neill's death is plausibly imagined in the poignant anguish of Georgie's schoolteacher, whose circumstances made it impossible for her to aid the boy in time. As well, it's also reasonable to infer the presumed uneasy consciences of Shropshire teachers who may have believed, after Dennis's death, that they too were guilty of having failed to intervene on his behalf.

The short story "Three Blind Mice," like her novel *The Mirror Crack'd*, is an example of Agatha Christie's way of righting, in her fiction, an anomalous but nevertheless grievous wrong, a morally "criminal" wrong that has gone insufficiently redressed in the real world. The "criminality" of the wrong is a type that, although it results in irreparable harm to victims and survivors, escapes what should have been, in some views, the full force of society's retribution. The crime then becomes eligible for the moral blame and moral punishment allotted to perpetrators of sins of omission or commission who, arguably, had no valid excuse for their lapses. In "Three Blind Mice" the Greggs pay the penalty that perhaps the Goughs did not meet in real life; Mrs. Boyle sustains the symbolic punishment that might metaphorically have been imposed on the carelessness of the Shropshire billeting divisions. Throughout the pages of the story, Christie imaginatively proceeds to "supply the deficiencies"—as Sherlock Holmes might have put it—of the stymied real-world justice system, using her storyteller's forum to "redress," fictionally, the real-life wrong, and thus to restore order.

# Chapter 7

# The "Little Man"
## Dr. Hawley Harvey Crippen and *Mrs. McGinty's Dead*

The novel *Mrs. McGinty's Dead* qualifies as another of Agatha Christie's "nursery rhyme murders," along with such fare as "Three Blind Mice"—although the McGinty rhyme seems to be much more obscure than others. The story appeared first in an American edition published by The Detective Book Club in 1951, with the title *Blood Will Tell*. The story is intricate despite Christie's deceptively straightforward way of telling the tale. She subtly shows her version of how the sins of the fathers (or mothers) affect succeeding generations. Parts of the novel *Mrs. McGinty's Dead* evoke the fascinating real-life crime of Dr. Hawley Harvey Crippen, hanged in Edwardian England for his sensational crime 42 years before the novel's advent.

## Dr. Hawley Harvey Crippen

In 1910, Dr. Hawley Harvey Crippen was accused of murdering his wife, Cora, by administration of the poison hyoscine, and then exacerbating the crime by dismembering and mutilating the body before burying it beneath his cellar floor.

The Crippens were Americans who had traveled to England in 1900 to make their home in London, each pursuing an individual goal. For Crippen's plump, forceful, and spendthrift wife Cora—who had misguided notions of her musical talents—the goal was a career in singing. For the bespectacled, reserved, and undersized Crippen, the goal was professional and economic opportunity. Born in Michigan in 1862, in 1884 he had completed a course in homeopathic medicine and styled himself "doctor." In 1894, Crippen had married his second spouse, Cora Turner, and had also begun working for Munyons, a patent medicine firm, in their American offices. By 1905, Crippen was working for Munyons in their London premises, while Cora, using the name "Belle Elmore," dabbled at making her dream of music-hall success come true.

The Crippen marriage was not a happy one. Mrs. Crippen's talent for music was minuscule, if not completely nonexistent; she did not attain her aspirations. This did not prevent her from sporadically trying to succeed, bankrolled by her compliant husband's earnings. Nor did it keep her from unwisely spending her husband's money faster than he could make it. Despite his efforts to please her, she berated her husband at every opportunity.

When Crippen's employment faltered with an accompanying decline in income, the couple began to take in lodgers at their home at 39 Hilldrop Crescent, into which they had moved in 1905. "Belle" had made friends with members of a music-hall guild, while unabashedly commencing to take lovers from the ranks of both her fellow actors and her lodgers. She did not do much to hide her infidelities, but Crippen, soon to be dubbed "the little man" by the presses because of his unimposing physical presence and his self-effacing behavior, seemed to endure quietly this state of affairs with characteristic and retiring restraint. However, the doctor came home one day in 1908 to discover his wife in bed with one of their lodgers, and that event apparently proved to be the final straw. The incident seemed to allow some resentment in the doctor to burst free of its inhibiting chains: he now felt justified in beginning his own affair with the young woman he had long ago begun to care for: Ethel Le Neve, bookkeeper and typist at his Munyons offices. Born Ethel Neave, she was a 19-year-old typist when Crippen first met her, and over the years the "quiet, ladylike, unassuming … [and] obedient" (Young, *Crippen* xix) girl came to mean more and more to the little man who was completely browbeaten at home.

They began their affair some two years before Cora Crippen's disappearance. At the time that Cora had found out about the relationship, she threatened to leave her husband and to elope with her lover, fellow actor Bruce Miller, if Crippen didn't immediately give up his liaison with Le Neve. In addition Cora vowed that she would take with her all her husband's money, which was held in a joint account, when she left. This would have been a serious blow to Crippen's economic survival, and therefore to his ability to continue the relationship with Ethel Le Neve in the style he wished to maintain. To prove she meant her menacing ultimatum, behind Crippen's back Cora had already begun preparing for acquiring the joint funds—just before she went suddenly missing.

The year 1910 was the fated one for the "little man" (Early 309), Dr. Crippen; he was not destined to live to see its end. He started on the path to his ultimate fate on that year's very first day. On January 1, Dr. Crippen placed an order with Lewis & Burrows, chemists, for five grains of the poison hyoscine, under the pretext that he was ordering it for his employers,

Munyons, as Lewis & Burrows was an establishment with which Munyons did regular business. On January 19, 1910, Crippen received the order, signing the poison book in the name of his employers. Later, at Crippen's trial for murder, Munyons' representatives firmly denied that their organization in any way authorized or desired that purchase; furthermore, Crippen was unable either to account believably for how the hyoscine had been used in his practice, or to produce the hyoscine itself.

On January 31, the Crippens' actor friends, Mr. and Mrs. Paul Martinetti, came to dine at 39 Hilldrop Crescent. The evening was more or less convivial, even though Cora several times found loud fault with her hapless husband, snapping nastily at him in the Martinettis' presence during the course of the evening. Just before the Martinettis departed, Cora angrily scolded Crippen for withholding some courtesy that, she felt, Crippen should have accorded their guests.

The Martinettis' departure from the Crippen home, sometime after midnight of February 1, marked the last time that anyone saw Cora Crippen alive—except for her murderer.

A day or so later, "Belle's" friends at the music guild received a hastily-written letter from her, in which she resigned her office as guild treasurer. She had been called suddenly back to America to see to a seriously-ill relative, the letter read; however, strangely, the note was in her husband's handwriting. Some two weeks later Crippen attended a Benevolent Fund ball with Ethel Le Neve—and she was wearing Cora Crippen's furs and jewelry. Gasps of amazement greeted this spectacle, and when Crippen answered Belle's music-hall associates' guarded questions with evasive or contradictory answers, the friends became more and more suspicious. To their repeated and ever more insistent inquiries as time passed, Crippen revealed that Cora had been writing to him that she too had fallen gravely ill. Crippen was careful to let it be seen that he had no expectations that she would recover.

Near the middle of March Ethel Le Neve openly moved into 39 Hilldrop Crescent as Crippen's "housekeeper," and continued to sport the missing Mrs. Crippen's clothes and jewelry, to the indignation of Cora Crippen's supporters. On March 23, the little man and his mistress prepared to leave London for a "recuperative" stay in Dieppe. From Victoria Station Crippen dispatched a telegram that reached the Martinettis, stating that Cora Crippen had died the night before in California. Cora Crippen's friends were stunned—and more suspicious than ever. On Crippen's return, they questioned him closely as to where Cora had died and been cremated, emerging from the disjointed interviews supremely dissatisfied. When one of the friends journeyed to Los Angeles, he attempted to verify the peculiar death and cremation information Crippen had given him—but with no success.

## Chapter 7. The "Little Man"

On his return to England, he went to Scotland Yard and divulged his increased apprehensions.

Cora's cohorts feared the worst, but Scotland Yard was not convinced on their evidence that any criminal circumstance had occurred. Nevertheless, the agency selected Inspector Walter Dew and Sergeant Arthur Mitchell to look into the matter. Their initial investigations and talks with Dr. Crippen yielded nothing especially suspicious. On July 8, they visited Crippen at his workplace, Albion House, where they also espied and questioned Ethel Le Neve. Crippen escorted the officers back to 39 Hilldrop Crescent, where the two policemen had a thorough look around without noting anything untoward. Suddenly, Crippen decided to "unburden" himself to Dew: he had indeed lied about his wife's disappearance, Crippen said, because he'd been too ashamed to tell the truth. Cora had run off, he said, with one of her lovers, actor Bruce Miller. To avoid ridicule, Crippen had invented the tales he told Cora's friends. By the time the Scotland Yard men departed, they were virtually convinced of the truth of Crippen's calmly plausible story. After all, it seemed far more likely than the dire imaginings of Cora's partisans.

But it transpired that something drew the Inspector back to 39 Hilltop Crescent the next day—and he was astonished to find that both Crippen and Le Neve had precipitately fled the city.

Startled into action, Dew immediately called in a crew to begin a massive scouring of the residence at Hilldrop Crescent, while descriptions and photographs of the couple were widely circulated in newspapers—and also by that recent invention, radio telegraphy. The pair had absconded from the Hilldrop Crescent premises in what could only be regarded as a guilty panic, and Dew felt there must have been a cogent reason for that panic. And for that guilt.

On July 13 the ostensible reason was discovered when human remains were found buried beneath the domicile's cellar floor.

It was a grisly, sickening discovery. The stage of decomposition indicated that death had occurred some time before. The head, bones, and limbs were missing, and the torso so minutely dissected that it was impossible to tell if the body was that of a man or woman. Accounts of the gruesome discovery ignited a media frenzy. Newspapers blazoned pictures of Crippen and Le Neve across their pages along with lurid details of the dismemberment-mutilation murder. The publications also carried sensational day by day coverage of the story, from the wildest "sightings" of the pair to the soberest comments on what the crime meant for society. Authorities issued warrants for the arrest of Dr. Hawley Harvey Crippen and Ethel Le Neve, who had by then fled the continent by boat. Obviously following a plan, they'd camouflaged themselves as "Mister and Master Robinson," a gentleman and his son—with Ethel disguised in boys' clothing. They'd booked passage on the SS *Montrose*, a liner heading from Belgium for landing at Canada's Father Point.

The ship sailed from Antwerp on July 20. The Montrose's captain, Henry Kendall, had been following the case closely by way of newspapers and wired reports accessed on the ship. The Robinsons had aroused his curiosity from the start, and he'd been watching them carefully: their affectionate behavior seemed inappropriate for a father and son, and Le Neve's "ridiculously altered men's suits" (Paine, "Hyoscine" 24) imperfectly disguised her feminine figure. The Captain became convinced that the wanted fugitives Crippen and Le Neve were traveling on the Montrose. On July 22, Kendall wired Scotland Yard that he strongly suspected that two passengers on his ship were the missing and highly sought-after duo. That communication would go down in history as the first time that wireless telegraphy was used to capture a criminal. Kendall made sure no English newspapers were available aboard ship and therefore the fugitives purportedly learned nothing of the sensation that their flight and the Hilldrop Crescent discovery had excited.

Immediately after finding the mutilated body, Dew and Mitchell gave chase, boarding a faster ship, the SS *Laurentic*, which was due to dock at Quebec's Father Point well before the arrival of the Montrose. After nerve-wracking, weeklong journeys by sea for both the unknowing but anxious runaways on one ship and their determined hunters on the other, Dew boarded the Montrose masquerading as a pilot-boat captain. He dramatically arrested the most famous fugitives on the planet before the astonished pair could disembark on New World soil. Crippen seemed to freeze the second he recognized his nemesis Inspector Dew in his seafaring guise. He then registered almost instant relief that the suspense was at last over, while Le Neve collapsed at once into bouts of fainting spells and hysteria. Hundreds of members of the public who'd eagerly followed the story and the pursuit in daily newspapers were gathered at the landing to witness this momentous event in criminal history. They were also there to get an avid first glimpse of the ferocious monster who had committed the savage murder depicted so horrifyingly in news accounts. Many of them, however, were disappointed at what they saw: Crippen was "a cringing figure," who "looked anything but the hypnotic marvel which cabled stories had held up" ("On This Day"). From the moment of arrest, all Crippen's concern had been focused on the prostrated Ethel Le Neve. While never confessing to murder, the little man also never ceased fighting for the woman he loved. His one focus was an anxious effort to exonerate Le Neve from any wrongdoing connected with any facet of the sordid affair.

On October 18, Hawley Harvey Crippen's trial for murder opened at London's famous courthouse, the Old Bailey. Already, in the minds of most of the multitudes engrossed in the unfolding affair, Crippen's guilt was a certainty. Lord Alverstone, Lord Chief Justice of England, presided over the trial; the redoubtable Richard Muir, K.C., led for the prosecution, with A. A. Tobin, K.C., heading Crippen's defense. The assured testimony of young Bernard Spilsbury for the crown helped to seal Crippen's fate. Spilsbury's long career as the star Home-Office pathologist of the era began with the tyro analyst's handling of the forensic evidence in Crippen's sensational trial. One of Spilsbury's almost insurmountable tasks was to make sure that the anomalous masses of human body parts found at Hilldrop Crescent were indisputably those of Cora Crippen. The missing bones, head, and limbs of the mutilated body were never found. Nevertheless Spilsbury testified that he'd been able to identify the badly decomposed remains by recovering abdominal skin tissue bearing a scar corresponding to one that Mrs. Crippen had been known to have. In recent times, however, modern forensic discoveries have stirred controversy over Spilsbury's identification of that scar tissue (Hodgson), which in turn has led to doubt in certain camps that Crippen did indeed murder his wife.

During the trial, Spilsbury also pinned down the means of the murder. The remains had yielded evidence of a massive dose of the vegetable alkaloid poison, hyoscine—a match exactly to the purchase that Crippen had artfully acquired from Lewis & Burrows, weeks before Cora Crippen's disappearance. It was also the exact poison and dosage that Crippen was unable to account for satisfactorily during his own courtroom testimony.

The thrilling spectacle of trial lasted five days. After the judge's summation on October 22 the jury retired, then promptly returned less than half an hour later, bringing in the expected verdict of Guilty. Crippen, still quietly protesting his innocence, was then duly sentenced to death by hanging. Doctor Hawley Harvey Crippen never confessed to murdering Cora Crippen, and after a fruitless appeal, he went somberly to the gallows on November 23, 1910, thinking only of Ethel Le Neve to the very end. At his request, her picture was buried with him.

Crippen's case was rich in sensationalism. Nearly all aspects of the case were exciting and bizarre—including the doctor's dramatic attempt at escape across the seas, with Le Neve accompanying him in disguise; the threshold-of-the-modern age radio technology that trapped the fleeing lovers; and Inspector Dew's determined pursuit by faster ship. Intense day-by-day news coverage kept the nation abreast of every move in real-time newspaper updates, much as audiences nearly a century later followed the gripping O. J. Simpson "white Bronco" car chase via television and other media.

On October 25, Ethel Le Neve was tried as an accessory after the fact in a perfunctory hearing that saw her acquitted of the charge. The public and the press speculated endlessly about Le Neve's part—if any—in that sensational drama of life and death, enacted all for love. Both she and Crippen maintained from beginning to end that neither of them knew anything of the alleged murder of Cora Crippen, either before or after the alleged deed. Many were skeptical of Le Neve's statements that she had never read English newspapers after their July 9 flight from London, either in Antwerp or elsewhere—and so was unaware of Crippen's wanted status, and therefore guiltless of abetting him after the fact. Still, no one could prove that she had either seen or read any such publications. Many other doubters of her innocence went further in their surmises: they believed that Le Neve not only knew of Crippen's murder of his wife, but had herself planned and goaded the erstwhile mild little man into that murder. But no one could show her supposed complicity with any certainty or real proof. Latter-day researchers, though, have come up with recent arguments for that scenario, typically offering "new evidence that suggests it was Crippen's mistress, Ethel Le Neve, who was the driving force behind the murder" ("Mistress").

And there were other questioners who went even further in their speculations about Le Neve's guilt or innocence in the case. They were convinced that there was cause to believe that Ethel Le Neve herself could have committed the actual murder, and that a horrified but besotted Crippen only afterwards did what he did to clean up, and cover up, her crime. But no hard evidence of any of these speculative notions was ever produced in either of the trials.

And so a question remained in the minds of many after the trials in 1910, and still remains in the minds of many students of the crime a century later: did Ethel Le Neve get away with murder?

Immediately after Crippen's execution, Le Neve had used an assumed name and boarded ship for Canada, where she took up residence and began to make a new life for herself. In 1915, unheralded and unrecognized, she returned to England. There she found work and marriage, leading a humdrum domestic life far different from the tense, perilous and prolonged drama of five years earlier. It wasn't until after her death in 1967 that what was known of her notorious part in one of the most notorious crimes of the century was once again revealed. She, too—like her paramour decades before her—went to her grave without shedding any new light on the slaying of Cora Crippen.

## *Mrs. McGinty's Dead*

On the eve of his retirement from the Kilchester constabulary, a troubled Superintendent Spence visits Hercule Poirot. Though not wishing to impose, the painstaking Spence has steeled himself to ask for the little

## Chapter 7. The "Little Man"

Belgian's help on a recent case whose outcome has worried him. Spence was instrumental in convicting one James Bentley for the sordid robbery and murder, in the little village of Broadhinny, of the man's aging, working-class landlady, Mrs. McGinty. But Spence has an uneasy feeling that despite convincing evidence, the convicted man did not commit the crime for which he's very shortly to be hanged. Poirot is disconsolately bored and at loose ends in his own retirement, and agrees with alacrity to look into the matter.

Mrs. McGinty's body had been discovered on the parlor floor of her cottage home, her head bashed in by a hatchet-like weapon that police had never recovered. Missing was £30 of her hard-earned money; but the notes were quickly found where they'd been hastily buried under a stone near the house. Mrs. McGinty's sole lodger, James Bentley, was immediately suspected of the crime. Before moving into Mrs. McGinty's cottage, Bentley had lived meagerly but respectably with his mother, to whom he was devoted, until her death; however he had steadily come down even further in the world by the time of Mrs. McGinty's slaying. When questioned he'd shown a tendency to lie to investigators about his movements at the time of the murder. His alibi for the time of the killing was weak in the extreme, and his own unprepossessing appearance and unfortunate slyness of manner did nothing to dispose anyone in his favor. It seemed that no one—except Superintendent Spence—doubted at all that James Bentley had killed Mrs. McGinty for her money. But when Poirot interviews the prisoner, he, like Spence, comes to think there might be reason to doubt the inevitability of Bentley's guilt. He arrives at this conclusion despite the young man's hang-dog and resignedly defeatist attitude. But if Bentley didn't do it, then who did? And would there be time enough for Poirot to ferret out the identity of the true murderer before the wretched Bentley is executed?

At the beginning of his investigations Poirot meets 30-year-old Maude Williams, a typist who had worked with Bentley at the office of estate agents Breather & Scuttle. The detective discovers in the decisive young woman someone else who has misgivings about Bentley's guilt, and who moreover had been drawn romantically to the awkward young man. The unattractive Bentley had nonetheless managed to attract this vital young woman, and she volunteers to help Poirot in his efforts to find the truth of the McGinty murder.

Continuing his inquiries, Poirot repairs to Broadhinny, where he encounters detective-fiction novelist Ariadne Oliver, an old acquaintance and sometimes fellow-sleuth. She is visiting Broadhinny to collaborate with Robin Upward, an up-and-coming young playwright on the brink of huge theatrical success; the two were adapting one of her detective works for the stage. Poirot enlists her cooperation in his quest. Ariadne is sojourning with Robin and his wheel-chair bound but autocratic and wealthy mother at

Laburnums, their country house; Mrs. Oliver's placement there provides for Poirot a means of social access to the Upwards—and beyond them to others in Broadhinny as well.

He finds he must put up at Long Meadows, the ramshackle and comically ill-run home of Maureen and Johnnie Summerhayes. Though Maureen had grown up an adopted child, Johnnie Summerhayes was descended from old-line stock and longtime gentry of Broadhinny. Despite his pedigree, they are now forced by modern-era poverty to take paying guests into their once-grand home. Poirot learns that Mrs. McGinty had charred for the Summerhayes ménage as well as for most of the "very nice" social-elite families of the small town.

Poirot further ascertains that several of those families had come to Broadhinny after the war and had no real roots in the village. By the time of Mrs. McGinty's demise they had lived there for several years, and were accounted neighbors and social leaders of the area. Mrs. McGinty had cleaned house diligently for all their households: the Upwards—mother and son; the newly-wed Carpenters; Dr. Rendell and his wife; and the Wetherby family. Laura Upward, relict of a rich northern lumber tradesman, had come to Broadhinny with her son Robin by way of Australia after the war. Young and politically ambitious Guy Carpenter, partner in an engineering works and the wealthiest resident of the village, resided at his estate, Holmeleigh, with his recently-acquired and glamorous wife Eve. She herself had come to Broadhinny as the impoverished widow of an officer killed in the war, and her marriage to Carpenter had elevated her status both financially and socially.

Mrs. McGinty had also worked for the blandly affable Doctor Rendell and his thin, nervy wife Shelagh. The couple had migrated to Broadhinny some years prior from the doctor's northern England practice. The Wetherby family—a husband and wife getting on in years, and Deirdre, the thirtyish daughter of Mrs. Wetherby by a previous marriage—had also employed and valued the hard-working Mrs. McGinty. Poirot is surprised to find that the somewhat stolid and awkward Deirdre, who is fiercely devoted to her mother, like Maude Williams had also been attracted to James Bentley—perhaps because he too had been as dedicated to his mother as she was to her own.

Poirot senses, from reluctantly or warily granted interviews with Broadhinny's residents, that nearly all are carefully hiding from him some secret or fear or reticence of their own; he also pieces together a picture of what Mrs. McGinty had been like. She had been a domestic jewel, a real treasure in those days of scarce and hit-or-miss domestic-servant reliability. She had been a good worker and thoroughly dependable. She was thought to be honest, if also a bit of a snoop, prying sometimes into the desk drawers and other belongings of her employers. Mrs. Sweetiman, the habitually talkative shopkeeper and village postmistress, also supplements the background information that Poirot gathers. The postmistress provides gossipy tidbits about Mrs. McGinty. While doing so, her cheerily casual, run-on comments furnish the detective with one of the most valuable clues of the novel. Following up on the promise of those comments Poirot unearths viable motives for murder other than those attributed to Bentley—and therefore other viable murder suspects.

While checking through the murdered woman's effects, Poirot finds that Mrs. McGinty had read and clipped out a feature from the sensationalist tabloid, *The Sunday Companion*, the week before her death. The article had showcased four women who'd been embroiled in four notorious past murder cases but who had dropped out of the public view: Eva Kane, Lily Gamboll, Janice Courtland, and Vera Blake. Accompanying the piece were photographs of each woman. Eva Kane had been the pregnant mistress—and possible accomplice—of an infamous wife-killer at the time he'd been hanged for his crime. There were some who believed that it was Eva herself who had done the murder, and her infatuated lover had taken the blame. Quoted in the article, she had vowed that "my daughter shall grow up happy and innocent" in a new country, completely ignorant of her parents' past. Lily Gamboll had been 12 years old when in a fit of temper she had slain her aunt with a meat chopper. Janice Courtland had been the wife for eight years of a fiendishly abusive husband; her young and impressionable "admirer" had impulsively but brutally killed that husband to protect her. Vera Blake's swain had been discovered to be a wanted killer; then the husband she subsequently married had turned out to be a thief. Other misfortunes showed she seemed destined to suffer disastrous human relationships.

Had Mrs. McGinty, while prying, unearthed a link between one of her employers and one of the women of the article? All of the people in Broadhinny were "very nice"; their social—and financial—survival depended on maintaining their façades of respectability. Once tear that away, and they were vulnerable to exposure—and unthinkable consequences. Murder had been done before, time and again, in the name of preserving respectability. Had the charwoman then for reasons of her own revealed her knowledge to one of those "nice" people? And had that person then killed Mrs. McGinty—who would have posed an intolerable threat to her status and wellbeing—and then gone on to frame the entirely frameable Bentley for the murder? If so, which "notorious woman" of the article was now living in Broadhinny, passing herself off under a respectable alias as a lady of blameless past?

Poirot decides there are likely candidates in Broadhinny who fit requisite age categories for the women depicted in the article. Eva Kane, Janice

Courtland, and Vera Blake would now be in their sixties; Mrs. Upward and Mrs. Wetherby, for instance, matched that age bracket. Eve Carpenter, Shelagh Rendell, and the adopted Maureen Summerhayes, among others would fit as Lily Gamboll or even the daughter of Eva Kane, who would be in the thirties. And when it came right down to it, what was actually known of the true histories of Broadhinny's inhabitants before they came to that part of the world? All anyone really knew of their origins was what each of them had claimed those origins to be. Nearly every household that McGinty worked for could have harbored an inmate fitting the description of a woman featured in that *Sunday Companion* article; therefore nearly every household harbored someone who could possibly have had a motive for murder.

With time running out for Bentley, Poirot hopes to startle the true murderer into making a revealing mistake. At a party hosted by the Upwards, many of Mrs. McGinty's former employers are in attendance. At that propitious gathering the detective suddenly exhibits photographs of the women featured in the article, thereby throwing down the gauntlet by strongly hinting he's close to exposing the killer. His quick perception espies an unguarded reaction; he urgently entreats anyone who knows anything at all about the pictures to divulge that knowledge immediately. To withhold even the smallest piece of information, he warns, could result in deadly peril. But his warnings and pleas go unheeded. Someone decides to play a lone hand—and in consequence the desperate killer strikes again. In the end, however, the inimitable Belgian detective uses his little grey cells and carefully puts pieces of the puzzle together, interspersing dogged labor with flashes of intuitive insight. The murderer goes too far in ever more desperate bids to escape detection, and is trapped at last by Poirot's infallible ingenuity—and attention to detail.

# Dr. Hawley Harvey Crippen + *Mrs. McGinty's Dead*

Agatha Christie's detective novel *Mrs. McGinty's Dead* was first published under that title in 1952 and featured the brilliant Belgian detective, Hercule Poirot. As the novel begins, there were doubts about the guilt of James Bentley, the man convicted of and soon to be executed for the robbery murder of his landlady, Mrs. McGinty, in the preceding November. She had been an elderly and harmless, if a bit nosy, charwoman of the South Devon village of Broadhinny. Poirot had been commissioned to unearth the identity of the true killer before it was too late for the singularly unappealing young Bentley—if indeed he *was* innocent.

## Chapter 7. The "Little Man"

Christie uses an article from the tabloid *Sunday Companion* not only as an indicator of Mrs. McGinty's cast of mind, but also as a vehicle for alluding to several categories of prominent domestic crime. These types were familiar to the populace, and well-chronicled in established as well as sensationalist newspapers of Christie's day. Reports of gullible women, swindled and victimized for gain by recently acquired "fiancés" or "husbands" who were little more than strangers, were all too numerous; and disturbing accounts of sociopathic or brutalized children of the slums who committed terrible crimes also made the headlines with disturbing regularity. Stories of adulterous wives, whose jealous paramours acted out violently against the husbands who were their rivals, never failed to fascinate the public. Nor did chronicles of adulterous husbands who poisoned their inconvenient spouses to cleave to younger mistresses: and the Eva Kane story within the tale echoes one of the most infamous "adulterous husband" true-crime histories of all—that of Dr. Hawley Harvey Crippen.

Crippen was executed in 1910 London for the gruesome poisoning, mutilation, and dismemberment slaying of his disparaging wife, Cora—a murder done for love of Ethel Le Neve, his young inamorata. Christie's approach to the Crippen affair, via her novel, offers a change of angle on the story. Most commentators on the case focused their attention on the motives and character of the enigmatic Dr. Crippen. Christie approaches the notorious crime by fixing her gaze on the even more enigmatic Le Neve, thus giving pride of place to suspicion and conjecture surrounding the role Crippen's mistress had played in the slaying of Cora Crippen—if any. Though little doubt exists that Mrs. Crippen was killed to clear the path to happiness for the lovers, to the present day a haze of mystery still surrounds the actual events of the actual slaying itself. The doctor's very name, however, has entered popular culture as an epithet for a husband who murders his wife.

In *Mrs. McGinty's Dead*, the eternal-triangle story of fictitious Alfred Craig, Mrs. Craig, and Eva Kane equates to that of true-life Dr. Crippen, Cora Crippen and Ethel Le Neve, and is chiefly elucidated through Hercule Poirot's brief retrospective rumination on the fictional event. The main characters of both dramas—the imagined Craig and the very real Crippen—were middle class professionals of a sort: Crippen had earned a homeopathic medicine degree in the United States, whence he and his stage-struck wife Cora came as permanent transplants to England; Alfred Craig was Town Clerk of Parminster.

Crippen was a small man, mild-mannered and self-effacing, a counterpart of the novel's fictional Alfred Craig. Christie had limned her unimposing bureaucrat in Crippen-like image, as a "conscientious, rather nondescript little man, correct and pleasant in his behaviour" (Christie,

## Dr. Hawley Harvey Crippen + *Mrs. McGinty's Dead* 133

*Mrs. McGinty* 65). Mrs. Craig was another story. Like the buxom extroverted Cora Crippen, who bullied her slightly-built introvert of a husband and spent his money profligately, she too had been a "tiresome" and "temperamental" spouse; her main preoccupation seemed to have been intimidating and nagging Craig much as Cora had intimidated and nagged Crippen. But whereas Cora's absorbing concern in life had been to continue, as "Belle Elmore," her pursuit of a music-hall career in England, Mrs. Craig's other defining trait was a fretting hypochondriac focus on her health. She appeared to have few, if any, real friends, while Cora Crippen had, perhaps, a few too many. The lady was quite a gregarious type, and was known to be unrepentantly promiscuous.

The background stories of *Mrs. McGinty's Dead* describe Eva Kane as the 19-year-old nursery governess of the Craig household, which included three young children. Significantly, a large part of the novel's intriguing storyline consists of an interplay of motive, means, and opportunity among other possible children of other possible parents. In the Crippen household, however, there had been in fact no minor children, although the doctor had a son living elsewhere—his offspring by his first wife.

The "Eva Kane" character of Christie's story is an alter ego of Ethel Le Neve. Their personalities were of a similarity: Kane was depicted as "pretty, helpless and rather simple" (65); Le Neve, age 19 when she became Crippen's secretary, was described in many newspaper accounts as petite, quiet, even mousy. In both the unreal case of Craig and the real drama of the Crippen case, doubts about the true "helplessness" of these ladies fuel noteworthy speculation in the aftermath of each murder investigation.

Not long after Crippen began his own affair with Le Neve, the situation took a deadly turn. Cora Crippen disappeared after the late night hours of January 31, 1910, from the Crippen home, nevermore to be seen by friends or family. In Christie's tale, Mrs. Craig inexplicably vanished overnight from the Parminster scene. Pressured by curious neighbors, Craig told a tale of her hasty departure to the continent, for, he said, health reasons: Mrs. Craig had been rushed to the South of France on doctor's orders. Correspondingly, Cora Crippen had vanished in much the same way. The day after her disappearance from the scene, Cora's theatre friends, who knew her as Belle Elmore, received a missive which she had supposedly penned, explaining her unexpected departure to America as due to a kinsman's sudden and serious illness. Still later, when Crippen judged it prudent to justify further his wife's extended absence, he told "Belle's" associates that he'd been receiving letters from her with sobering news: she herself had now fallen gravely ill.

Time and again Crippen was forced to fend off increasingly perturbed questions from Belle's associates by providing increasingly somber tidings. The word from America, he told them, was that his wife's health continued to worsen. Just so did the novel's town clerk put off inquiries regarding Mrs. Craig's health and wellbeing. Her letters, he explained to inquiring neighbors, contained unhopeful reports: her condition was not improving. Eva Kane had moved into the Craig home as "housekeeper" soon after her mistress's disappearance, as Ethel Le Neve had done in real life: weeks after Cora had last been seen, Le Neve had abandoned her own residence to establish herself in the Crippen home as housekeeper. Soon after, Crippen left town briefly for France, accompanied by Le Neve—ostensibly after receiving word that Cora had died abroad a short while earlier. On his return, he showed a solemn face to Belle's friends and reported that her body had been cremated in Los Angeles. Similarly, Craig of the novel claimed to have been notified that his wife had died in France. Craig also took the brief journey from Parminster to France, echoing the real-life diversionary journey to France that Crippen took after Cora's disappearance. Echoing Crippen's motives, Craig also hoped the ploy would give verisimilitude to lies aimed at satisfying suspicious neighbors. On his return from France, Craig announced that Mrs. Craig had been buried in a resting place on the French Riviera.

In neither the fictional nor the factual scenario were the victim's associates taken in for a moment by the proffered factitious explanations. Crippen's accounts of his wife's death and funerary arrangements were met with deep skepticism. When Belle's theatre colleague took a trip to the United States, he made a point of investigating the information Crippen had supplied. There were no records, official or otherwise, of Cora Crippen's demise or of her cremation. It was obvious the events Crippen had described had never taken place. Scotland Yard, notified of these findings, sent an investigating officer to question Crippen at his home. The doctor then suddenly "confessed" to the official that he'd lied about Cora's death and cremation to save face: his humiliatingly promiscuous wife had actually deserted him and run away with her lover. The officer was inclined to believe Crippen's tale, but Crippen himself had apparently been more unnerved by the questioning than officials had known. Almost immediately after the police visit, the doctor had panicked and fled, taking Le Neve with him.

Authorities reacted immediately, scouring the Crippen residence over and over for evidence of whatever it was that the pair was fleeing. Finally, they made a discovery: a mutilated, dismembered, and decomposing human body had been deposited under the boards of the cellar floor. Autopsies on the unearthed remains, famously performed by fledgling pathologist Bernard Spilsbury, ultimately determined them to be those of Cora Crippen, and showed that she had died from a large dose of the vegetable-alkaloid poison hyoscine. Crippen and Le Neve were finally captured after a dramatic and sensational ship chase across the seas. The man and his mistress were brought back to England for separate trials: the doctor for murder and

Le Neve as accessory. Le Neve was ultimately acquitted; Crippen, however, was found guilty of his wife's murder and hanged for it on November 23, 1910.

In the pages of *Mrs. McGinty's Dead*, Craig's story follows a similar pattern. His neighbors contact friends in France to investigate the unconvincing tale Craig had told about his spouse's burial on the Riviera, and discover that there was no evidence of any such death or interment ever having taken place. The alarmed neighbors go to the police, just as their real-life counterparts had done; and investigators eventually find Mrs. Craig's dismembered corpse buried beneath the cellar floor of the Craig home. As in the Crippen affair, an autopsy on fictional Mrs. Craig's remains also revealed that death resulted from a vegetable-alkaloid poison. When confronted with the fact that police had found the body, Craig, unlike his real-life alter ego, immediately made a full confession, giving officials no trouble at all. But he, like Crippen, remained steadfast in protecting his paramour: he swore that Eva Kane had had nothing at all to do with the murder. Craig was eventually tried and convicted and hanged; the charges against Eva Kane as accessory to murder were dropped; and the young woman, pregnant with Craig's child, left England by boat after her ordeal, heading for "the New World" and a new life. Immediately after Crippen's execution and her own ordeal by trial, Ethel Le Neve had also sailed from England to North America, leaving in disguise and under another name. By the conclusion of *Mrs. McGinty's Dead*, the story of Alfred Craig's paramour Eva Kane has proved to have meaning for Poirot's investigation into Mrs. McGinty's murder—but in clever twists and in unexpected ways. Agatha Christie displays once again the skill at adroit misdirection that has indisputably made her detective and mystery fiction's past-master of pleasurable deception.

# Chapter 8

# The "Balham Mystery"
## The Case of Charles Bravo
## and *Ordeal by Innocence*

In 1958's *Ordeal by Innocence*, Agatha Christie tries her hand at revealing the deleterious psychological effects on members of a household when each one of that household is deemed capable of having murdered one of its own. One of them is, indeed, the true culprit—but which one? Each therefore suspects the others, and all trust and relationships are destroyed.

Like several of her other novels (for example, *Five Little Pigs*; *Elephants Can Remember*), *Ordeal by Innocence* investigates a murder committed in the past, in order to reveal at last the crime's perpetrator. Unlike the others, however, *Ordeal* makes it a point to foreground the mental anguish of innocent bystanders caught up in the nightmare of suspicion. Facets of the celebrated cases of Charles Bravo ("The Balham Mystery") in 1876, and the extraordinarily strange Croydon Poisonings of 1928 and 1929—two histories which have become veritable icons of classic true-crime lore—are reflected in Christie's novel, published some 80 years after the first crime and nearly 30 years after the second.

## The Case of Charles Bravo

Charles and Florence Bravo were young socialites from well-to-do and prominent upper-middle-class backgrounds. Their lurid story was the story of a marriage gone awry from the start; of the specter hovering over the marriage in the form of the wife's past love affair with eminent and elderly Dr. James Manby Gully; and finally of the violent death by poison of the furiously jealous husband. Was it murder? Was it accident, or even suicide? The circumstances surrounding Charles Bravo's death were so balanced that any of the three possibilities could easily have prevailed as the correct one. But the scandal, and the smoldering and volatile emotions that surrounded the affair, all tilted the scale of public and official opinion toward murder. Then who within the Bravo household had committed the artful crime?

The unsolved mystery of Charles Bravo's death in 1876 reads more like an Agatha Christie country-house murder plot than the shocking real-life tragedy that it actually was. As P. D. James notes, "Nearly everything about the case is extraordinary" (36). The case continues to reign in British annals as one of the most sensational domestic-crime *causes célèbres* of England's Victorian Age; aficionados from that time to this remain fascinated by the possible permutations in the intriguing puzzle's circumstances. In many ways it was the very definition of the quintessential Victorian domestic murder—if murder it was...

On April 18, 1876, ambitious young barrister Charles Bravo sat down to dinner with his household at The Priory, their grand home in Balham, a southwest area of London. At table with Bravo were his beautiful and wealthy wife of four months, Florence, and Florence's plain, middle-aged and unobtrusive companion, Mrs. Cox. The meal was not a cheerful one—Bravo was bruised and out of sorts from a horseback-riding fall; Florence was weak and frail as she recovered from a recent, disabling miscarriage; and the self-effacing Mrs. Cox, aware that Bravo was pressuring Florence to dismiss her to save money, was even more subdued and withdrawn than usual.

Bravo dined well enough, though it seemed he did so without pleasure, accompanying his meal as was customary for him with a good deal of the burgundy which he alone drank. Due to the recent tension in the home, Florence too had taken to imbibing more and more of the wine she favored, despite Bravo's disapproval and his attempts to curtail her intake. The tension was largely occasioned by Bravo's escalating and violent paranoia over his wife's past affair with Gully, whose very presence near The Priory drove Bravo mad with jealousy. After the meal, all had retired to bed as usual that night: Charles moodily, to his bedroom, alone; Mrs. Cox quietly and Florence shakily, to a room Florence temporarily shared with her companion in order to evade Bravo's advances—for despite Florence's second miscarriage in only a few months, her husband insisted they try again for a pregnancy as soon as possible.

Some hours later the silence was rent by a fearful cry from Bravo as he burst from his room, shouting for "hot water! hot water!" His vomiting and other distressed symptoms proclaimed he'd been poisoned, and from that moment a nightmare of desperate attempts to save the doomed man had taken over the lives of everyone at The Priory. Three days later, after incredible suffering, he was dead: poisoned by a fatal dose of tartar emetic, a product of antimony. With his death, Charles Bravo's ordeal—whatever it was and however it was caused—had ended; but the ordeals of Florence

Bravo, Jane Cox, and Dr. James Gully had just begun. And in a sense, those ordeals have never ended.

Their lives had all fatefully converged mere months earlier. Florence Ricardo, a young and rich widow, lived in luxury at her grand London home, The Priory, with Mrs. Cox, her companion and confidante. Mrs. Cox had left her plantation in Jamaica for better economic opportunities in England, and she counted herself very fortunate to have secured a position with a mistress as wealthy and generous as Mrs. Ricardo. Florence had carried on an affair with the much older Dr. Gully for years before buying and moving into The Priory, and the married doctor had left his famous and profitable hydrotherapy practice in another region to move to an area discreetly near his love. But one of their reckless sexual escapades had come to light within their upper class circle, and Florence had taken fright at her resultant loss of social standing. She broke off the romance with Gully, who, deeply in love with his young mistress, was hard hit by the break. It was just as hard for Florence: despite the near forty years difference in their ages, she dearly loved the successful and magnetic doctor, who was irrevocably tied to a mentally ill wife by the laws of the times. But Florence loved social acceptance even more, and she now wished to regain her lost respectability. In that strict and straitlaced age, the only way for a woman in her position to accomplish that goal was through an eligible marriage. Charles Bravo was "clever and handsome, [and] seemed an eminently suitable choice" (36). He came of an unexceptionable family, and was unfailingly charming to the young widow. And so Florence convinced herself to accept an alliance with Charles Bravo, a man she hardly knew, as a passage back to the life she loved. To start their marriage off honestly, before the wedding she confessed to him the affair with Gully, and Charles had magnanimously forgiven her.

But four months later, someone had poisoned Charles Bravo on that April evening. Judging by the time it took for the symptoms to take hold, the deed had been done with a probable dose of poison in his dinnertime burgundy or in his bedside drinking water. Who had committed that deed? Florence had been suffering her husband's bitter and vicious rages over her liaison with Gully almost since the day she had been foolish enough to confess it to Bravo. In addition she had determined to keep control of her own fortune, to her husband's deep and bitter resentment. He wanted an heir; and she was genuinely terrified that another enforced pregnancy would kill her. Had Florence killed him to rid herself of a brutally jealous, grasping and controlling tyrant of a husband? Had Mrs. Cox poisoned the man who was trying to discharge her from a situation she desperately needed? Or had the poisoning been orchestrated by the nearby Dr. Gully, with the help of a willing accomplice? Had Charles killed himself—either by deliberate suicide, or by accidentally taking poison?

All four had motive, all four had opportunity—and access to means. Tartar emetic was kept in the stables and any one in the household could have laid undetected hands on it. Gully was a doctor: the toxin would have been easily available to him, and, still desperately in love with his former mistress, he may have decided that murder was the only way back to her. Mrs. Cox, far from rich, felt the threat of losing an influential and comfortable position. The thwarted Charles may have been out for revenge: he was violently jealous and felt publicly humiliated by Florence's affair and by his own inability to subjugate his wife. There was even a farfetched other possibility. At the time of the Bravo marriage, Priory stable hand George Griffiths had predicted that Charles Bravo wouldn't live four months. Four months later, Bravo was indeed dead—and Griffiths had also had access to tartar emetic since he kept it for stable use.

Investigation into the strange death of Charles Bravo "electrified the country and exposed the dark side of upper-class Victorian society" (Sherwin 19). The unprecedented scandal lit a firestorm of lurid sensationalism in the press and excited a furor of avid speculation among members of the fascinated populace. The titillating story had everything: murder and adultery in high places; a mysterious poisoning; salacious misbehavior in the moneyed classes; disgrace and dishonor of the respected and the prominent. The public lapped it up. Florence Bravo's worst nightmare—public exposure of her affair with the doctor—was now blazoned all over the pages of rapacious tabloids. Two inquests later, with Florence's and Dr. Gully's sexual liaison shamefully bared, with Mrs. Cox's belated and shocking statement that Bravo had told her he'd taken the poison deliberately because of his wife's affair with the doctor, and with Bravo's relatives baying for Florence's blood, the official verdict was the worst possible for actors in the drama who had had nothing to do with Bravo's demise. The inquest jury found that Bravo had been murdered by someone at the Priory that night, but the available evidence was inconclusive as to which of the main suspects had done it.

Yet each of them had suffered thereafter as if he or she had indeed been found solely guilty of Charles Bravo's murder. Mrs. Cox, reviled in England where many believed her Bravo's killer—and expressed that belief by speeding many hate letters to her by post—fled back to Jamaica. Even there, everyone must surely have looked askance at the now-notorious woman who had spent much of her life striving not to be noticed. Doctor Gully's social and professional reputations were in irreparable ruin: he died in quiet but permanent and bankrupt dishonor years later. And Florence—ostracized by her family, shunned by society, indelibly labeled a scarlet woman and a probable murderess—died a solitary death as an alcoholic less than two years after her husband's demise. The tale lives on, one ribald view of it embodied forever in a little parody of Oliver Goldsmith (Goodman 83) that

## Chapter 8. The "Balham Mystery"

was tremendously popular at the time of the Bravo case, and is still remembered today:

> When lovely woman stoops to folly
> And finds her husband in the way,
> What charm can soothe her melancholy,
> What art can turn him into clay?
>
> The only means her aims to cover
> And save herself from prison locks,
> And repossess her ancient lover,
> Are Burgundy and Mrs. Cox.

## *Ordeal by Innocence*

Who killed the rich and philanthropic matron, Rachel Argyle, by brutally striking her down in her sitting-room at Sunny Point, her family's luxurious home? Who had watched and waited that night until she was separated from the rest of her household, then had gained admittance to the room where she was momentarily alone? What violent interloper attacked and robbed her, and afterwards fled undetected into the night? Surely it must have been some conscienceless, dangerous passerby: someone with a hard-luck story to whom Mrs. Argyle had innocently opened her door, someone who had then taken cruel advantage of her kindness. The lady assuredly had no enemies: she was a beacon of charitable light, years earlier having acted to share her home and her generosity with the young wartime wards she'd rescued from New York poverty, or London slums, or from the very real World War II dangers of the blitz. Yet, these credentials notwithstanding, it didn't take long for authorities and the Argyle family itself to realize that, unbelievable as it seemed, the ghastly crime had most likely been perpetrated by a member of the murdered woman's own household.

Mrs. Argyle had lived a quiet, rather ordinary life at Sunny Point with her family and staff. On the premises near the time she was killed was her abstractedly intellectual husband, Leo, as well as three of her now-grown children, who either lived at home or happened to be visiting Sunny Point that day. Other members of the Argyle ménage were there at some point during that night: Leo's secretary, the efficient and earnest Gwenda Vaughan, who was quietly devoted to her employer; and Kirsten Lindstrom, the plain middle-aged household factotum, who had nursed and cared for the Argyle children from the day each had arrived. Though "Kirsty" was blunt of manner, each child had held a special place in her heart.

Rachel Argyle had hoped permanent adoption of several of her foster sons and daughters would appease the grief of her life: her inability to bear children. The adoptions further attested to Rachel's optimism and charity across social and cultural lines, for the children were of disparate backgrounds and dispositions. There was Mary, the angelic blue-eyed, fair haired child who quite willingly and calculatedly left her family in New York to make her home with the rich, indulgent Mrs. Argyle. There was the belligerent and unhappy young Michael, who never quite forgot the shallow, poor but frivolous mother who didn't care at all that he was parted from her. There was Tina, the quiet little "half-caste" (Christie, *Ordeal* 68) whose prostitute mother had no use for her. There was pretty and otherworldly Hester, the youngest and most emotionally hectic of the children. And then there was Jacko. Jacko had charm and quick wit, but his rough-and-ready slum origins told. He was unscrupulous, untruthful, violent, greedy for money; but Rachel Argyle had tried to apportion to this unsatisfactory but somehow attractive child the same careful if somewhat unimaginative attention she bestowed on his siblings. She had run all their lives according to her lights, and had done her best to do right by each of them. Yet despite her efforts, and despite the passage of time, there was an uneasy awkwardness that marked the atmosphere of Sunny Point. That unease never completely disappeared as the years passed and the children grew to adulthood: it simply became the accepted normality. Rachel Argyle, vaguely feeling the gulf, was at a loss, her hidden hurt and puzzlement half-acknowledging the truth that, try as she might to reach them, her children did not love her as she wished.

Then came the fateful night of Rachel Argyle's murder. Kirsten's discovery of the battered body left the family horrified. Jacko had been with Mrs. Argyle earlier, hotly pressuring his mother for badly-needed funds, but he had stormed out in anger after she'd refused his demands. Rachel Argyle had certainly been alive at that juncture. But after initial murder investigation, officials informed the Argyles that Jacko had been picked up—and he had undeniably been in possession of money stolen from his mother at the time she was killed. Jacko was promptly arrested, but the swaggering young man confidently advanced an alibi: during the time the crime had been committed, he had been hitching a ride with a man who would surely come forth to support his statement when he heard of his rider's predicament. But no such deliverer was ever found or brought to the notice of the authorities; and Jacko Argyle, the ungrateful, unsatisfactory son of the esteemed Rachel Argyle, was ultimately charged, tried, and convicted for the murder of his mother. Clinging to the alibi that no one believed, he died in prison six months after receiving a life sentence.

For two years after the murder and trial, the residue of the household struggled to get on with their lives, healing as best they could. And then came the bombshell. A stranger suddenly presented himself one day to the Argyle family, a stranger clearly overwhelmed by horror and guilt. His name, he told them, was Arthur Calgary, and he had indeed been the man that had given Jacko a lift that night of the murder, just as the young man had claimed—and at a time which made it impossible for Jacko to have killed Rachel Argyle.

Calgary explained he had suffered a bad accident soon after giving Jacko the lift; concussion and amnesia had then wiped all memory of the encounter with Jacko from his mind. He had left England shortly thereafter, unaware of the slaying or of Jacko's arrest. Calgary had been a scientist taking part in an expedition which had departed immediately for out of the way places—places so isolated that he had neither read nor heard of the tragedy of Rachel's murder, or of Jacko's conviction, until his recent return to civilization. A chance sighting of Jacko's picture in an old newspaper suddenly brought back his memory; prostrate with contrition, he had hastened to bring his consoling news to the grieving family. Even if knowledge of his innocence could not bring Jacko back, they surely would be happy for proof that their Jacko's story had been true: he had not, after all, been so unnatural a son as to have murdered his mother.

But Calgary was taken aback by the distressed reception accorded his news. The Argyle family, having literally and figuratively buried their dead, was indeed stricken by the import of his revelations. But their emotion was not due to bitterness or grief because Jacko had died for a crime he hadn't committed. They had long known that Rachel Argyle must have been killed, not by a transient vagrant, but by someone in her household that night. Jacko, the unsatisfactory, violent-tempered troublemaker of the family, had been the most likely, the most palatable and acceptable candidate among them. He'd been apprehended with Rachel Argyle's money, after all; and so after his death the family had moved on, tacitly relieved to be able to believe it had been the unscrupulous Jacko who, among them, had committed the awful deeds. They'd even been able to pity him, since he'd obviously been born with the crooked mentality that led him to his own destruction.

And now, suddenly, devastatingly, they had discovered that Jacko could not have been Rachel Argyle's killer. Now, suddenly, devastatingly, they were again plunged into the nightmare turmoil of the murder and the havoc it had wrought on their lives. For, if Jacko had not killed his mother, *which of the other household members had done it?* Rachel Argyle had been unwavering in directing their lives in the paths she steadfastly believed was right for them, whether they had wanted direction or not. Each of them had had some sort of motive or resentment of one kind or another, hidden or otherwise, which could have smoldered into violence against the woman who had been incapable of inspiring any deep affection in any of them. And at that late date it wasn't likely that the true killer would be easily unmasked.

Who could it be—who was it that the rest of them had trustingly lived with, ignorant of the blood on his—or her—hands? Now they would be doomed to suspect and fear each other forever—and, too, the rest of the world would always cast sidelong glances at each and every one of them, glances hard with speculation and suspicion. The innocent would suffer as horribly as the guilty—*more* horribly than the guilty. Now perhaps the important question for them all had become, not which of them killed Rachel Argyle, but which of them did not?

## The Case of Charles Bravo + *Ordeal by Innocence*

"One of the pleasures of writing detective stories," Agatha Christie wrote in *An Autobiography*, "is that there are so many types to choose from" (425). She characterizes one of these pleasurable types as "the detective story that has a kind of passion behind it—that passion being to help save innocence. Because it is innocence that matters, not guilt." She demonstrated her passion in several of her works, of which the novel *Ordeal by Innocence* (1958) is the most outspoken exponent of her philosophy: the very title trumpets her theme.

In the novel Christie fascinates readers with imaginative possibilities inherent in a situation of murder. *Ordeal* is an entertaining example of her closed-circle mysteries, where the unknown perpetrator could only be a member of a defined set of persons, confined to a defined space reasonably inescapable by insiders and reasonably impenetrable by outsiders. Yet the novel offers something in addition. There's an intriguing twist, a reversal of the "normal" mystery-detective story convention of putting forward, as the principal motivation of the tale, hunting out and confounding the guilty party. *Ordeal* gives pride of place to validating attention to besieged guiltlessness. The story graphically demonstrates how the insidious and inescapable gangrene of deadly, lifelong suspicion of guilt could eat relentlessly away at the spirits, the lives—and even the deaths—of the wrongly-suspected. While never losing sight of solving the robbery-murder of wealthy matriarch Rachel Argyle, in *Ordeal* Christie nevertheless deftly manages to shift philosophical focus equally and skillfully between the importance of finding out who is guilty and the imperative of freeing who is innocent.

Christie's preoccupation with two very famous true-crime cases is very evident in *Ordeal by Innocence*: the Victorian-era Bravo case and the 20th-century Croydon Poisonings. The author demonstrated her deep interest in each case by penning articles for London newspapers on the issues involved in each incident, dealing with the Bravo mystery in a *Sunday Times*

*Magazine* segment written nearly four decades later, in 1968 ("Great"). The nightmare quality of never being able to escape or to be rid of the terrifying taint of suspicion, coupled with the bleak burden of ostracism, is at the heart of the survivors' fates in both the Balham case—the mysterious poisoning of Charles Bravo—and in the Croydon murders. It is that exact nightmare quality Christie recaptures and elucidates so vividly in *Ordeal by Innocence*.

*Ordeal* opens two years past the time moneyed matron Rachel Argyle was robbed and brutally bludgeoned to death while briefly alone in a room of her mansion, Sunny Point. The shocked and shaken family is soon aware that the timetable of her death made it virtually impossible for an outsider to have committed the crime; and it would later become apparent that nearly everyone in the Sunny Point ménage seemed to have had some sort of motive for murder.

The setting for the factual Bravo affair much resembled the fictional setting in Christie's novel.

Charles Bravo was poisoned to death at his luxurious home, The Priory, as Christie's character Rachel Argyle was slain at her luxurious home, Sunny Point. The time it would have taken to mete out the poison to Bravo, and then for the toxin to have taken effect, mandated a timetable that severely restricted the number of possible perpetrators. The inhabitants of The Priory at that period were therefore all indicated as suspects. They included various servants as well as Bravo's wife Florence; her companion, Mrs. Jane Cox; and even Bravo himself. Also indicated was Dr. James Manby Gully, who lived nearby. After the poisoning, investigators minutely interrogated the household servants, with several of them offering valuable or suggestive information. No staff member was seriously or lastingly considered as a person of interest in the case.

It was far otherwise with the others.

Official inquiries uncovered layer after layer of intrigue at The Priory, revealing secret, desperate skirmishes for position, and exposing submerged resentments seething beneath the surface of supposed domestic harmony. All of the principals had viable opportunities and harbored credible motives for slaying Charles Bravo. He had frightened the impecunious Mrs. Cox by pressuring his wife to get rid of the companion. Florence, an independently rich widow, was bullied and terrified by her spouse. Before her marriage to Bravo, she had been carrying on a long-term secret affair with the unhappily married Dr. Gully, who still loved his former mistress and hated Charles Bravo.

Christie's fiction tale skillfully and effectively reproduces the resentment-filled closed-circle ambience that was perfectly exemplified in the true-crime Bravo affair. Members of the Argyle household at Sunny Point around the time of the fictional crime include Rachel's intellectual husband; his secretary; and "Kirsty," middle-aged mainstay of the domestic staff. Three of Rachel's children had also been on hand that fatal day: young Hester, coolly elegant Mary, and the crooked but somehow charming Jacko. Subsequent developments within the novel would show that almost every member of Rachel's household, on the scene or not, harbored simmering resentments and motives that could ostensibly have led to murder.

A similar gathering of key individuals had marked the Bravo episode. The scenario was simple: on the evening of April 18, 1876, Charles Bravo had dined with his household at The Priory, the family's grand home in a southwest area of London. Later that night, Bravo began vomiting and shouting out for an emetic, indicating he knew he'd ingested poison. Three days later, he was dead—poisoned by a fatal dose of tartar emetic. The aftermath of his death forever poisoned the lives of the surviving household members as well.

The angst in the atmosphere at The Priory had been generated largely by the imperious demands of Charles Bravo. By the same token the anger in Christie's fictional Argyle home was due to Rachel Argyle's own softer and unintended version of Bravo's overt aggression. She had held firmly to the conviction that, whether they themselves believed it or not, or wanted it or not, her choices for the welfare of her household were always best for them.

The Argyles had barely survived the trauma of the murder and Jacko's death when the impossible happened: two years after the slaying, Jacko's mystery stranger—scientist Arthur Calgary—had suddenly and stunningly materialized; and he had duly verified the young man's alibi beyond a doubt. For the surviving family, Jacko's electrifying moment of vindication was also the moment that the Argyle household's second and even more horrible ordeal had begun.

Calgary's verification that Jacko could not have been Mrs. Argyle's slayer now undeniably meant one of the remaining members of the group was the secret, unsuspected killer. Like the recurring nightmare that it was, the family and household, including those who were supposedly nowhere near Sunny Point at the time of the murder, were once again to be endlessly tormented by not knowing who had slain the matriarch of Sunny Point—or who had not. Similarly, the real-life conundrum left behind for posterity in the Bravo affair has become the case's true legacy. Who killed Charles Bravo? By accident or design, Bravo could very well have killed himself; and Florence certainly had motive enough. Mrs. Cox, too, had motive: far from rich, she'd felt the threat of losing a lucrative and influential sinecure. Or had the murder been planned by Dr. Gully, and executed with inside help?

Two inquests after the young barrister's death, the beleaguered principals in the affair had been so pilloried by widespread sensationalized publicity that, afraid of the noose, they began to turn on each other. In the tumult of this unprecedented situation, the official second inquest jurors reached a verdict declaring that Bravo had been murdered by someone at The Priory that night, but they were unable say which one. By that damning verdict each of the survivors had thenceforward been indelibly branded. Each suffered thereafter as ceaselessly as if he or she alone had indeed murdered Charles Bravo that April night.

Christie posits the inevitability of similar fates for the protagonists of the novel—if Mrs. Argyle's killer is never unmasked. The psychological focus of *Ordeal by Innocence* remains primarily on the killing of Mrs. Argyle and the impact of that killing, and that primary focus both overshadows and precipitates ensuing crimes. In the aftermath of Calgary's revelation of Jacko's innocence, the acid of suspicion eats into the characters' interrelationships as effectively as it had done to those of real-life survivors in the Bravo mystery. Christie shows the effects of the rot of doubt, distrust, and fear as it sets in and does its work. Nagged by gnawing suspicion of each other, Leo and Gwenda drift miserably away from their engagement to marry. Kirsty warns the frightened Hester not to trust even her. Mary's husband, knowing what his quiet wife is really capable of beneath that calm exterior, casts uneasy sideways glances in her direction. Other members of the family, now aware of each other's motives, also struggle against but inevitably succumb to suspecting each other of the worst. So, too, had the members of the Bravo household regarded each other.

The Argyle murder in Christie's novel had been a "family affair": so, too, were the between-the-wars anomalies of the Croydon poisonings.

The case encompassed the slayings of three members of the Duff and Sidney (or Sydney) households. All of whom were related to each other by marriage or by blood. All of whom were presumably poisoned off with arsenic, one at a time, in one home at a time, and over a sporadic period of a year. The victims were, first, middle-aged former civil servant Edmund Duff; then Vera Sidney, sister of Tom Sidney and of Duff's much younger wife, Grace; and finally the siblings' mother, elderly Violet Sidney. Spinster Vera and semi-invalid Violet shared a home, while other subsets of the family lived in abodes that were in close proximity to each other. Circumstances in fact dictated that the unknown killer was a family member or a servant of the households—someone with ready access, someone very familiar with the comings and goings and domestic routines of each victim.

The Duffs and Sidneys would visit and dine with each other often, making it quite easy for one or more of them to bide their time, and then to turn knowledge of the victims' habits to murderous account. Lack of suspicion in the death of Edmund Duff enabled the culprit to remain invisible in the background, engaging in a furtive hit-and-run approach to the remaining killings. But the sudden death of Vera sparked an unconscious warning note. Her symptoms resembled too closely those that had prostrated Duff months before, causing a certain uneasiness in some quarters. When Violet's unexpected death followed Vera's so swiftly, and followed as well the same symptomatic patterns as had attended Vera's dying, officials' doubts transmuted into action. The remains of all three relatives were eventually exhumed and examined, with Home Office experts Sir William Willcox and Sir Bernard Spilsbury called to the case. Arsenic was detected in each body.

Tom Sidney, Grace Duff, and the family cook all came in for their share of suspicion and grueling interrogation. Other theories also arose for consideration, among them conjecture that Violet, who had disapproved of and disliked her son-in-law, murdered both Duff and Vera, and then turned to suicide.

The most virulent winds of speculation, however, swirled around the figure of Grace Duff, who was rumored—but not proven—to have carried on an affair with the young family doctor, which would have given her a fair motive for killing her spouse. Moreover, authorities were able to impute to her a financial motive of sorts for the murders of her sister and mother. Yet after intense investigation, no truly clear suspect or cogent motive ever emerged from the mists of what seemed an inexplicable series of slayings. A July 1929 inquest jury in the cases of Vera and Violet felt compelled to bring in a verdict of murder by persons unknown. In August 1929, inquiry into the bizarre events was officially suspended. No one was ever charged with or tried for the deaths, earning the perplexing business a permanent place on the list of Britain's most intriguing unsolved murder cases. Christie was extremely interested in the affair, deploring its horrific effects on the guiltless. Christie biographer Laura Thompson comments "In 1929 [Agatha Christie] wrote in the *Sunday Chronicle* about the 'Croydon Murders' ... in which three members of the same family were poisoned: the murderer clearly came from within the family circle but the case was—and remains—unsolved. It always fascinated Agatha ... because 'It is a case where the innocent suffer most horribly for sins they have never committed. They live in a haze of publicity; acquaintance and friends look at them curiously.... Any decent happy private life is made impossible for them.' The idea in this article would later be written into one of her best detective novels, *Ordeal by Innocence*" (266).

Christie's short fiction narrative "Sing a Song of Sixpence" also dwelt on the theme of "saving innocence." It was published late in 1929, close to the time of the unfolding Croydon case. The timing of the short story makes it highly probable that the Croydon mystery directly influenced her approach to "Sing a Song of Sixpence" and its setting. Miss Lily Crabtree, rich and eccentric aunt of the story's characters, is violently murdered in a room of the Chelsea house they all share, and at an hour when only the four members of her family and her longtime faithful servant are at home. Each of the potential suspects is—supposedly—alone at the time of the murder, engaged in his or her separate preoccupations in separate areas of the house. Money is the likely motive; the logistics and circumstances inevitably point to a household member as the culprit. But which of them did it? Realizing the implications of never knowing who actually committed the crime, their fear and suspicion of each other begins to poison their lives. Christie's brief tale served as forerunner to the fuller treatment to come in *Ordeal by Innocence*, both fiction pieces delving into the same philosophical territory as that attending the true-crime Bravo and Croydon murders. The author's words in the mouth of her character Magdalen, the young ingénue of the short story, reveal Christie's preoccupation with the very real deleterious impact of wrongful distrust on lives of ordinary people. Magdalen speaks of the destructive uncertainty that mutual suspicion has planted in the minds of the four members of her own family, fearing that the authorities, as well, believe that "it's one of us four. It must be. They don't know which—and we don't know which...." She goes on to characterize the reactions of the household: "We don't know. And we sit there every day looking at each other surreptitiously and wondering..." (Christie, "Sing" 143). Her faltering but expressive thoughts foreshadow the more developed fears and observations, decades later, of characters in *Ordeal by Innocence.*

In the novel, Agatha Christie makes it clear that if the true killer of Rachel Argyle was never unmasked, the same type of destructive legacy that marked the Bravo case awaited surviving members of the fictional Argyle family. Some of the novel's characters are instantly and acutely aware of that danger; others are loath to acknowledge the torment that Jacko's belated exoneration will unleash anew on their existence. Christie allows readers an inkling of what that would mean to the protagonists' lives, laying bare their churning thoughts and feelings throughout the novel's pages. The horror of the situations, in both the fictional *Ordeal* and the factual Balham and Croydon mysteries, was succinctly articulated by the novel's Dr. MacMaster as he ruminated on the meaning of the Bravo case: "Someone was guilty—and got away with it. But the others were innocent—and didn't get away with anything" (Christie, *Ordeal* 80).

Agatha Christie was always fascinated by the Bravo case's possibilities. Even though the Croydon mystery shared points of similarity with the Bravo case, and therefore with *Ordeal*, it is the neatly compacted action and setting of Mrs. Argyle's murder that marks *Ordeal* as patterned along the lines of the Balham episode. The Croydon slayings had featured a set of murders linked and limited to two families, but committed at an almost meandering pace. The three killings occurred one by one, each separated by uneven stretches of time, and perpetrated in two separate locations. Moreover, the perpetrator had had more than enough time between killings to obscure or muddle the trail, and the murders themselves didn't come to light until months after the initial crime.

The "Balham Mystery" on the other hand followed an almost classic unity of time, place, and "action." It was instigated at one circumscribed time; it involved only one, instantaneous strike: an instantly sensational slaying by poison. It was committed within the walls of one luxurious home, and there were four instant suspects more or less on the spot—each one having almost equally compelling motives and opportunities for murder. So, too, was the case with the principal murder in *Ordeal by Innocence*. Although the true resolution of the novel's slaying occurred two years after the fact, during that interim while it lay dormant, it was assumed by everyone—including the real malefactor—that Jacko's conviction had insured an end to the case, and to any continuing danger. *Ordeal*'s principal murder had been a single occurrence, committed at a single time at a single place and with, so to speak, a single attack; and it remained so, a completed "package" despite the passage of time.

Beyond exploring the Bravo case's dynamics in the novel, *Ordeal by Innocence* allows Agatha Christie to illustrate imagined but possible consequences of a destructive type of social inertia. She gives a voice and a form to a certain situation: the unheard pleas and the unheeded suffering of persons who are guiltless of crime, but caught and tainted by circumstance in webs from which they are virtually powerless to extricate themselves. Christie allows readers to witness and imagine a fictionalized version of their torments through the forum of her detective-story creations, where the characters and scenarios of the tales make a strong case for "saving the innocent." Christie repeats that theme throughout the novel, in the words and musings of her characters. Hester in *Ordeal* maintains heatedly to Calgary, "It's not the guilty who matter. It's the innocent" (24). And later Dr. MacMaster echoes her feeling in an attempt to bring home a sense of the enormity of it all to a bemused Arthur Calgary: "It reminds me, you know, of the Bravo Case.... Books are still being written about it; making out a perfectly good case for his wife having done it, or Mrs. Cox having done it, or Dr. Gully—or even for Charles Bravo having taken the poison in spite of the Coroner's verdict. All quite plausible theories—but no one now can ever know the truth" (79).

CHAPTER 9

# "Poor Little Rich Girl"
## The Life of Gene Tierney and *The Mirror Crack'd*

Deemed the last of Agatha Christie's "village cozy" detective tales, *The Mirror Crack'd* portrays the unsettled and unsettling social and economic changes wrought on England by World War II—in the most genteel of fashions, and as seen through the experiences of an aging Miss Marple. The novel was published in England in 1962 as *The Mirror Crack'd from Side to Side*. In America, the story was also published the same year as its United Kingdom counterpart under the abridged title *The Mirror Crack'd*. The novel tells the story of Miss Marple's reluctant inquiry into the murder of a harmless if officious village resident, Mrs. Heather Badcock. Christie here scrutinizes and depicts the anguish suffered by survivors of needless tragedies, and that suffering's possible consequences, allowing readers glimpses of the psychologies that caused snowballing sets of tragedies. A main plot and storyline faithfully recalls dramatic and tragic events in the life of a major film star of the 1940s and beyond, the lovely Gene Tierney, 20 years after those events.

## The Life of Gene Tierney

"Life," film star Gene Tierney pensively asserted in her 1978 autobiography, *Self-Portrait*, "is not a movie" (Tierney 211). That was the difficult lesson her difficult life experiences finally succeeded in teaching her, and at terrific cost.

But that was not how things had begun for the stylish, sophisticated, and dazzlingly attractive actress. At first Gene's own personal life had seemed to unfold, in approved cinematic fashion, very much like a movie, a romantic Hollywood success movie. If any young woman seemed to have it all, it was Gene Tierney: striking beauty, intelligence, charm, affluent background, private education, privileged social standing—all were hers. Fortune appeared to smile on her every circumstance and endeavor. Not for her the penury, the scheming, the clawing and scrambling struggle to survive endured by countless starstruck hopefuls awaiting that first lucky break in the Hollywood of their dreams. Gene Tierney never had to fight for or chase after Hollywood stardom; it seemed she only had to show her face for Hollywood stardom to chase eagerly after *her*.

Gene Eliza Tierney, whose first name derived from a maternal uncle who had died in his teens, was born November 19, 1920; she was destined to become one of America's most glamorous screen stars in Hollywood's most glamorous movie era, the 1940s. Her cool, elegant good looks assured her inclusion on many lists of "filmdom's most beautiful women" during her motion picture career. She was the middle child of three offspring born into the well-to-do family of Brooklyn insurance broker Howard Tierney and his wife Belle Lavinia Taylor Tierney. Gene enjoyed a close relationship with her parents, especially her father, whose oft-professed belief in honor and in practical wisdom she deeply respected. When Gene was a small child the family moved from Brooklyn to a mansion-type home in Connecticut, where they lived an upper-class lifestyle. Howard and Belle Tierney were extremely determined in their aspirations to high society, and this was evident in their plans for their children. Gene's schoolgirl days, for instance, were spent in exclusive boarding and finishing schools in the U.S. and abroad. She was first a pupil at prestigious St. Margaret's School for Girls (afterwards the coed St. Margaret's–McTernan School, and then Chase Collegiate School) in Waterbury, Connecticut. Gene learned French in Switzerland as she pursued a traditional upper middle class education in 1936 at Brillantmont International School in Lausanne, and then capped her studies on returning to America at that fashionable institution for girls, Miss Porter's School in Farmington, Connecticut—the establishment, incidentally, which Jacqueline Bouvier would also later attend.

During a tour of Warner Brothers studios on a family trip to California, her beauty attracted the attention of company bigwig Anatole Litvak, who wanted to sign her immediately onto the studio's rosters; however, the young girl's parents declined the offer. Howard Tierney wanted his daughter to move into the highest circles of society attainable for her before she made a choice as to a career or profession. Gene duly made her society debut in September 1938. Mere months later the debutante, who appeared to be having the time of her life in the season's social whirl, stunned her father by telling him that she was not only bored with society life but that she had also indeed decided to become an actress. Bowing reluctantly to her wishes, her parents steered her towards the more "genteel" legitimate stage rather than to the silver screen. Her first theatre roles in 1938 and 1939 were little more than walk-on or small parts, but her attractiveness brought her to the notice of leading critics and commentators who were kind to the newcomer, though more effusive about her looks than her acting talent.

Gene's father utilized his business expertise as a successful east coast insurance broker to set up a family corporation, "Belle-Tier," putting the financing and finances of his daughter's acting career on a professional footing. Gene signed on with Columbia Pictures in 1939, but delays in casting sent her back to Broadway when her six-month contract expired. She then starred in the 1940 hit play *The Male Animal*, whose acclaim and success placed her suddenly and squarely in the limelight. Her highly photogenic looks earned the ingénue picture spreads in *Life* and other leading mainstream periodicals of the day, as well as in popular trade magazines. During the run of that play, Gene was "discovered," in true Hollywood style, when famed 20th Century–Fox executive Darryl F. Zanuck spotted the fledgling stage actress and signed her to a studio contract. This was the beginning of a highly successful period in Gene's acting career, which was to last off and on for well into four decades.

The young actress took her work seriously. After the first few times she heard herself speaking onscreen, she commented that she "sounded like Minnie Mouse," and took up heavy smoking to lower her voice. She graduated from smaller movie parts to substantial lead roles, and then moved on to the films which were destined to define her place in, and contribution to, motion picture history: *Laura* and *Leave Her to Heaven*.

These two motion pictures, among all of the ones in which she appeared, garnered most of the popular and critical acclaim she was to enjoy for her body of work. Substantially lifted above the ordinary by her very presence and by her outstanding portrayals, these films rightfully stood out from the rest. She was nominated for a Best Actress Academy Award for her stunning depiction of the jealous sociopath Ellen Harland in the 1945 melodrama *Leave Her to Heaven*, but she enjoyed more fame for the elusive haunting beauty of her lead role in *Laura*, the 1944 Otto Preminger *noir* drama in which she co-starred with Clifton Webb, Dana Andrews, Judith Anderson and Vincent Price. In effect, she also co-starred with her character's own portrait—and with composer David Raksin's yearningly evocative soundtrack and title theme. The film's music, to this day, is nearly synonymous with the movie itself.

Her love life, befitting fans' popular conceptions of what a lovely and glamorous young movie star's amorous adventures ought to be, also appeared to develop along the lines of a Hollywood romantic drama. She dated glamorous co-stars such as Tyrone Power and Clark Gable. Other prominent swains included highly eligible, successful—even royal—socialites and powerbrokers, numbering Howard Hughes, Prince Aly Khan, and a young senator named John F. Kennedy among the admirers who courted her. She ultimately fell in love with and married fashion designer Oleg Cassini, himself a scion of European nobility.

But darkest clouds were gathering over Gene's seemingly fairytale existence. Howard and Belle Tierney disapproved almost violently of her relationship with Cassini ("Mother" 3). Much against her parents' wishes, and despite her father's threats to have her declared "mentally unstable" if she went ahead with her plans, Gene had determined to wed the designer—especially when she discovered in April 1941 that her father was having an affair with a divorcee friend of her mother. Shocked and disillusioned, Gene finally eloped to Las Vegas with Cassini in June 1941. An enraged Howard Tierney attempted an annulment, as much due to his financial situation as to his daughter's choice of husband: Gene's marriage ousted Belle-Tier, the family corporation run by Howard to manage his daughter's earnings, as Gene's agent. She had acquired a husband, and Howard Tierney was legally no longer automatically positioned to receive the 25 percent agent's cut of Gene's earnings he had been raking in before. To recover that position, Howard Tierney sued his daughter for breach of contract—and $50,000. In the course of the proceedings, Gene was stunned to learn that the corporation had been shorn of its assets: the father she had trusted with her finances had secretly spent all her money on his own numerous debts. Her ultimate winning of the lawsuit proved almost a pyrrhic victory. Coming on the heels of discovering his adultery, the revelation of her father's further treacheries and frauds compounded the blow, planting insidious seeds of loss and an almost unconscious, creeping realization that the family values on which she had founded her lifelong sense of self and security were shams.

On top of these discoveries, Gene's own domestic situation was weakening—as her parents had predicted. The closeness of marriage revealed clashes of goals and personality that surfaced as they hadn't before; and almost from the beginning, the union had shown signs of heading for trouble. Gene was separated often from her new husband by the demands of her work; and even when they were together, she was often too tired to participate in the social activities in which he reveled. Then too, the fact that his wife was the major breadwinner of the marriage became more and more irksome to the proud young designer; arguments and recriminations ensued and abounded. In March 1943, however, when the couple found they were to have a child, their happiness about that life-altering wonder seemed to banish other considerations and to draw them closer together. But what should have been a joyful event, and the beginning of a new and wonderful chapter in their marriage, was destined to prove instead the harbinger of one of the major tragedies of their lives.

There was a war going on in 1943. *The* War: World War II. Both Gene and her husband did their parts to help with the war effort. Cassini was stationed at Fort Riley, Kansas, where he had been commissioned as a lieutenant of the U.S. Army. Gene, as did many of the nation's top entertainment stars, performed morale-boosting shows for the men and women of America's armed forces at the Hollywood Canteen. Gene dutifully performed one such turn in March, just before she was to join her husband at Fort Riley. When she came down later with a mild case of what her doctor called German measles, the actress was assured that the red, splotchy rash on her face would disappear and the indisposition itself would last only a few days. The illness duly passed off, and Gene resumed her plans to rejoin Oleg, with the added excitement of anticipating and preparing for the child that would be born at the end of the year.

Gene went into premature labor, however, and on October 15, 1943, the dream of motherhood seemed to come true for her when she gave birth to a beautiful daughter, Antoinette Daria Cassini. Though the child weighed a mere 3½ pounds, and was scheduled for six weeks of monitoring in a hospital incubator, the infant seemed to weather her anxiety-making start in life well enough. But worse was yet to come.

During the year or so after Daria's birth, the Cassinis gradually became aware that their daughter was not developing as she should. In her autobiography Gene recalls that she "felt a chill" as, one day, she happened to peruse a "newspaper article reporting that an epidemic of German measles in Australia had, a year later, produced a generation of defective babies" (96). In an agony of apprehension, she consulted Daria's pediatrician. Examination of the child confirmed the parents' worst fears: as a result of Gene's exposure to and suffering from German measles—or rubella—in March 1943, the first month of her pregnancy, Daria had indeed not only been born with hearing loss and some sight loss, she was also severely intellectually and developmentally disabled. Reeling from the blow of this diagnosis, Daria's parents then learned that the conditions were incurable and irreversible. The Cassinis were advised to place their daughter in an institution. Gene rebelled at this advice, and fought desperately against it until Daria was four, when Gene and Cassini, mentally and physically exhausted from the efforts to care for their child, maintain their marriage, and pursue their careers, had yielded at last to the inevitable. Daria was placed in a home. Sick with worry and self-blame over Daria's condition, Gene's own psychological state deteriorated. Endless and fruitless speculations chased themselves in her fevered mind. How had it happened? Why? "Daria's birth had been the beginning of a darkening time for me," Gene would later write. "I wondered why God had punished me by afflicting my child. I felt guilt I could not explain, and self-pity that I could not throw off" (101). But there seemed to be no answers to any of her questions.

And then, one day, totally out of the blue, some of the questions *were* answered—suddenly, without warning, with all the deep, sharp, unbearable devastation of a death-dealing stab to the heart. "A year after Daria was born, I attended a tennis party on a quiet Sunday afternoon in Los Angeles," Gene relates. "A young woman approached me.... She said she was in the women's branch of the marines and had met me at the Hollywood Canteen.... Then she said, 'Did you happen to catch the German measles after that night?' I looked at her, too stunned to speak. 'You know,' she went on, 'I probably shouldn't tell you this. But almost the whole camp was down with German measles. I broke quarantine to come to the Canteen to meet the stars. Everyone told me I shouldn't, but I just had to go.' She beamed, then added, 'And you were my favorite.' I stood there for a very long minute. There was no point in telling her of the tragedy that had occurred. I turned and walked away very quickly" (101).

Gene, heartsick, delved deeper and deeper into her work, driven to earn enough to maintain Daria's care. Separations from her husband became more frequent and for longer periods—and neither of them fought the effects of this estrangement on their marriage as they had before Daria's birth. By the end of 1946, the couple had officially separated. Gene met John Kennedy when he visited the set of *Dragonwyck*, the movie Gene was making at the time. The lonely young woman fell in love with the charming young politician; but her hopes of life with him were devastated when he, a Catholic—moreover, one with political ambitions—suddenly revealed to her on a dinner date that he could never marry her, a divorcee. Gene, though staggered, immediately ended what she had in effect just been told was, from her point of view, a hopeless relationship. She bid John Kennedy good-bye then and there at the restaurant table, and with that goodbye the relationship was over. In March 1948, Gene's uncontested divorce from Cassini was decreed final. But after Gene's breakup with Kennedy in 1946, she and Oleg had been able to draw nearer to each other; the separation period had given them room to view the differences and pressures of their marriage from a calmer vantage point. By summer 1948, the couple decided their divorce had been a mistake, and reconciled in August. On November 20, 1948, her own birthday, Gene gave birth to their second child, Christina Cassini, "Tina," who was a healthy infant.

But Gene's mental state was increasingly fragile. First weakened by the shock of her Daria's maladies, and then by the sudden and painful blow of learning their cause. Her marriage to Cassini faltered again, ending finally in a second divorce in 1952. In 1953 Gene fell in love with another charmer, and began a hectic love affair with Aly Khan, ex-husband of Rita Hayworth. But the prince's father forbade their marriage, and the relationship was permanently terminated by the end of that year.

The mounting stress made her unable to focus on her work, and she dropped in and out of several movie projects during the ensuing few years. By 1955 she was worried enough that she sought out psychiatric help, checking herself into facilities where she underwent a series of shock-treatment therapies. She afterwards declared that, far from curing or helping her, these frightening and painful treatments had actually destroyed some of her memory.

During the next few years Gene floated in and out of anguish and depression, culminating in a December 1957 suicide attempt from her mother's New York high-rise apartment window. She was committed to the Menninger Clinic in Kansas where she underwent a year-long treatment regimen for her depression. On her release, she attempted to resume her normal life, but a mental vulnerability and anxiety at the back of her mind held her fast in chains of psychological insecurity. A breakthrough of sorts, however, had occurred by this point, and during this portion of her life, Gene Tierney seemed at last to learn to make tentative peace with herself.

After 1958, she seemed better able to come to grips with reality and her own abilities to cope with it. Although she dropped out of several more movie projects, in 1962 she finally made a successful return to films in the movie *Advise and Consent*, helmed by Otto Preminger, who had also directed her in *Laura* almost twenty years earlier. "I can no longer doubt that the main cause of my difficulties stemmed from the tragedy of my daughter's unsound birth and my inability to face my feelings, trying instead to bury them," she would later muse (Tierney 209).

By the time of a major outbreak of rubella in the U.S. in 1964, some twenty years after Daria's birth, the story of the Cassini family's traumatic experience with rubella-caused birth defects had long been public knowledge, complete with details of how it had occurred. The sad tale was recalled when Hedda Hopper, famed Hollywood gossip columnist, commented in a newspaper article that "if people had listened to Gene Tierney's story about German measles, the tragedy of all these defective babies being born following last year's epidemic could have been averted. During the war, Gene, pregnant with her first child, was helping out at the Hollywood Canteen. A woman marine told Gene she had violated a quarantine for German measles just to come and meet her. Gene caught the measles, and her child was born retarded..." (Hopper 38).

Gene had again fallen in love in 1958; this time fate was kinder to her. W. Howard Lee was a Texas oil man, still tied in a failed marriage to actress Hedy Lamarr at the time that he and Gene first met. After an acrimonious divorce from Lamarr in 1960, he and Gene were then free to marry; they tied the knot in 1961. They remained together in apparent marital harmony until his death in 1981.

By the 1970s, Gene had gained enough perspective to be able to examine her experiences with relative objectivity. The self-knowledge gained from the healing and clarification afforded by time and distance from major traumas provided a hard-won but cautious serenity that endured, with careful guarding, for the rest of her life. "I regretted too many things: finding out that a father who taught me that honor was everything was not an honorable man. Marrying against my parents' wishes and proving them right. Twice falling in love with men with whom I had no future" ("Gene Tierney" A3).

Gene Tierney, at age 70, died of the emphysema resulting from her smoking habits on November 6, 1991, having traversed, survived, and overcome a lifetime of experiences marked by great good fortune and, in some ways, even greater misfortune.

## *The Mirror Crack'd*

Agatha Christie's *The Mirror Crack'd*, published in 1962, treats of the absorbing mystery surrounding the poisoning death of Heather Badcock, and of Miss Marple's detective prowess in solving the baffling case.

After the demise of her husband Arthur, the widowed Dolly Bantry (good friend of that noted elderly sleuth, Miss Jane Marple) began her new life by selling Gossington Hall, her sprawling Victorian home, and moving into a small lodge neighboring the property. The Hall had changed hands a few times before being purchased, surprisingly, by the famous and beautiful long-time Hollywood glamour movie queen, Marina Gregg and her fourth (or fifth) husband, the prominent movie director Jason Rudd. The location of Mrs. Bantry's new lodging, and her status as both former owner of Gossington and a prior acquaintance of Miss Gregg, later placed her in an ideal position to help Miss Marple when she was called upon to unravel the mystery about to unfold in Gossington Hall—the second since a body had been discovered in its library years earlier.

Marina Gregg's fame had kept her in the public eye for many years. Her intriguing life story had been marked by achievement and misfortune, triumph and tragedy. Despite acclaim, glamour, and success, her unstable life had been tainted by much restive unhappiness and, as was to be expected of anyone who had succeeded in a survival-of-the-fittest arena, she had undoubtedly inspired both absolute devotion in some associates and bitter enmity in others. The actress had callously shed at least one unwanted husband and ruthlessly broken up at least one marriage. On the other hand, in a mood of largesse she had adopted three orphans, introducing the impoverished children to a lifestyle of heady privilege. She wanted to have children of her own, but was distraught when her son was born mentally and physically disabled due to a minor ailment that Marina had unwittingly contracted while pregnant. The blow had been too much for Miss Gregg's highly-strung nature and she had suffered a mental breakdown. Now, after a dozen years of struggle and healing it was hoped that the beautiful and alluring actress was well on her way to complete recovery. Although still rather emotionally fragile, her improvement was evident as she was attempting a comeback in a highly anticipated film directed by her husband. Much was riding on the venture, and her spouse, reputedly deeply in love with his fascinating if restless wife, seemed as anxious for its success as was the actress herself.

The urbane Hollywood couple had duly arrived in St. Mary Mead and proceeded to modernize, glamorize, and take up occupancy in Gossington Hall, complete with *de rigueur* Hollywood-celebrity entourage. Their descent upon the village gave every initial sign of being auspicious, despite any trepidation the locals might have felt about movie-star morals and temperaments. The couple had even been generous enough to allow a charity fête to be held on the grounds of the Hall. The event was in aid of St. John's Ambulance Corps, and the association's secretary, Mrs. Heather Badcock—a longtime great fan of Marina Gregg and a sunnily tireless hard worker—had thrown herself heart and soul into arranging and organizing the fête.

But on the day of the fête, Heather Badcock had died—very suddenly and very shockingly, only minutes after appearing at a private reception inside Gossington Hall. She had carried on a cheerfully longwinded and effusive if largely one-sided conversation with Marina Gregg, her greeter and hostess, but had collapsed a short while later, just after having drunk a cocktail meant for the glamorous star. The drink had been poisoned. Authorities soon came to the inevitable realization that the dose of poison had been deliberate—and that it must have been meant for the famous actress, not for the simple local visitor who had by tragic mischance swallowed it instead. The inoffensive and generous if single-minded Mrs. Badcock had, sadly, died by a bizarre, unforeseeable accident, but the mistake had given police a cogent though tragic forewarning: the task now would be to waylay the murderer of Mrs. Badcock before he—or she—could succeed at a second attempt on the life of Marina Gregg.

When the tragedy occurred at Gossington Hall, Miss Marple was recovering from a debilitating bout of bronchitis and an accompanying slight despondency of mind. She herself had met and interacted with Heather Badcock only once before. During that sole encounter Mrs. Badcock had come to Miss Marple's aid when the old lady had taken a fall. Mrs. Badcock's strange and sudden death reawakened the elderly spinster's interest in sleuthing, and as she had not been present at the fête's scene of the tragedy, she turned to her village and metropolitan "intelligence corps" for information.

Dolly Bantry was eager to share her experiences with St. Mary Mead's own home-grown sleuth, recapitulating excitedly for Miss Marple all that had struck her as noteworthy at the fête reception. Miss Marple's old ally, Scotland Yard's Chief Inspector Dermot Craddock, had been assigned to the case since it involved an international celebrity. He too collaborated with Miss Marple, supplying her with reports on the official progress of the investigation. When she had pieced together the various accounts, Miss Marple had acquired not only a mental picture of salient circumstances of the tragedy at Gossington Hall, but also of events leading up to it. A few months before the fatal event, Marina Gregg's advent had hit the sleepy little village of St. Mary Mead like a sudden cultural windstorm. By the day of the fête it seemed that the entire population of St. Mary Mead and environs had been agog to attend, if only to see the marvelous new alterations wrought to the venerable pile. In an additional act of diplomacy, Rudd and Miss Gregg had arranged a small private reception in the Hall for guests of honor. Among these privileged few had been Dolly Bantry, who had briefly socialized with Miss Gregg once before during a visit to California, and Heather Badcock, who had not only organized the present charity event, but had also served during the war as a driver for St. John's Ambulance.

This second social encounter between Dolly Bantry and Marina Gregg was mirrored in what had seemed to be a similar duplicate felicity for Heather Badcock. A devoted fan of Miss Gregg, she had first met the star at a wartime charity occasion years before during the war. Heather, even then, had been determined not to miss what could have been a once-in-a-lifetime opportunity to encounter the talented and beautiful Marina Gregg. She had defied an annoying but not incapacitating illness and gone on to the event—coincidentally, one also in aid of St. John's Ambulance. By the time of the Gossington Hall fête, Heather had been thrilled at the prospect of once again meeting her favorite star face to face. She had no inkling that her innocuous devotion would end in her death.

Mrs. Badcock had succeeded Dolly and the Vicar in the reception line near the top of Gossington's stairway landing. Mrs. Badcock, excited at once again seeing her idol, had been unable to resist buttonholing the star and breathlessly reliving that long-ago moment when she had first met the actress. Her enthusiasm had effectively halted the stairway progress of invitees behind. She indulged in an interminable, tedious (to everyone else) recital, but Miss Gregg had been gently charming about it all. Later, while informing Miss Marple of all she knew about the reception's tragic occurrence, Dolly described Heather's misplaced enthusiasm about having defied a bout of chicken pox in order to be introduced to the actress. Mrs. Bantry had also noticed with complete sympathy and understanding when Miss Gregg's smooth veneer of flattering attention at last began to slip a bit. She had allowed her attention to wander towards the staircase while Heather had gone eagerly on, recalling her boast that "I won't be beaten!" (Christie, *Mirror* 45). She was determined not to miss the chance of meeting her favorite actress, and about her pluck in accordingly getting herself up from a sickbed, making herself up to look presentable, and triumphantly going out to greet the star.

If she had expected her confidences to flatter and impress the actress, Mrs. Badcock must have been greatly disappointed. By the time she'd reached that point in her story, Marina's attention had all at once, without warning or apparent reason, been completely diverted from focus on the guest before her. The actress's gaze seemed riveted by the sight of something—or someone—that she was staring at over Heather's shoulder, in the direction of the stairway landing. Marina Gregg's whole demeanor underwent a dramatic instantaneous change. Whatever she saw had, for the briefest moment, completely horrified and immobilized her. Mrs. Bantry described the expression on Marina Gregg's face to Miss Marple in terms of dramatic if slightly misquoted words from a Tennyson poem: "She had a kind of frozen look.... Do you remember the Lady of Shalott? 'The mirror crack'd from side to side. "The Doom has come upon me," cried the Lady of Shalott.'" (61). This fleeting moment, the dreadful frozen look on Marina Gregg's face, and the configuration of people and objects on the landing were to become significant for Miss Marple's later investigations into the tragedy that followed so soon after.

At the time, a startled Dolly Bantry had quickly cast a surprised glance in the direction of Marina Gregg's gaze, and thought that the view in the actress's line of sight seemed hardly likely to cause such a look of horror. The stairway landing alcove held the harmless photographic gear of a London photographer, as the photographer herself swiftly and intently snapped pictures of the unfolding scene. There was a scattering of household employees stationed or roaming there with various hospitality-dispensing paraphernalia. The alcove's wall was graced by an inoffensive painting that was thoroughly familiar to Marina Gregg: an image of a Madonna and child. Also, there were a few fête visitors patiently making their way up to be greeted by their hosts. To be sure, a slightly jarring note had been sounded by the uninvited, unexpected, and unwelcome appearance on the landing of two of Miss Gregg's Hollywood studio colleagues—but they were well-known if not wholly beloved associates of their hosts. Was the sight of one or both of them the reason for Marina Gregg's extraordinary reaction?

Dolly assured Miss Marple that the moment of reaction had been quickly over, and Marina Gregg had been swift to resume a demeanor of gracious aplomb. Later, Miss Marple would hear additional and slightly different versions of the same incident from other sources—and more besides.

She learned of the key instant when, scant moments after Miss Gregg's "frozen" look, someone among the milling guests had accidentally jostled Heather's elbow and caused her to spill her own cocktail: a daiquiri that Jason Rudd had urged on her as the same type that Marina Gregg preferred. The cocktail had splashed onto both Heather's and Marina Gregg's dresses. The now-recovered Miss Gregg made a swift soothing hospitable effort to mitigate the awkwardness of the incident, impulsively replacing Heather Badcock's lost cocktail with her own untouched drink. Though unaccustomed to sophisticated cocktails, Heather had gamely managed to down the drink. Minutes later she was dead—poisoned, it turned out, by an overdose of the tranquilizer Calmo, which had somehow been surreptitiously added to Marina Gregg's glass. Calmo, it transpired, was a drug in widespread use among many of Gossington Hall's current fashionable inhabitants. Almost anybody at the reception could have added it to Marina's unattended glass during the general mingling and movement and bustle associated with a successful social gathering.

Miss Marple's intelligence corps keeps her apprised of other startling developments. Among them was the news that Marina Gregg had finally revealed that she'd been receiving death threats even before Mrs. Badcock's death—threats that she'd kept secret even from her husband—and that someone had laced her coffee with arsenic on the movie set.

But before the mystery of Heather Badcock's poisoning could be solved, more murders are committed, and surprising and ominously coincidental relationships are uncovered. Miss Marple, however is back in fighting form, and in true armchair detective fashion arrives inevitably at the extraordinary key to the affair, expounding her solution and her judgments from the clear-sighted, no-nonsense yet sympathetic perspective that only she can deliver.

# The Life of Gene Tierney + *The Mirror Crack'd*

Agatha Christie's full-length tale, *The Mirror Crack'd*, features the detective abilities of Miss Jane Marple, that impressive spinster sleuth from the little English village of St. Mary Mead.

Within the novel's pages Christie again works the magic of adeptly incorporating the pathos of a tragic true-life event into her own original story of detection fiction. The narrative reflects inspiration from a poignant event in the life of American movie star Gene Tierney. Both the central plot of Christie's cautionary tale, and the tragic occurrence in Gene Tierney's life, revolve around the far-reaching destructive results of a well meant, but ultimately self-centered and tunnel-visioned act. That act's ripple of dire consequence constituted a lesson in awareness and self-awareness, in both the real world of Tierney's tragedy, and in the fictitious parallel situation of the novel.

The special advantages conferred on Gene Tierney by her beauty, wealthy background, and near-effortless stardom did not prepare her for the upheavals and sudden hardships that, at the peak of her success, seemed to gather and overwhelm her existence. The beloved father she'd believed in all her life had betrayed his family's trust; the marriage for which she'd defied her parents was disintegrating; each of the prominent men she afterwards fell in love with effectively abandoned her. But she was hardest hit by the unexpected blow of discovering her daughter was born with permanent disabilities. That tragic circumstance comprises the most striking direct similarity between Tierney's real life ordeal and the fictional sufferings of "Marina Gregg," the restive, highly strung personage of Christie's novel. The major plotline of Christie's tale centers around the cause of Marina Gregg's past mental illness—and its unforeseeable repercussions. Mirroring Gene Tierney's experience, the collapse of Marina's fragile mental health had been largely induced by the shock of her child being born with severe physical and mental disabilities.

Although mental depression and personal calamities nearly destroyed Gene Tierney, in time she grew enough in self-knowledge to come to terms with her losses, and even in some measure to rise triumphant above them. Her imagined counterpart, Marina Gregg, undergoes several of the same trials, but does not choose to go down all the same paths that her true-life alter ego traveled. As a storyline device Christie elects to attribute actions and characteristics to Marina Gregg that serve to sharpen the mystery and detection aspects of the novel. The stories of Gene Tierney and of "Marina Gregg" resemble each other in some particulars and diverge radically in others—as readers of the novel appreciate by the conclusion of the work.

The central plot of *The Mirror Crack'd*, with its ultimate unveiling of an unorthodox killer for an intriguing, unorthodox motive, is quite good Christie fare. But a curious feel of distance and disengagement also pervades the tale, beginning with Miss Marple's odd absence from many key scenes, even after she's been introduced into the story. Although she has had a brief prior encounter with the first murder victim in the novel, throughout the tale Miss Marple gleans quite a bit of her information only indirectly, interacting in person with few of the story's major characters.

Much of the action of the novel, including the principal murder itself, has occurred behind the scenes by the time the narrative reveals it. Although it's not unusual for Miss Marple—or for any detective—to arrive on the scene of a slaying until after the crime has been committed, Miss

Marple's detectival technique usually gets going thereafter, featuring her patented "busybody" methodology of investigation. The wily spinster of St. Mary Mead customarily positions herself to mingle innocently among suspects and potential suspects, culling information by employing her deceptive, dithering, "prying-old-lady" tactics; however, in *The Mirror Crack'd* Christie applies this trademark approach rather sparingly. Christie returns to form by the novel's next slaying, portraying a second and important murder with more of her customary style and onstage immediacy of action; while a third killing, although also onstage, seems to have a "once-removed" feel: it occurs due to a fairly "secondhand" type of blackmail. Other strangely offstage instances crop up in the story: the arrest of a surprising suspect, and the exposure of that suspect's even more surprising past relationship with Marina Gregg; the spiriting away of a character who, unwittingly, has seen too much; the peculiarly sudden death, late in the novel, of a key player in the drama.

In the novel, middle-aged Heather Badcock, an enthusiastic, generous, and hard-working resident of St. Mary Mead, drinks a poisoned cocktail and dies at a reception just before a village charity fête at St. Mary Mead's Gossington Hall—once the grand home of Miss Marple's longtime friends, Colonel Arthur Bantry and his wife Dolly. The cocktail had been originally meant for beautiful and glamorous Marina Gregg, the famous but psychologically fragile American film star. It is therefore obvious to investigators that the unknown killer's plans had gone awry. It was theorized that some unidentified enemy of Marina Gregg, present at the reception, had chosen that time and place to poison the star, but an innocent bystander had imbibed the deadly drink instead.

Acting on that theory, authorities had begun inquiries into the case. Why, and by whom, had the star been targeted for murder? Marina Gregg had only recently bought and moved into Gossington Hall with her movie-director husband Jason Rudd and her Hollywood retinue. The new owners had generously lent the Hall's grounds for the charity occasion, inviting Heather as event organizer and Dolly as past Gossington owner to a small private foregathering on the day of the fête. Marina Gregg had undoubtedly earned resentment and enmity from some associates in her life as she climbed the ladder to stardom, but from others she had as well earned the expected adulation and sycophancy accorded to glamorous celebrity. The temperamental but alluring star had married five times. She had unceremoniously dumped her commonplace and completely forgotten first spouse; and she had broken up at least one marriage.

But Marina Gregg had suffered calamities of her own as well. Over a decade earlier she had been delighted to find she was finally pregnant—but the health of her long-awaited son had been compromised by a mild illness that Marina had caught during the early stages of her pregnancy. Marina Gregg was shattered, never knowing how or when she had been exposed to the destructive disease. Her pain and devastation had sent her over the edge. She had fallen victim to a severe nervous breakdown, from which now, years later, she had only recently begun to recover enough to feel her way tentatively back to a normal life. She was in fact attempting to crown that recovery by making a comeback film at a studio near St. Mary Mead, working under the direction and vigilant protection of her adoring current husband. The fragile star, happy in her new life, had been doing quite well—and then the murder of Heather Badcock, along with the subsequent realization of her own life being in jeopardy, had taken their toll on her still-brittle state of mind.

On the day of the fête, tragedy had struck soon after Marina Gregg had greeted Heather Badcock in the reception receiving line, situated near a Gossington stairway landing. The guests had been filing up the steps to be greeted by their hosts, Miss Gregg and Jason Rudd. When her turn came to be greeted by the star, Mrs. Badcock had hijacked Miss Gregg's attention, despite the queue of excited guests behind her. Dolly Bantry, nearby, inwardly smiled in sympathy with the actress's graciously concealed boredom with what Dolly thought of as Heather Badcock's runaway "chicken pox" story.

Then all at once Mrs. Bantry's amusement was startled into alarmed attention. Marina Gregg's whole demeanor had undergone a sudden and drastic change. The star had in fact ceased to listen at all, and was now staring over Mrs. Badcock's shoulder, in stark transfixed horror, at something—or someone—she saw on the stairway landing beyond. And then, as swiftly as it came, that frozen look had vanished. Christie uses this "startled and portentous recognition" device to great effect in *The Mirror Crack'd*, and successfully repeats the gambit two years later in 1964's *A Caribbean Mystery*. Moments after Marina Gregg's strange behavior, someone in the cheery reception throng accidentally jostled Heather's arm. The unaccustomed cocktail Heather was holding spilled onto her own dress, and onto Marina Gregg's dress as well; however, the tactful hostess had graciously pressed her own untouched daiquiri on her flustered guest—and scarcely minutes after reluctantly downing the cocktail meant for her famous hostess, Heather Badcock had died.

The calamity in the fictional life of Marina Gregg—the permanent disability of her newborn son—parallels that of the real-life American film star Gene Tierney, whose cool elegant beauty graced many films. From 1940 onward, Hollywood moguls impressed by her beauty practically handed Tierney a movie-star-career on the proverbial silver platter. She married Oleg Cassini, future designer to future First Lady, Jacqueline Kennedy. The

World War II years saw the flowering of Gene's popularity, and in March 1943, she had volunteered to help the war effort on the home front by participating, as did many other famous entertainers of the era, in the Hollywood Canteen—a social club where ordinary servicemen and women could freely dine, dance, and hobnob socially with the entertainment world's elite. It was also in that month Gene discovered she was pregnant. Like the novel's Marina Gregg, Gene Tierney had longed for a child; when she and her husband learned that a baby was coming, the signs were happy and propitious for their beginning-to-be-troubled marriage. Their daughter Daria Cassini was born prematurely in October 1943, but still seemed outwardly perfect. During the year or so after her birth, however, it began to dawn on the parents that their baby was not progressing as she should.

In the first weeks of her pregnancy, Gene had come down with a minor ailment normally contracted in childhood. At first, reassured by doctors that the child she was carrying would not be affected by the indisposition, her main concern as an actress was the ailment's accompanying mild rash and its impact on her looks. But there were to be far more terrible consequences from the sickness than cosmetic ones. Gene Tierney had not made the connection between her brief bout with the slight ailment and her daughter's developmental delays until, one day, she chanced to read an article detailing effects of an illness which a number of Australian women had contracted at the beginning of pregnancy. The women had been exposed to rubella, better known as German measles—the same disease that Gene had contracted in the first months of her own pregnancy. Like many in that era, Gene and her husband had been unaware of the dangers the mild-seeming disease could inflict on a child in gestation. Now thoroughly frightened, the Cassinis consulted physicians who confirmed that Daria was permanently physically and mentally disabled due to exposure to German measles in the womb. Daria's stricken parents were nearly crushed by grief. Gene brooded feverishly, blaming herself, wondering endlessly how and when she had come in contact with the disease. But a shattering, almost unendurable enlightenment was awaiting her.

Her daughter was about a year old when, by an almost incredible quirk of fate, Gene was at a social function in Los Angeles where a smiling young woman, an enthusiastic fan, approached her. She told Gene that she had been in the military and had met the star once before at the Hollywood Canteen. And then she added a devastating rider, whose words and effects Gene describes calmly, dispassionately, but nonetheless poignantly in her 1978 autobiography, *Self-Portrait*: "The [young woman] said, 'Did you happen to catch the German measles after that night?'" The young woman then went on to tell Gene she'd broken a rubella quarantine that evening to come and meet the stars.

## Chapter 9. "Poor Little Rich Girl"

With this cataclysmic bolt from the blue, Gene Tierney had finally learned the answer to the most anguished question of her life. Dazed, without speaking one word to the woman about the tragedy her ill-advised action had brought into at least three lives, Gene Tierney turned and walked rapidly away.

Agatha Christie deplored the injustice of society's seeming to "care" more about perpetrators of crimes than about their victims or their victims' survivors, and it shows in *The Mirror Crack'd*. The author contrives an alternate ending in her fictional tale to Gene Tierney's true-life encounter, an ending that reflects Christie's belief, as exemplified in several of her tales, that moral crimes should not go unpunished. And although the "crime" that desolated the existence of Gene Tierney's counterpart Marina Gregg—a catastrophe caused by a willful if oblivious headstrong act—was not one punishable by law, the destruction wrought on several lives by that act was depicted as real. It was as devastating and irremediable as any deliberately violent act of aggression.

In *An Autobiography* Agatha Christie decried the amount of time, attention, and publicity given to the plights of wrongdoers as opposed to that given to the plights of those they'd harmed. "It frightens me that nobody seems to care about the innocent," she wrote. "When you read about a murder case, nobody seems to be horrified by the picture, say, of a fragile old woman ... being attacked and battered to death. No one seems to care about her terror and her pain.... Nobody seems to go through the agony of the victim; they are only full of pity for the young killer, because of his youth" (425). If chastisement for such transgressions could not be brought about in real life, she could in some measure remedy that unfairness through the plots of her made-up tales. Christie brought closure of a certain kind by creating "justice"—or simply by creating more satisfying, "eye for an eye," wish-fulfillment scenarios—for certain cases. In addition, by "righting" unrighted real world wrongs—if only in the imaginary settings of her detective fiction—she also symbolically re-imposed and reasserted needed order to society.

*The Mirror Crack'd*, Agatha Christie's work of imagined mystery-detection, therefore sympathizes in great part with the victim's point of view, as the author subtly considers issues of morality behind both the principal crime, and the eventually-revealed, background "crime" that incited it. Christie does not, however, allow that sympathy to overpower the tenor of her tale. In her own understated fashion, she also zeroes in on baring faults in the different mentalities that created each criminal situation, past and present.

Within the pages of her story, Christie deftly clothes and re-echoes true-life situations with events of her imagined plot and storyline. The author's character Marina Gregg had wed and shed a number of husbands, while Gene Tierney married only twice. She and Oleg Cassini finally divorced in 1952, but ensuing glamorous romances with the likes of Tyrone Power and Howard Hughes came to nothing. Gene suffered terribly from sad endings to other high-profile, more serious love affairs with a young John F. Kennedy, and then with Prince Aly Khan. During succeeding months and years after Daria's birth, still shocked and embittered by financial and marital betrayals by the father she'd adored, and demoralized by the parade of relationship failures, Gene's state of mind slid further into mental illness. Despite giving birth to a healthy second daughter, Christina Cassini, in 1948, Gene continued to fall prey to manic depressive episodes. She was unable to focus on making films—or even on surviving in day to day reality. This situation finds echo in the correspondingly troubled life of Marina Gregg.

In 1955 Gene Tierney began treatment in psychiatric institutions, undergoing shock treatment—to no real avail. "Marina Gregg" of the novel had also suffered a nervous breakdown. After a suicide attempt in 1957 Gene was committed to a clinic where she underwent a year-long successful treatment for depression. Having gained a tentative foothold on the ladder back to wholeness, Gene thereafter left the clinic, and strove to climb her way slowly back to normality, as her counterpart Miss Gregg had begun to do in *The Mirror Crack'd*. In 1958 Gene met the man who was to become her second husband, Texas oil baron W. Howard Lee, while he was still married to the glamorous and famous actress Hedy Lamarr. After a bitterly fought divorce, Lee was finally able to wed Gene in 1960. Christie echoes this circumstance in her novel with the fact of Marina Gregg's having broken up the marriage of Lola Brewster, a character in the novel who was, like Hedy Lamarr, also a famous actress. Marina then subsequently married Lola's ex-husband—but only for a while.

Tierney's personal life seemed to settle down after her marriage to Lee, and in 1962, strongly supported by director Otto Preminger, she made a triumphant comeback to the silver screen in the film *Advise and Consent*. Marina Gregg's comeback effort under the guidance of her adoring husband, Jason Rudd, closely resembles this phase of Gene's difficult journey to recovery. Tierney retired almost completely from show business after 1964, electing for the most part to live quietly away from Hollywood with her husband until his death in 1981. Having at last found a measure of stability and tranquility in her later years, Gene Tierney died of emphysema in 1991.

The ultimate fate of the fictional Marina Gregg in *The Mirror Crack'd* differs from that of Gene Tierney. After Mrs. Badcock's death, Dolly Bantry brings details of the poisoning at Gossington Hall to the interested attention of Miss Marple, who had not been present at the reception. When retelling to Miss Marple all that she knew of events preceding the tragedy—including

## Chapter 9. "Poor Little Rich Girl"

Heather Badcock's longwinded "chicken-pox" tale—Mrs. Bantry described the ghastly frozen look on Marina Gregg's face in the words of a slightly misquoted Tennyson passage: "The mirror crack'd from side to side, 'The doom has come upon me!' Cried the Lady of Shalott." The quote later gives Miss Marple valuable insight into the case as she delves into its implications.

For Miss Marple's information, Dolly also described the stairway landing toward which Marina Gregg had directed that "basilisk" stare. There had been no one and nothing there either unfamiliar to the actress, or likely to strike that perceived momentary horror into Marina Gregg's whole expression. The stairway or landing area held photographic gear, the photographer herself, a smattering of household staff, a Madonna and child painting on the wall, and ascending guests waiting to be greeted. But Marina Gregg had been stricken with horror on looking toward that stairway landing. Had she suddenly espied there some deadly enemy, come expressly to harm the world-famous actress? Had that enemy later silently and secretly doctored Marina's momentarily unattended drink with a fatal dose of poison?

Scotland Yard sends one of Miss Marple's old friends, Chief-Inspector Dermot Craddock, to investigate the high-profile case. Strangely, the Gregg camp seems unwilling to work with authorities on finding the slayer of Mrs. Badcock, or on protecting Marina Gregg from future murder attempts. In spite of the Gregg household's lack of cooperation, Miss Marple, Craddock, and Dolly Bantry collaborate and manage to amass significant information about Marina Gregg's past as well as her present. They uncover details about her history of mental illness and about her institutionalized child; they unearth specifics of her varied matrimonial history—including the fact that one of her discarded spouses was actually present, unrecognized, in St. Mary Mead. Even more significantly, Marple and company find that more than one attempt has been made on the actress's life.

Miss Marple, oddly remote from the scene of the crime and the major characters until the novel's final pages, nevertheless is able to apply her own brand of logic to the mystery and therefore to unravel its complications. But two more murders, and a thwarted third were to occur before the elderly crime solver of St. Mary Mead pieced together enough of the puzzle to decipher its intricacies, and to bring the truth at last to light.

Agatha Christie makes it clear in *The Mirror Crack'd* that there were no real excuses or exonerations for any of the wrongdoings within its pages, including the years-old inciting crime of the past: the culprit had been well aware that actions taken could be injurious to others. Christie paints a vignette of subtext with her words, illustrating for the reader not only the fictional offenses and the moral evils she treats in the tale, but their consequences as well—deftly driving home an interpretation of the biblical decree that "the wages of sin is death." There being no true excuses for any of the malefactions in the novel, there were no valid reasons why they should not have been dealt with; and, within the pages of *The Mirror Crack'd*, dealt with they were. By the pensively melancholic conclusion to the novel, the author has seen to it that two sets of morally complicated but totally human sins had indeed been punished by death. While doing all this she remains true to her mission imperative, never losing sight of the fact that ultimately, her aim is first of all to create, for the innocuous pleasure of her readers, not a polemic but an intelligent, enjoyable, and entertaining work of mystery fiction.

## Chapter 10

# The "Brides in the Bath" Murderer
## George Joseph Smith and *A Caribbean Mystery*

The novel *A Caribbean Mystery* finds Miss Marple transplanted, rather surprisingly, from her beloved village of St. Mary Mead to foreign soil as she investigates the mystery of a fellow guest's death at a West Indies resort. Unlike that gadabout, Hercule Poirot, who regularly found himself solving mysteries in such exotic locales as France, Jerusalem, Rhodes, Egypt, and other glamorous venues, *A Caribbean Mystery* represents Miss Marple's sole venture away from England—yet she manages to bring the flavor of her sedate little village along with her. Christie muses on the psychology of her killer, having Miss Marple carefully dissect the mentality of slayers whose arrogance and unvarying mindsets trap them into the exposure they were so sure of evading. In intricate fashion Christie artfully weaves into her story, published almost 50 years after George Joseph Smith's execution, powerful echoes of major aspects of the incredible true-life tale of the "Brides in the Bath Murderer."

## George Joseph Smith

George Joseph Smith was 43 when he was hanged on August 13, 1915, in Kent for the murders of the "Brides in the Bath." The son of working class parents, the "lonely hearts"/"Bluebeard" killer had been in and out of prison from the age of nine years, spending most of his adult life preying on women for their ready money, their life insurance proceeds, or their inheritances. So shocking and fascinating to the public were the revelations of investigations into Smith's crimes and subsequent trial that they took over the headlines of British newspapers up to that time featuring the horrors of the "Great War," which was then raging in Europe.

Smith's only legal marriage was to a Caroline Thornhill, who had soon after run away from England to escape her spouse. He did not slay *every* woman that he wooed or bigamously married: the fortunate ones he merely robbed and left penniless. There was even one woman for whom he seemed actually to care. In 1908 he "wed" unsuspecting Edith Pegler and remained with her for the rest of his life—when he was not traveling out and about, swindling or murdering other women. At the time when he was at last apprehended and charged with his horrific crimes, Pegler loyally stood by him. But Smith had not been as kind to at least three other ill-fated women as he had been to Edith Pegler.

Smith "married" and murdered for gain. He was methodical only in his process for committing his type of crimes, and his method for murder was simple and deadly: at seaside locations he targeted susceptible, lonely, and unprotected spinsters of some sort of means—women who were eager for matrimony, and ripe for his kind of animal magnetism. In his career, Smith went through bigamous marriage ceremonies with at least seven victims, each time in a different locale, often using an alias. With the lucre netted from his crimes, Smith seemed to be playing out some muddled dream of attaining respectability and prosperity, a "gentlemanly" existence. In certain quarters after his exposure, his erstwhile pretensions earned him the derisive nickname of "Gentleman George" Smith. He would open a bakery here, an antique shop there; with the proceeds from one particularly profitable murderous foray, he ventured into real estate by buying up several houses. But his business acumen was as muddled as his dreams, and he would inevitably wind up a bankrupt—and again on the prowl for another victim to replenish his depleted coffers.

With each of the three trusting "brides" that he murdered, Smith would go through a marriage ceremony, and quickly locate a lodging house, taking a set of rooms for which he had one immutable requirement: it must have a bathtub. The newlyweds would by then have made mutual wills leaving everything to each other, and in the latter cases Smith would have taken out life insurance on his spouse.

The next step in his grim program was extremely crucial to his plan. He would take his new wife to a local doctor, one to whom they were both strangers, to have the woman treated for fitful "headaches" and blackouts. Smith would thereby smoothly plant in the physician's mind a most necessary lie: the bride was prone to sudden "spells" or fits. On an evening soon after, the ill-starred bride would drown in the bathtub—ostensibly while alone, and ostensibly as a result of one of her random and therefore incalculable seizures. Smith, "suitably horrified and distraught when she was found drowned in the bathtub" ("Serial" 9), would then fetch the physician consulted for headache a few days before, who would in good faith issue a certificate of accidental death. Smith would then walk away to collect his profit from the unfortunate woman's demise. The callous killer had disposed of three known brides in this way by the time he was arrested: Bessie Mundy at Herne Bay in 1912, Alice Burnham at Blackpool in 1913, and Margaret Lofty in London in 1914.

Beatrice "Bessie" Mundy was the first unfortunate bride. She and Smith—using the alias "Henry Williams"—had married in 1910, but on finding that her money was not as readily available to him as he'd thought, he promptly and summarily abandoned her. But two years later, when Bessie by accident espied her "husband" on a beach at Weston-super-Mare, she joyfully welcomed him back into her life. Taking advantage of the circumstance, opportunist Smith saw that she made out a will and took out life insurance on herself in his favor—and sent her out to rent a bathtub for their lodging. He also brought her to a physician who was unacquainted with either of them, telling the medical man that Bessie seemed prone to "headaches" and fainting "fits" at odd moments, about which she afterwards remembered nothing. On July 13, she was found drowned in the bathtub of their Herne Bay lodging by her distraught husband. The sympathetic doctor who had so recently treated her signed unsuspectingly a certificate of death by misadventure. Smith in due course collected the monies from Bessie's estate, and resumed his life with Edith Pegler.

Smith encountered the second bride in Blackpool in September 1913. Plump and pleasant Alice Burnham was 25. Her discerning parents distrusted and disliked Smith on sight, but Alice was smitten. When she announced her intention to marry a man she hardly knew despite her family's objections, they did their angry utmost to dissuade her. Defiantly, she married him on November 4, 1913, with Smith this time undergoing the bigamous ceremony using his own name. The couple rented rooms in Blackpool, Smith having made sure there was a bathtub available to them at the boarding house. He found a local doctor who was a stranger to them both, and sought treatment for his new wife's "headaches" and sporadic "fits." On December 12, 1913, Alice Burnham was found drowned in the bath; the doctor who had treated her at Smith's request and the inquest jury found that her death had been accidental.

The multiple murderer had known how to pick his targets, who all seemed more than willing to be dominated by him. When Alice Burnham's parents demanded more information on his background, the brazen Smith fired off a retort by postcard: "my mother was a Bus horse, my father a Cab-driver, and my sister a rough rider over the Arctic regions. My brothers were all gallant sailors on a steam roller. This is the only information I can give to those who are not entitled to ask such questions. Your despised son-in-law, Geo. J. Smith" (Watson 321). Such was Smith's hypnotic—or menacing—sway over her that Alice Burnham took his part over that of her family at every turn, placing herself completely in his power. Each of his other two murder victims had also similarly cast her lot with his, effectually isolating herself to the power of a monster.

George Joseph Smith was using the alias "John Lloyd" when he met 38-year-old Margaret Elizabeth Lofty in November 1914. He married her in London mere weeks later, on December 17. The groom had made sure that the honeymoon lodging they chose had a bathtub, and that a nearby doctor was immediately consulted about the bride's tendency to unaccountable headaches and seizures. And on December 18, Smith drowned Margaret Lofty in her bath.

When Smith's third bride's drowning was reported with its attendant details in the widely circulated London newspaper, *News of the World*—one of Britain's most popular Sunday tabloids of that or any era—the article caught the eye of relatives and friends of the second bride, Alice Burnham. The details were so strikingly like the details of Alice's case that two different sets of Alice's associates alerted police. Scotland Yard promptly opened an investigation. In a police ruse on February 1, 1915, Smith was lured to the insurance agency where he was set to collect on Margaret Lofty's life insurance policy. He was arrested on the minor charge of falsifying information on a marriage certificate—and George Joseph Smith's days of freedom, murder, and life itself were numbered.

Newspapers around the country immediately picked up on the story and began to proliferate accounts of the sensational investigation into the two deaths. A police official in Herne Bay saw the similar pattern between the deaths of Burnham and Lofty and that of Bessie Mundy in 1912, and got in touch with Scotland Yard. Officials sent photographs of Smith to the Herne Bay authorities, who promptly identified the photographs as those of "Henry Williams." Armed with this strong evidence of serial slaying, authorities charged George Joseph Smith with murder on February 15, 1915. Edith Pegler remained sincerely unbelieving at the time he was arrested and charged with the horrific crimes, convinced that the police had made a terrible mistake. The revelations of the trial, however, couldn't be denied, leaving her aghast and shaken.

The trial also launched a legal landmark. As was the procedure pertaining at the time, Smith was tried for one murder, Bessie Mundy; however, an interpretation of the law allowed admissibility of evidence in the slayings of Burnham and Lofty to show Smith's "system" for murder, proving "two non-character issues: absence of mistake and common scheme or plan" (Paine, "Brides" 26). The admissibility was upheld on appeal, and the ruling set a significant legal precedent, one since applied to a multiplicity of other cases.

During the trial, the Crown used dramatic means to prove their case against Smith. The principal hurdle was proving to the jury that the death of Bessie Mundy—and those of the other brides—had not been accidental, when there had been absolutely no signs of a struggle. Bessie Mundy's "bath[tub] was brought into the court and used for demonstrations" ("Ten" 7) so that the prosecution could use a bathing-suited policewoman to stage a reconstruction. The demonstration of Smith's alleged surprise-assault technique for drowning his unsuspecting victim was so successful that the policewoman herself also very nearly drowned.

Renowned pathologist Bernard Spilsbury had also been called onto the case to clarify the cause of death. His ingenious proofs convinced the jury that the deaths of the women—whose corpses on exhumation had exhibited no obvious signs of having been violently drowned—had indeed been caused by murder, made forensics history, and effectively sealed the fate of George Joseph Smith.

The "Brides-in-the-Bath Murderer" earned his place of infamy with the pattern he developed to murder for gain. He followed his blueprint faithfully each time, because time and again that blueprint had worked—but "George Smith's blunder was that he adopted precisely the same villainous technique" ("Why" 4) too many times in his known ventures into murder. And therein lay his undoing: his pattern, repeated twice, was recognizable to any outside observer who twice was exposed to its workings—as had been individuals who, after Smith's last venture into murder, recognized those patterns in newspaper articles. Not being especially imaginative, Smith saw no reason why his blueprint should not keep on working: death-dealing had become, for him, just a routine habit.

## *A Caribbean Mystery*

Agatha Christie's *A Caribbean Mystery*, published in 1964, begins as Miss Marple is convalescing from a severe bout of pneumonia at a sunny Caribbean beach resort, the Golden Palm Hotel in St. Honoré. She had established a daily routine and was out sunning herself as she usually did, that day seated a little in front of the young and eager-to-please new owners of the hotel, who were companionably absorbed in working together on hotel accounts. Sitting with Miss Marple as she rested near the beach with her knitting was the inescapable Major Palgrave, "purple of face, with a glass eye, and the general appearance of a stuffed frog," (Christie, *Caribbean* 2) who was maundering on as usual to anyone who would listen about his past exciting adventures and travels.

The Major was demonstratively as fond of Planters Punches as he was of sharing his adventures. He had managed to latch onto Miss Marple for one of his interminable sessions of storytelling, but the forbearing Miss Marple had kindly allowed him to do so, absently half-listening and responding to him as her needles clicked and her mind dwelled on other things. The Major told his usual stories of safari hunts, military campaigns, and hair-raising situations he'd encountered, and today somehow the topic wandered off to include murderers and murders. As her attention drifted in and out of the conversation, Miss Marple caught certain phrases. Then the Major added that while they were on that subject, he had a story to tell of a strange thing that had happened to a physician friend of his.

Encouraged by Miss Marple's absent-minded agreeableness, Major Palgrave enlarged on his theme. His physician friend had treated a young wife who'd tried to hang herself after suffering recent bouts of despondency. Her adoring husband, who had found her in just the nick of time, had been distressed and broken up and panicky, but the physician had been able to save her. The Major's friend had been an enthusiast of certain botanicals, and when he afterwards followed up on his patient he noticed a plant of interest to him near the couple's door. He had seized the opportunity to take a quick snapshot of it just when the young husband, unaware he was being photographed, showed up as the shutter clicked.

The woman's progress had appeared to be satisfactory, but unfortunately a month or so later, she tried killing herself again, and this time was successful. A year or so afterwards a fellow doctor happened to tell the Major's physician friend about a case he'd had of his own: an unhappy young wife had tried to kill herself, but her young husband had found her just in time. The colleague doctor had managed to pull her through, but some weeks later the poor woman had made another suicide attempt that succeeded in putting an end to her life. Startled, the Major's physician friend recalled his own involvement in such a case. The two medical men then compared notes and were struck by the similarities in occurrences involving different people at different times in different locations. It might have passed off as just an interesting coincidence, but the physician friend remembered he had saved his snapshot of the first bereaved husband; he showed it to the second doctor, who was bowled over to recognize in the photograph the picture of the shattered young husband of his own case.

The physician friend had later given the photo to the Major as a novelty, and Palgrave had duly added the picture and the story behind it to his own store of interesting accounts. Would Miss Marple, the Major now asked, "like to see the picture of a murderer?" (10). On her acquiescence, the Major had fumbled among the papers in his overstuffed wallet, muttering to himself the while, and had then looked up from his searches and made as if to present to her the snapshot he had at last managed to locate.

Suddenly an extraordinary change came over him: he seemed to be staring in fixed fascination over her right shoulder, and it was obvious that he had seen something that had momentarily stunned him. He hastily stuffed the snapshot back into his pocket. Miss Marple, alerted, quietly looked over her right shoulder to see what it was that had so transfixed the Major. Four people were continuing their advance onto the scene while the Major suddenly began speaking loudly in flustered tones. The foursome was made up of two married couples getting toward middle age, repeat guests at the Golden Palm. Big, bluff Greg Dyson and his glamorously blonde and edgy wife Lucky were American; quiet, darkly spare Edward Hillingdon and his decidedly unglamorous wife Evelyn were typically English. Beyond them was only the villa of another party of St. Honoré habitués: the old, rich, irascible, and invalid businessman Mr. Rafiel, accompanied by his valet and secretary. There seemed nothing sinister in anything or anyone that she could see. But Miss Marple felt that, for the Major, there had been *something*...

The next morning brought the distressing news that Major Palgrave had died suddenly in the night. A bottle of pills, medication for a blood pressure disorder, had been found among his toiletries, and everyone generally supposed that the garrulous old boy had died from a combination of his medical condition and too much drink.

But Miss Marple wasn't so sure, for, oddly, the snapshot that the Major had so hastily stuffed back into his wallet had disappeared.

She rapidly went over events of the previous day in her mind: she and the Major had been casually discussing murderers. He had told Miss Marple a story of a probable serial wife-killer, and had cheerily offered to show her a snapshot of that killer, with the air of one who had told that story and presented that snapshot many times before. Or had he been preparing to show a picture of a *woman* who was a killer? He had looked up—and had frozen in momentary astonishment at something he'd seen over her right shoulder.

Miss Marple was vexed with herself for not having paid closer attention. Had the face in his snapshot suddenly loomed before him in real life, in the form of Edward Hillingdon or Greg Dyson? Or perhaps someone in the Rafiel household? It hardly seemed likely that the wheelchair-bound and aged Jason Rafiel could have anything to do with the subject of the Major's verbal meanderings. But Arthur Jackson, Mr. Rafiel's hired help? He was a dark horse indeed. To complicate matters, Miss Marple later discovered that the Major had told others stories of a woman who was a murderer. Miss Prescott, another guest, recounted to Miss Marple a disclosure the Major had made to her on one occasion about a woman who had poisoned someone, there with them that very moment on the island. Miss Marple's subsequent investigations found that the Major had talked to other guests about a murderess, a "Lucrezia Borgia" type who had poisoned her husband. If the hapless Palgrave had nosed out a murderer, man or woman, and that murderer had overheard his comments and acted to prevent exposure, then the possibility was very real that Major Palgrave himself had been victim of murder disguised as a natural death.

If Major Palgrave was slain to safeguard the identity of a wife-killer in the story, that killer's behaviors could well have replicated those of George Joseph Smith. Indeed the 1989 television adaptation of *A Caribbean Mystery*, starring Joan Hickson—for many the quintessential Miss Marple—showed a makeshift marker for the lonely Major's grave inscribed "G. J. Palgrave," though the Major's first names or initials were never revealed in the novel. Was it a play on George Joseph Smith's given names—the production's low-key manner of paying tribute in a way to the tale's relation to a classic true crime?

As *A Caribbean Mystery* nears its end, Miss Marple follows her instincts and goes on to investigate fully the death of the Major, employing her trademark "twittering, busybody old lady" subterfuges and enlisting the aid of some unlikely fellow sleuths. But two more murders and one attempted murder follow before Miss Marple has an epiphany and looks at the case with a new eye, enabling her at last to ferret out a canny murderer in true surprise-twist, Agatha Christie style.

## George Joseph Smith + *A Caribbean Mystery*

*A Caribbean Mystery* by Agatha Christie appeared in 1964, two years after the publication of *The Mirror Crack'd*. Both novels showcase the detective talents of Miss Jane Marple, notable but unlikely crime solver from the village of St. Mary Mead. Both novels also highlight an intriguing Christie plot device. In the middle of an ordinary conversation, a singularly curious incident occurs: one of the participants suddenly breaks off communication to stare thunderstruck over an interlocutor's shoulder, transfixed by a riveting sight—a sight triggering a realization not possible to make until that split second of awareness. The scene at which the momentarily stunned character stares is a perfectly ordinary and familiar one; the character has seen it many times before. Yet there is something tense, sinister, foreboding about this particular instance which impresses the onlooking witness as having ominous and chilling portent. And very soon thereafter, murders most mysterious begin to occur. Christie had employed this fateful "hook" two years earlier in *The Mirror Crack'd*; and other kindred though less extendedly dramatic flashes of startled recognition occur in such Christie tales as *Mrs. McGinty's Dead*.

The "Caribbean mystery" referred to in the novel's title derives from the demise of one Major Palgrave, a fellow guest at the West Indies island

## Chapter 10. The "Brides in the Bath" Murderer

resort where Miss Marple is staying. It is he, a wearingly voluble old campaigner, who experiences the dumbstruck moment of insight bridging the curious incident with the main plot; and soon it is he who winds up dead. It is possible that Major Palgrave may have died of natural causes—but he may equally well have been murdered.

If murder it was, Christie keeps readers on their mettle by serving up a buffet of references to classic, real-life, accused or convicted killers in the course of the novel. The story's villain may have modeled his or her own murder on those of the notorious real-word personages. The Borgias—especially the beautiful Lucrezia, cynosure of Renaissance Italy's poison intrigues—figures among the true-crime possibilities; as does a Victorian-age accused murderess who was barely acquitted of poisoning her husband. However, Christie refers most substantially in the tale to one of the most infamous killers in modern British history: George Joseph Smith, hanged in 1915 England for the notorious series of slayings dubbed the "Brides in the Bath" Murders. While the Borgias and other real-life crime figures are sparingly sketched in the novel, Christie infuses her narrative throughout with frequent expressed or implied allusions to Smith or to his methods. The references artfully woven within the fabric of the story give it a hint of familiarity for many readers knowledgeable about the affair, imparting a *déjà vu* sensibility to the storyline. Yet so skillful is the author that readers who know nothing of Smith's contribution to crime suffer no impairment of understanding or enjoyment of her engrossing tale. Christie re-creates piecemeal Smith's true crimes in a clever take on the "brides in the bath" scheme, referring to the case in subtle, oblique, or overt fashion practically from start to finish of her story.

As *A Caribbean Mystery* begins, Miss Marple is at fictional St. Honoré's Golden Palm Hotel in the West Indies, chatting with Major Palgrave, garrulous resort bore and inveterate imbiber, as she makes plausible pretense of attending to his longwinded tales.

The topic arises of killers he has known, and Miss Marple vaguely registers his references to a woman who was a murderer. Palgrave adds a tale about a friend's unwitting encounter with murder. It seemed that some years ago the friend, a physician, received an emergency call from a panicked young husband whose mentally unstable wife had just attempted to kill herself. The Major's doctor friend saved her, as the devoted young husband wept in relief.

When the physician followed up his visit, the wife now seemed well on her way to recovery. At the time, the doctor had accidentally taken a snapshot of the husband, a fact of which the young man was unaware. The wife's situation seemed to be resolved, but sometime later, the doctor learned that the unhappy young wife had tried suicide again, and this time did indeed end her own life.

A year or so after the sad incident, a colleague recounted a story to the first physician much like the one the first physician had experienced. Struck by similarities between the cases, the first doctor produced his snapshot of the distressed and devoted husband he had known, and the second doctor was shocked to recognize in the photograph the rattled young husband of his own acquaintance. The names were different, the wives were different, the times and locations were different—but the husband was the same, and the pattern of events was the same. It was obvious to the two medical men that, wildly coincidental as it seemed, they had just stumbled on a case of serial wife-killing—and there was no indication the killer had ever been caught.

Major Palgrave was now the owner of the telltale snapshot, and he offered to show Miss Marple his picture of a murderer. But when, with jolly alacrity, he made as if to present the shot, he suddenly froze in mid-motion, gaping in astonishment over her shoulder. To Miss Marple's surprise, he hastily stuffed the unshown snapshot back into his wallet. What was there about the harmless quartet of persons advancing on the scene behind her to evoke this time the Major's singular reaction of the moment just past? Or had it something to do with the villa beyond the foursome, where resided a wealthy old autocrat and his entourage?

In Chapter One of the novel, Major Palgrave's "picture of a murderer" tale initiates pointers to the true-crime case of George Joseph Smith, and Christie skillfully relates the wife-killer aspect of her novel's storyline to that case by referring to it via Palgrave's story. Through the device of Major Palgrave's second-hand account, she just as skillfully foregrounds the viewpoint of duped doctors who stumbled on awareness that they had unwittingly aided a serial wife-murderer. Deceived physicians had played important parts in the success of Smith's murderous schemes, and Christie's clever twist on exposition of Smith's crimes by way of the Major's story recognizes, appreciates, and features that importance. Her treatment offers a fresh vantage point from which to consider Smith's murders, since factual résumés of the sensational crimes were most often written or told from the perspective of investigators, reporters, or forensic commentators.

The morning after hearing the Major's story, Miss Marple learns that the old soldier had passed away suddenly during the night. Was it natural causes or murder? The elderly sleuth of St. Mary Mead begins investigating the problem. When she finds that the Major's "picture of a murderer" has unaccountably disappeared, her conviction of foul play firms and gathers strength. At this stage of her novel Christie reintroduces more robust consideration of George Joseph Smith and his methods. Major Palgrave himself had first mentioned the crimes of the notorious killer in Chapter One of the tale, although the killer himself is not referred to by actual name until

Chapter Sixteen. The Major spoke of Smith's murders by their famous appellation, invoking them, in ironic prophecy, just as he ends his wife-killer story to Miss Marple: "'Queer story, isn't it? Wouldn't think things like that could happen.' 'Oh yes, I would,' said Miss Marple placidly. 'Practically every day.' 'Oh, come, come. That's a bit fantastic.' 'If a man gets a formula that works-he won't stop. He'll go on.' 'Brides in the bath-eh?' [said Major Palgrave]" (10).

Smith and his crimes are cited specifically several more times in the novel, especially as Mr. Rafiel and Miss Marple rehash the story Major Palgrave had told her about a serial wife-slayer. They compare it to Smith's infamous *modus operandi* for his "Brides in the Bath" murder schemes. Their discussions amount to both an exposition of the novel's main plot, and also of the premise from which the plot was derived:

"The story Major Palgrave told me concerned a man whose wife died under suspicious circumstances. Then, after a certain lapse of time, there was another murder under exactly the same circumstances ... and [he was recognized] as the same man, although he'd changed his name. Well, it does look, doesn't it, as though [the murderer identified by Major Palgrave] might be the kind of murderer who made a habit of the thing?" "You mean like Smith, Brides in the Bath, that kind of thing. Yes?" (146).

Their conversation continues, reviewing the salient features of Smith's methods and mindset—a refresher for those readers familiar with the case, and an introduction for those new to his notorious story.

Miss Marple outlines her logic for her conclusions, wherein Christie deftly links the circumstances of her novel's plot with the circumstances of the Smith case; she also clearly delineates the departure point from the Smith events to her own scenario for her own story: "...if this-this person had got things all lined up for a murder out here, for getting rid of another wife, say ... the Major's story would matter because the murderer couldn't afford to have any similarity pointed out. If you remember, that was exactly the way Smith got caught. The circumstances of a crime attracted the attention of somebody who compared it with a newspaper clipping of some other case" (147).

Substitute the word "photograph" for the term "newspaper clipping" in the last sentence above and it becomes clear how simply, yet ingeniously, Agatha Christie effects the correspondence between the real-life means of exposing Smith, and the fictional means of exposing the fictional killer of her novel. Her own original mystery story—that of Major Palgrave's murder, its consequences, and its unraveling—revolve intriguingly around this correspondence.

In Christie's novel, a type of hubris similar to Smith's led to the eventual downfall of the villain of the work. Largely due to the resemblance between that villain's crimes and the crimes of George Joseph Smith, Miss Marple and Mr. Rafiel work out a "picture" of their own, an awareness of the killer's technique. That awareness eventually leads Miss Marple to solution of the novel's mystery.

For Agatha Christie and her contemporaries, it would not have been at all remarkable that Miss Marple and Mr. Rafiel were so readily conversant with the notorious Mr. Smith's history and methods. Christie would have expected no less from her sophisticated and criminologically literate characters—or from her readers of the era. She did not talk down to consumers of her detection concoctions, expecting them to be contemporaneous with her at all times: on the same page as she, both literally and figuratively. Her fictional characters and her real-life readers too would therefore immediately recognize the reference to the famous murder case of the brides in the bath as a matter of course, and by the conclusion would understand its applicability to the premise of the novel in hand. Miss Marple and Mr. Rafiel, the two most objective and experienced characters in the novel, are also the ones who elaborate most fully on Smith's techniques and why they worked— and why they ultimately trapped him. Through them the author makes certain that the novel's references to Smith take readers where she wants them to go. Christie craftily emphasizes how telltale, habitual patterns in Smith's methods were there in plain sight—if one were positioned to read them. At the same time in her novel's storyline, she ingeniously places the telltale patterns of her fictional murderer just as much in plain sight of her readers. It is so deftly done, however, that it is all too easy to miss it—and therefore to miss also the felicity of beating the novel's sleuth to identifying "whodunit."

Within the pages of the novel, before she reaches the solution, Miss Marple again permutes the possible configurations that could lead her to unmasking a killer. Palgrave had recounted stories at times of a Lucrezia Borgia type; a woman right there on the island. As a device, Christie uses Miss Marple's doubts to widen the field of possibilities: despite Palgrave's photograph and wife-killer tale, Miss Marple could legitimately ask herself if the Major's slayer had indeed been a woman instead.

Her sleuth's cogitations thus enable Christie to utilize variations on one of her enduring strengths, and one of her favorite ploys: casting doubt in all directions on the bona fides, guilt, or innocence of every viable character in the tale. She accomplishes this feat by skillfully planting clues that could implicate any number of characters almost equally. In these challenges to the sleuth and to the reader, Christie also casts doubt on the true personal identities of personages in the story: were the individuals at that hotel on that Caribbean island really who they said they were?

But at last Miss Marple reaches her goal, though not before misgivings and frustrations nearly mislead her. A hotel guest's comment on the Major points her at last in the right direction, and suddenly it all comes together for the elderly detective. But she senses that time is still running out for preventing another crime, and she hurries anxiously off to enlist the urgently needed aid of her new ally, Mr. Rafiel. The fluffy pink wool shawl across her frail shoulders belies her claim of representing Nemesis, the goddess of retribution, to the amusement of the wily invalid. But he trusts her instincts, and makes it possible for her to thwart, just in time, the obvious murder that the novel's ruthless killer had been driving toward all along, and the one that had been before their very eyes all the time.

Christie's narrative makes references to classic killers throughout the novel. Lucrezia Borgia's name is invoked several times, and in certain of the novel's scenarios, a woman poisoner could well have met the requirements for being the novel's ultimate culprit: the killer of Major Palgrave. But Christie alludes most often and most tellingly to Smith and his crimes. Certain scenes or events in her narrative correspond, subtly or overtly, to several facets of Smith's malefactions. The catalysts to killer Smith's exposure were telltale newspaper articles, revealing a *modus operandi* so graphic that it served as a metaphorical "photograph" for identifying the murderer. In Christie's tale, that telltale catalyst to the murderer's exposure becomes an *actual* photograph; a choice that showcases Christie's ability to retranslate the metaphor cleverly into the thing it represents—a picture in this case being the equivalent at least of the "thousand words" bestowed on Smith's transgressions in newspaper articles alone. The Major's snapshot of a killer also brings to mind the role that photographs played in connecting Smith to the murder of Bessie Mundy at the time when Scotland Yard knew only of the connection of Alice Burnham and Margaret Lofty's deaths to the suspected killer. A Herne Bay police official recognized, from newspaper accounts, Smith's pattern for murder in the circumstances of Bessie Mundy's death in Herne Bay years earlier. On receiving photos of Smith from Scotland Yard, he was able to link Smith undeniably with Mundy's now-suspicious demise—and it transpires that it was for Mundy's murder that Smith was ultimately tried.

Small as well as large reminders of Smith's methods and ways of life are sprinkled about the novel's unfolding expositions. When one of the characters in the novel declines to bring her lover to meet her family for their approval "just as though [he was] a horse," the words recall Smith's powerful ability to estrange his victims from the reasoned counsel of their families. More subtly and quite potently it also alludes to Smith's famous "my mother was a Bus horse" retort to his second bride's hostile family. Another character in Christie's tale, whose hidden fascination with a dangerous man prevents her from seeing through his lies and duplicity, is loyal even when he is exposed—much like the imposed-upon Edith Pegler.

The Caribbean island's sea-setting venue subtly evokes the seaside venues where Smith picked up or murdered his victims. Smith had used his blood money to dabble in real estate and other ventures. A poor businessman, he lost his money and went bankrupt time and again. This trait is reflected in Christie's narrative when a business in the novel heads for impending failure as visitors flee from an island where murder instead of pleasure seems to be the order of the day.

In the case of the "brides in the bath," Smith had probably drugged his "wives" to bring on headaches and giddiness: the illnesses served as pretexts to take his brides to local physicians. Smith's real-life "physical-illness" ploy with each doctor becomes the novel's "mental-illness" ploy with each doctor in the tale; the falsely bruited tendency to seizures in Smith's brides becomes the falsely bruited proneness to suicide attempts in the brides of the novel—as well as the artfully-spread lie about Major Palgrave's hypertension. Smith's successful "accidental" drownings of his spouses become *A Caribbean Mystery*'s successfully-engineered spousal "suicides." The sole murder by drowning in the novel turns out to be more of an accidental necessity for the killer, if exposure were to be avoided. Nevertheless, accidental necessity or not, the novel's murderous drowning in the sea recalls the true-life murderous drownings in the baths.

Agatha Christie's distinctive approach to creating the novel, in which she conveys a complex mixture of true and fictional crime themes in deceptively simple and accessible style, gives the tale a satisfying texture. The mix of direct reference and subtextual nuance combine to create a rich backdrop to Christie's original tale of murder, mystery, and detection, concocted as always in her own inimitable tradition. In addition the persistent haunting sense of lingering familiarity for some readers of *A Caribbean Mystery* enables double appreciation of the richness in this sturdy example of Christie's later creative period.

# Postscript

*The effect of a random **photograph** looms large in* A Caribbean Mystery. *In a handful of other stories, Agatha Christie also employs, equally well, the same device of having fateful snapshots lead to momentous—or murderous—events. While in the village of Broadhinny investigating the slaying of the titular character in* Mrs. McGinty's Dead, *Hercule Poirot happens on a tabloid newspaper's sentimental article in Chapter 8 which highlighted four women "victims" of bygone crimes. Each of the crimes had touched somehow on murder—and murder was what had brought the detective into the little village of Broadhinny in the first place. Four faded photographs of the said* women illustrated the newspaper article. Mrs. McGinty had read the article, and mere days later had been killed. Was there a connection? Had she recognized someone in the photographs who didn't want to be recognized? The newspaper pictures, Poirot muses, might well provide clues that help him unmask a brutal and ruthless killer—or they may prove to be completely useless and unrelated to his quest.

Christie uses the mystery and lure of a photograph in a different way in the novel Why Didn't They Ask Evans? While keeping watch over the body of a stranger accidentally fallen off a cliff, young Bobby Jones happens to espy the photograph that drops out of the victim's pocket. The face in the picture— that of a hauntingly beautiful young woman—captivates Bobby's imagination; it was a face "not easy to forget" (7). Soon thereafter strange and deadly events begin to dog Bobby and "Frankie"—his childhood friend, Lady Frances Derwent—as they look further into the fall victim's past. When the woman pictured in the photograph puzzlingly materializes—in two different incarnations—Bobby and Frankie are led into dramatic and perilous adventures that not only uncover cold-blooded murder but also puts their own lives at risk as well.

In A Murder Is Announced, it's not the presence of snapshots that puzzles Miss Marple as she inquires into the seemingly senseless murder of a seeming robber. It's the absence of photographs from an album that intrigues the spinster sleuth (157–8). Family photographs suddenly go missing from the albums of the robber's intended victim, elderly Letitia Blacklock of the village of Chipping Cleghorn. Miss Marple figures out the significance of the vanished pictures on her way to solving the case and revealing the surprising identity of the killer.

# Appendix A: Christie Chronology of Mystery Novels and Story Collections

(*Alternate titles are in parentheses*)

1920 *The Mysterious Affair at Styles*
1922 *The Secret Adversary*
1923 *The Murder on the Links*
1924 *The Man in the Brown Suit*
1924 *Poirot Investigates*: Collection
1925 *The Secret of Chimneys*
1926 *The Murder of Roger Ackroyd*
1927 *The Big Four*
1928 *The Mystery of the Blue Train*
1929 *Partners in Crime*: Collection
1929 *The Seven Dials Mystery*
1930 *The Murder at the Vicarage*
1930 *The Mysterious Mr Quin*: Collection
1931 *The Sittaford Mystery* (*Murder at Hazelmoor*)
1932 *Peril at End House*
1932 *The Thirteen Problems*: Collection (*The Tuesday Club Murders*)
1933 *The Hound of Death*: Collection
1933 *Lord Edgware Dies* (*Thirteen at Dinner*)
1934 *The Listerdale Mystery*: Collection
1934 *Murder on the Orient Express* (*Murder in the Calais Coach*)
1934 *Parker Pyne Investigates*: Collection (*Mr. Parker Pyne, Detective*)
1934 *Why Didn't They Ask Evans?* (*The Boomerang Clue*)
1935 *Death in the Clouds* (*Death in the Air*)
1935 *Three Act Tragedy* (*Murder in Three Acts*)
1936 *The A.B.C. Murders*
1936 *Murder in Mesopotamia*

# Appendix A

1936  *Cards on the Table*
1937  *Death on the Nile*
1937  *Dumb Witness* (*Poirot Loses a Client*)
1937  *Murder in the Mews*: Collection (*Dead Man's Mirror*)
1938  *Appointment with Death*
1938  *Hercule Poirot's Christmas* (*A Holiday for Murder*; *Murder for Christmas*)
1939  *And Then There Were None*
1939  *Murder Is Easy* (*Easy to Kill*)
1939  *The Regatta Mystery*: Collection
1940  *Sad Cypress*
1940  *One, Two, Buckle My Shoe* (*An Overdose of Death*; *The Patriotic Murders*)
1941  *Evil under the Sun*
1941  *N or M?*
1942  *The Body in the Library*
1942  *Five Little Pigs* (*Murder in Retrospect*)
1942  *The Moving Finger*
1944  *Towards Zero*
1944  *Death Comes as the End*
1945  *Sparkling Cyanide* (*Remembered Death*)
1946  *The Hollow* (*Murder after Hours*)
1947  *The Labours of Hercules*: Collection (*The Labors of Hercules*)
1948  *Taken at the Flood* (*There is a Tide*)
1948  *Three Blind Mice and Other Stories*: Collection
1948  *The Witness for the Prosecution and Other Stories*: Collection
1949  *Crooked House*
1950  *A Murder Is Announced*
1951  *They Came to Baghdad*
1951  *The Under Dog and Other Stories*: Collection
1952  *Mrs McGinty's Dead* (*Blood Will Tell*)
1952  *They Do It with Mirrors* (*Murder with Mirrors*)
1953  *After the Funeral* (*Funerals are Fatal*)
1953  *A Pocket Full of Rye*
1954  *Destination Unknown* (*So Many Steps to Death*)
1955  *Hickory Dickory Death* (*Hickory Dickory Dock*)
1956  *Dead Man's Folly*
1957  *4:50 from Paddington* (*What Mrs. McGillicuddy Saw!*)
1958  *Ordeal by Innocence*
1959  *Cat Among the Pigeons*
1960  *The Adventure of the Christmas Pudding*: Collection
1961  *Double Sin and Other Stories*: Collection
1961  *The Pale Horse*
1962  *The Mirror Crack'd* (*The Mirror Crack'd from Side to Side*)
1963  *The Clocks*
1964  *A Caribbean Mystery*
1965  *At Bertram's Hotel*
1966  *Third Girl*
1967  *Endless Night*

# Chronology of Mystery Novels and Story Collections

1968  *By the Pricking of My Thumbs*
1969  *Hallowe'en Party*
1970  *Passenger to Frankfurt*
1971  *The Golden Ball and Other Stories*: Collection
1971  *Nemesis*
1972  *Elephants Can Remember*
1973  *Postern of Fate*
1974  *Poirot's Early Cases*: Collection
1975  *Curtain*
1976  *Sleeping Murder*
1997  *The Harlequin Tea Set*: Collection

# Appendix B: Alphabetical List of Christie Mystery Novels and Story Collections

4:50 from Paddington (*What Mrs. McGillicuddy Saw!*)
The A.B.C. Murders
The Adventure of the Christmas Pudding: Collection
After the Funeral (*Funerals are Fatal*)
And Then There Were None
Appointment with Death
At Bertram's Hotel
The Big Four
The Body in the Library
By the Pricking of My Thumbs
Cards on the Table
A Caribbean Mystery
Cat Among the Pigeons
The Clocks
Crooked House
Curtain
Dead Man's Folly
Death Comes as the End
Death in the Clouds (*Death in the Air*)
Death on the Nile
Destination Unknown (*So Many Steps to Death*)
Double Sin and Other Stories: Collection
Dumb Witness (*Poirot Loses a Client*)
Elephants Can Remember
Endless Night
Evil under the Sun
Five Little Pigs (*Murder in Retrospect*)
The Golden Ball and Other Stories: Collection
Hallowe'en Party

## Mystery Novels and Story Collections

*The Harlequin Tea Set*: Collection
*Hercule Poirot's Christmas* (*A Holiday for Murder*; *Murder for Christmas*)
*Hickory Dickory Death* (*Hickory Dickory Dock*)
*The Hollow* (*Murder after Hours*)
*The Hound of Death*: Collection
*The Labours of Hercules*: Collection (*The Labors of Hercules*)
*The Listerdale Mystery*: Collection
*Lord Edgware Dies* (*Thirteen at Dinner*)
*The Man in the Brown Suit*
*The Mirror Crack'd* (*The Mirror Crack'd from Side to Side*)
*The Moving Finger*
*Mrs. McGinty's Dead* (*Blood Will Tell*)
*The Murder at the Vicarage*
*Murder in Mesopotamia*
*Murder in the Mews*: Collection (*Dead Man's Mirror*)
*A Murder Is Announced*
*Murder Is Easy* (*Easy to Kill*)
*The Murder of Roger Ackroyd*
*The Murder on the Links*
*Murder on the Orient Express* (*Murder in the Calais Coach*)
*The Mysterious Affair at Styles*
*The Mysterious Mr Quin*: Collection
*The Mystery of the Blue Train*
*N or M?*
*Nemesis*
*One, Two, Buckle My Shoe* (*An Overdose of Death*; *The Patriotic Murders*)
*Ordeal by Innocence*
*The Pale Horse*
*Parker Pyne Investigates*: Collection (*Mr. Parker Pyne, Detective*)
*Partners in Crime*: Collection
*Passenger to Frankfurt*
*Peril at End House*
*A Pocket Full of Rye*
*Poirot Investigates*: Collection
*Poirot's Early Cases*: Collection
*Postern of Fate*
*The Regatta Mystery*: Collection
*Sad Cypress*
*The Secret Adversary*
*The Secret of Chimneys*
*The Seven Dials Mystery*
*The Sittaford Mystery* (*Murder at Hazelmoor*)
*Sleeping Murder*
*Sparkling Cyanide* (*Remembered Death*)
*Taken at the Flood* (*There Is a Tide*)
*They Came to Baghdad*
*They Do It with Mirrors* (*Murder with Mirrors*)

*Third Girl*
*Three Act Tragedy* (*Murder in Three Acts*)
*Three Blind Mice and Other Stories*: Collection
*Towards Zero*
*The Thirteen Problems*: Collection (*The Tuesday Club Murders*)
*The Under Dog and Other Stories*: Collection
*Why Didn't They Ask Evans?* (*The Boomerang Clue*)
*The Witness for the Prosecution and Other Stories*: Collection

# Works Cited

Abrams, Fran. "Age of Innocence."*newstatesman.com*, 22 Nov. 2012, www.newstatesman.com/culture/culture/2012/11/age-innocence. Accessed 4 Feb. 2016.
"Actress's Tragic Death." *Birmingham Daily Mail*, 3 Dec. 1918, p. 3.
Adam, Hargrave L. "Madeleine Smith-Mme. Steinheil." *Woman and Crime*. T. Werner Laurie, 1912, pp. 301–18.
"Baroness Libelled: Famous Trial Recalled in Detective Story." *Times of London*, 16 Nov. 1938, p. 4.
"Beautiful 'Billie Carleton': Her Strange Weird 'Life' and Sudden and Lamentable Death; Allegations as to 'Amazing Orgies'; Did 'Billie' and Her 'Unholy' Associates Try to Revive Madame de Montespan's 'Black Mass'?" *New Zealand Truth*, 29 Mar. 1919, p. 8.
"Billie Carleton's Death: Final Act in Drama." *New Zealand Herald*, 7 June 1919, p. 2.
"Billie Carleton's Tragic Death." *Dundee Evening Telegraph*, 3 Dec. 1918, p. 1.
"The Case against de Veulle: Sir R. Muir's Opening Statement." *Times of London*, 1 Feb. 1919, p. 3.
"Chinatown Opium Traffic: Man and Woman Arrested; Charge of Supplying Drugs to Miss Carleton." *Times of London*, 14 Dec. 1918, p. 5.
Christie, Agatha. "The Affair at the Victory Ball." *The Under Dog and Other Stories*. Dodd, Mead, 1951, pp. 109–30.
———. "The Ambassador's Boots." *Partners in Crime: A Tommy and Tuppence Collection*. Morrow, 2012, pp. 231–50.
———. "The Augean Stables." *Hercule Poirot: The Complete Short Stories*. Morrow, 2013, pp. 718–33.
———. *An Autobiography*. Dodd, Mead, 1977.
———. *A Caribbean Mystery*. Dodd, Mead, 1964.
———. "A Christmas Tragedy." *Miss Marple: The Complete Short Stories*. Morrow, 2011, pp. 153–73.
———. *Death in the Clouds*. Berkley, 2000.
———. *Hickory Dickory Death*. The Winterbrook Edition. Dodd, Mead, 1987.
———. "The Horses of Diomedes." *Hercule Poirot: The Complete Short Stories*. Morrow, 2013, pp. 775–90.
———. "The Lernean Hydra." *Labours of Hercules*. Collins, 1947, pp. 40–62.
———. *Lord Edgware Dies*. Greenway Edition. Dodd, Mead, 1970.
———. *The Mirror Crack'd*. Dodd, Mead, 1962.
———. *Mrs. McGinty's Dead*. Dodd, Mead, 1952.
———. *The Murder at the Vicarage*. Winterbrook Edition. Dodd, Mead, 1986.
———. *Murder in Mesopotamia: A Hercule Poirot Mystery*. Harper, 2011.
———. *A Murder Is Announced*. Berkley, 1991.

# Works Cited

———. *The Murder of Roger Ackroyd. Masterpieces of Murder.* Dodd, Mead, 1977, pp. 1–188.
———. *The Murder on the Links.* John Lane, The Bodley Head, 1923.
———. *Murder on the Orient Express.* Dodd, Mead, 1934.
———. *The Mysterious Affair at Styles: A Detective Story.* New York: John Lane, 1920.
———. *Ordeal by Innocence.* Dodd, Mead, 1958.
———. *Peril at End House: A Hercule Poirot Mystery.* Harper, 2011.
———. *A Pocket Full of Rye.* Dodd, Mead, 1988.
———. *Sad Cypress.* Dodd, Mead, 1940.
———. "Sing a Song of Sixpence." *The Witness for the Prosecution and Other Stories.* Morrow, 2012, pp. 143–65.
———. "Three Blind Mice." *Three Blind Mice and Other Stories.* Dodd, Mead, 1948, pp. 1–93.
———. *Why Didn't They Ask Evans?* St. Martin's Paperbacks Edition. St. Martin's Press, 2002.
"'Dope': Drug Fiends of London; Alarming Growth of the Habit." *Marlborough Express,* 28 Jan. 1919, p. 3.
Douglas, John, and Mark Olshaker. *The Cases That Haunt Us.* Scribner's, 2001.
"Drug Cocaine from an Egyptian." *Birmingham Daily Mail,* 12 Dec. 1918, p. 3.
"The Drug Scandal." *Press* (Canterbury), 15 Mar. 1919, p. 10.
"A Drug Victim: Death of an Actress." *Hawera & Normanby Star,* 27 Jan. 1919, p. 5.
Duke, Winifred, editor. *Trial of Harold Greenwood.* Hodge, 1930.
Early, Julie. "Technology, Modernity, and the 'Little Man.'" *English Victorian Studies,* vol. 39, no. 3, Spring 1996, pp. 309–37.
"Farmer Gough Denies Allegations: 'Boys Very Happy: Four Meals a Day, Sometimes Five.'" *Aberdeen Journal,* 17 Mar. 1945, p. 3.
Fisher, Jim. *The Lindbergh Case.* Rutgers UP, 1987.
"Foster-Parents Charged: Doctor on Death from Violence." *Times of London,* 14 Feb. 1945, p. 2.
"The Freedom of the Seas." *Times of London,* 2 Aug. 1918, p.9.
"Gene Tierney Dies at 70." *Los Angeles Times,* 8 Nov. 1991, p. A3.
Goodman, Jonathan. *Bloody Versicles: The Rhymes of Crime.* Kent State UP, 1993.
"Gough, in Box, Declares Boys Were Happy: Pig Bench Incident Was Joke." *Dundee Courier,* 17 Mar. 1945, p. 3.
"Great Unsolved Mysteries." *Sunday Times Magazine,* 20 Oct. 1968.
"Hermit Life of Greenwood: The Finger of Scorn." *The Straits Times,* 18 Feb. 1929, p. 12.
Hertog, Susan. *Anne Morrow Lindbergh: Her Life.* Anchor Books, 2000.
Hodgson, Martin. "100 Years On, DNA Casts Doubt on Crippen Case." 16 Oct. 2007, www.theguardian.com/uk/2007/oct/17/ukcrime.science Accessed 18 June 2017.
Hopper, Hedda. "Helen Says She'll Give Tony Party." *Los Angeles Times,* 24 Apr. 1965, p. B8.
James, P. D. "Who Killed Charles Bravo?" *Sunday Times,* 23 Sept. 2001, p. 36.
Kennedy, Ludovic. *The Airman and the Carpenter: The Lindbergh Kidnapping and the Framing of Richard Hauptmann.* Viking, 1985.
"Kidnaping Laid to Capone Men." *Los Angeles Times,* 16 Mar. 1932, p. 2.
Knott, George H., editor. *The Trial of William Palmer.* Hodge, 1912.
Kohn, Marek. *Dope Girls: The Birth of the British Drug Underground.* Granta, 1992.
Logan, Guy B. "More Deadly Than the Male." *World's Greatest Detective Stories,* edited by Howard Spring, Syndicate, 1934, pp. 961–970.
Macdonald, John F. "Paris and Mme. Steinheil." *The Fortnightly Review,* vol. 86, Dec. 1909, pp. 1103–1114.

# Works Cited

Martin, Benjamin F. *The Hypocrisy of Justice in the Belle Époque*. Louisiana State UP, 1984.
Matlock, Daniel. "Dr. Smiles and the Counterfeit Gentlemen: Self-Making and Misapplication in Mid-Nineteenth Century Britain." *Victorian Literature and Culture*, vol. 46, issue 1, Mar. 2018, pp. 83–94.
"Miss Carleton's Death." *Times of London*, 13 Dec. 1918, p. 3.
"The Mistress Who Drove Crippen to Murder. *"Daily Mail*, 29 Oct. 2005, www.highbeam.com/doc/1G1-138118777.html. Accessed 3 Feb. 2018.
*The Most Extraordinary Trial of William Palmer for the Rugeley Poisonings, Which Lasted Twelve Days—(May 14–27, 1856)*. Fourth ed. rev. Clark, 1857.
"Mother Refuses to Forgive Gene Tierney for Marrying." *Los Angeles Times*, 4 June 1941, p. 3.
"Mrs. Gough Tells Court She Was Afraid: On Brink of Collapse in Witness-Box." *Sunday Post*, 18 Mar. 1945, p. 2.
"Mystery of a Famous Poisoning: Welsh Crime Classic." *kidwellyhistory.co.uk*. 8 July 2009, kidwellyhistory.co.uk/Articles/Greenwood/Murder.htm. Accessed 7 Mar. 2017.
"Night Orgies." *Western Mail*, 21 Dec. 1918, p. 6.
"Not Guilty! My Life's Tragedy: Harold Greenwood Tells His Sensational Story." *The World News*, 15 Jan. 1921, pp. 12–13.
"On This Day: The Arrest of Dr. Crippen." *Times of London*, 2 Aug. 2001, p. 19.
"Opium Orgy." *Wairarapa Age*, 12 Apr. 1919, p. 3.
Paine, Donald F. "The 'Brides in the Bath' Case: The Other Crimes of George Joseph Smith." *Tennessee Bar Journal*, vol.41, no. 5, May 2005, pp. 26–7.
\_\_\_\_\_. "Hyoscine and Old Lace: The Trial of Hawley Harvey Crippen." *Tennessee Bar Journal*, Nov. 2006, vol. 42, no. 11, Spring 1996, p. 24.
"Poison-Tongue Gossip." *Auckland Star*, 6 Jan. 1934, p. 4.
"Prison Cell to Prosperity." *Auckland Star*, 16 Aug. 1924, p. 24.
"Producers of New Play Warned by Solicitors." *Newcastle Morning Herald and Miners' Advocate*, 18 Oct. 1949, p. 1.
*Report by Sir Walter Monckton on the Circumstances Which Led to the Boarding Out of Dennis and Terence O'Neill at Bank Farm, Minsterley, and the Steps Taken to Supervise Their Welfare*. Presented by the Secretary of State for the Home Department to Parliament by Command of His Majesty. London: H.M.S.O., 1945.
"Rugeley Doctor's Turf Downfall." *Nambour Chronicle and North Coast Advertiser*, 6 June 1941, p. 12.
"Rugeley Poisoner Worst of All." *Brisbane Telegraph*, 11 Oct. 1950, p. 19.
"Rugeley Poisoning Cases." *Adelaide Observer*, 30 Aug. 1856, p. 7.
"Serial Killer Smith Convicted." *History Today*, vol. 65, no. 7, July 2015, p. 9.
Sherwin, Adam. "Was It the Wife, the Lover, the Stableman or the Maid Who Poisoned Charles Bravo?" *Times of London*, 11 Oct. 2004, p. 19.
Sly, Nicola. *Shropshire Murders*. History P, 2009.
Steinheil, Marguerite. *My Memoirs*. New York: Sturgis & Walton, 1912.
"Steinheil Case: Acquittal of the Prisoner." *Times of London*, 15 Nov. 1909, p. 5.
"Suit to Prove That She Lives: Baroness Gets Big Damages." *Morning Bulletin*, 7 Jan. 1939, p. 5.
"Ten Remarkable Pieces of Evidence." *Times of London*, 22 Jan. 2008, p. 7.
Thompson, Laura. *Agatha Christie: An English Mystery*. Headline Review, 2007.
Tierney, Gene, with Mickey Herskowitz. *Self-Portrait*. Book Club Edition. Wyden, 1978.
"Tragedy of an Artist's Flat." *Auckland Star*, 18 July 1908, p. 15.

Underwood, Terry. *Foul Deeds and Suspicious Deaths around Newport.* Wharncliffe, 2005.
"Unholy Rites." *Liverpool Echo,* 15 Mar. 1919, p. 5.
Watson, Eric R., editor. *Trial of George Joseph Smith.* Hodge, 1922.
"Why Britain Fights: Hitler's Technique Is That of George Joseph Smith." *Courier-Mail,* 8 Apr. 1940, p. 4.
"William Palmer: England's Wickedest Man." *Morning Bulletin,* 9 Jan. 1923, p. 10.
Young, Filson, editor. *The Trial of Hawley Harvey Crippen.* Hodge, 1920.
―――. *The Trial of Herbert Rowse Armstrong.* Glasgow: Hodge, 1927.

# Index

Abinger, Baron *see* Scarlett, Robert Brooke Campbell
"The Affair at the Victory Ball" 6, 59–62, 65–71
"L'Affaire de l'Impasse Ronsin" 29, 34–35, 37, 40
Allen, William 79
Alverstone, Lord Chief Justice 126
antimony 137
Armstrong, Herbert Rowse 99, 104
arsenic 89, 95–99, 101, 103–104, 146–147, 161
"The Augean Stables" 105
*An Autobiography* 49, 51, 115, 143, 166

"Balham Mystery" 136–137, 149
Bamford, William 11–12, 25–26
Bank Farm 108–109, 115, 117
Barney, Elvira 68
Belcher, Lionel 61–62, 65–67, 71
*Blood Will Tell see Mrs. McGinty's Dead*
Booker, May 65–66
Bowater, Thomas Vansittart 90
Bravo, Charles 136–140, 143–149, 192–193
"Brides in the Bath" 49, 170, 174, 178, 180–181, 183; *see also* Burnham, Alice; Lofty, Margaret; Mundy, Bessie; Smith, George Joseph
"Bright Young Things" 68
Burnham, Alice 172–173, 182

Capone, Al 75
*A Caribbean Mystery* 164, 174–183
Carleton, Billie 59–69, 70–71
Cassini, Christina 155, 167
Cassini, Daria 154–155, 165
Cassini, Oleg 153–155, 164, 167
Castle, Irene 60
"Cemetery John" 78–80
Children Act of 1948 111, 119
"A Christmas Tragedy" 106
Cochran, Charles B. 60
*commedia dell'arte* 68, 71
Compton, Fay 60–61, 67
Condon, John F. 78–80

Cook, John Parsons 9–14, 24–28
Cox, Mrs. Jane 137–140, 144–145, 148
Crippen, Cora 121–122, 126–127, 132–134
Crippen, Hawley Harvey 121–127, 131–135
Cronshaw, William 71
Croydon Poisonings 136, 143, 146–148

Darling, Justice Charles 44, 62
*Death in the Clouds* 71
Defence of the Realm Act of 1914 61
de Veulle, Reginald 60–63, 65–71
Dew, Walter 124–125
DORA *see* Defence of the Realm Act of 1914
Dreyfus, Alfred 30–32, 35–36, 50
Dreyfusards 32, 36, 50
Duff, Edmund 146
Duff, Grace 147

Edwards, Eirlys 108, 110, 115
"Elmore, Belle" *see* Crippen, Cora

Faure, Felix 30–36, 40, 50

German measles 54, 156, 165; *see also* rubella
Gough, Esther 108–111, 115–116
Gough, Reginald 108–111, 115–116
Gow, Betty 74–76, 86–87
"Great War" *see* World War I
Greenwood, Harold 5, 88–99, 102–104
Greenwood, Irene 98
Griffiths, George 139
Griffiths, May 90–94, 96–97
Griffiths, Thomas 90–94, 96–97
Gully, James Manby 136–139, 144, 149

Hauptmann, Bruno 79–80, 85
Hayworth, Rita 155
*Hickory Dickory Death* 72
Hollywood Canteen 154–156, 165
Hopper, Hedda 156
"Horses of Diomedes" 72
Hughes, Howard 152, 167
hyoscine 121–123, 126, 134

**195**

# Index

*J'Accuse* 30
"Jafsie" *see* Condon, John F.
*John Bull* 99
Jones, Elizabeth 91–95, 104
Jones, Gladys 92, 94–95, 97, 104

Kempton, Freda 68
Kendall, Henry 125
Kennedy, John F. 152, 155, 167
Khan, Aly 152, 155, 167

Lamarr, Hedy 156, 167
SS *Laurentic* 125
Le Neve, Ethel 122–135
"The Lernean Hydra" 5–6, 100–104
Lindbergh, Anne Morrow 74, 84
Lindbergh, Charles Augustus, Jr. 74
Lindbergh, Charles Augustus, Sr. 74
Lindbergh kidnapping case 5, 74–81
Lofty, Margaret 172–173
*Lord Edgware Dies* 72

*The Man They Acquitted* 99
Marshall Hall, Edward 96–99
Miller, Bruce 122, 124
*The Mirror Crack'd* 150, 157–168
The Monckton Report 111
SS *Montrose* 125
*Mrs. McGinty's Dead* 121, 127–131, 177, 183
Muir, Richard 66, 126
Mundy, Bessie 172–174, 182
Munyons 121–123
*Murder in Mesopotamia* 106
*Murder in the Calais Coach* see *Murder on the Orient Express*
*A Murder Is Announced* 106, 184
*The Murder of Roger Ackroyd* 71
*The Murder on the Links* 29, 44–58
*Murder on the Orient Express* 5–6, 74, 81–88
*The Mysterious Affair at Styles* 7, 9, 14–28

Neave, Ethel *see* Le Neve, Ethel
Newport Education Authority 108, 110, 115, 119
Newton, Charles 12, 28

Oddie, Ingleby 64–65
O'Neill, Dennis 2, 107–110, 114–120
O'Neill, Frederick 107, 108–109, 115, 117

O'Neill, Terence 107, 108–109, 115, 117
*Ordeal by Innocence* 136, 140–149

Palmer, William 2, 9–14, 23–28
*Partners in Crime* 72
Paul, Brenda Dean 68
Pegler, Edith 171–173, 182
*Peril at End House* 72–73
"The Priory" 137–139
The "Purple Gang" 75

Reilly, Ed 80
rubella 154, 156, 165
"The Rugeley Poisoner" 9–28

Scarlett, Robert Brooke Campbell, 6th Baron Abinger 41, 44, 56
Schwarzkopf, H. Norman, Sr. 75–76, 78, 87
Sharpe, Violet 76–78, 85, 87
Shropshire Council 108, 110, 115, 119, 120
Sidney, Tom 146–147
Sidney, Vera 146–147
Sidney, Violet 146–147
Simpson, O.J. 126
"Sing a Song of Sixpence" 147
Smith, George Joseph 170–181
Snyder, Ruth 44
Spilsbury, Bernard 126, 134, 147, 174
*Spirit of St. Louis* 75
Steinheil, Adolphe 29–32, 40, 49–50, 54
Steinheil, Marguerite 29–58
Stevens, William 13, 26
strychnine 9, 2, 13–14, 20–22, 25–28

tartar emetic 137, 139, 145
Taylor, Alfred Swaine 13, 26–28
telegraphy *see* wireless telegraphy
"Three Blind Mice" 5, 88, 107–120
Tierney, Gene 2, 150–169

Veulle, Reginald de *see* de Veulle, Reginald

*Why Didn't They Ask Evans?* 184
Willcox, William 147
Williams, Hannah 90, 95–96, 98, 104
Williams, Orville 79
wireless telegraphy 124–125
World War I 15, 60, 68, 89, 170
World War II 109, 140, 150, 153, 165

Zola, Emile 30